Aestheticism

AESTHETICISM

The Religion of Art
in Post-Romantic Literature

LEON CHAI

COLUMBIA UNIVERSITY PRESS
NEW YORK

The author and publisher gratefully acknowledge the support toward publication given them by the University of Illinois Research Board.

COLUMBIA UNIVERSITY PRESS
New York   Oxford
Copyright © 1990 Columbia University Press

Library of Congress Cataloging-in-Publication Data
Chai, Leon.
Aestheticism : the religion of art in post-romantic literature /
Leon Chai.
p.   cm.
Includes bibliographical references.
ISBN 0-231-07224-4 (alk. paper)
1. Aestheticism (Literature)
2. English literature—19th century—History and criticism.
3. English literature—20th century—History and criticism.
4. French literature—19th century—History and criticism.
5. French literature—20th century—History and criticism.
6. Art and literature—Great Britain.
7. Art and literature—France.
I. Title.
PR468.A33C44   1990
820.9′008—dc20
90-35132
CIP

Casebound editions of Columbia University Press books are Smyth-sewn and printed on permanent and durable acid-free paper

Printed in the United States of America

c 10 9 8 7 6 5 4 3 2 1

CONTENTS

ACKNOWLEDGMENTS

I would like first of all to thank Jonathan Arac, whose watchful spirit, as always, has hovered over this project from its beginnings.

My sister, Jean, has (once again) given me indispensable assistance by procuring some of the photographs employed for illustrations, and by helping to suggest others.

I owe something to the timely assistance of several kind friends who helped at crucial moments: Eugene Hill, Cary Nelson, and Richard Wheeler.

I have benefited a great deal from the suggestions and comments of the anonymous readers for Columbia University Press; I would like to take this opportunity to record my gratitude to them.

I am also the beneficiary of support from the following institutions: the Center for Advanced Study at the University of Illinois, the University of Illinois Research Board, and the University of Illinois (Urbana-Champaign) English Department.

Finally, I would like to thank Cara Ryan, whose tireless and unfailing efforts at all stages have done more than anything else to help bring this work into existence.

PREFACE

In a letter to a friend Marcel Proust once wrote: "Si je n'ai pas la Foi, comme tu dis, en revanche la préoccupation religieuse n'est jamais absente un jour de ma vie." [If I do not have the Faith, as you say, on the other hand the preoccupation with religious things is never absent even a day from my life.] And in a sense all of Aestheticism might be said to emerge out of the twilight of a waning religious faith in the later nineteenth century. At the heart of the Aesthetic movement is a desire to redefine the relation of art to life, to impart to life itself the form of a work of art and thereby raise it to a higher level of existence. In tracing the history of such a movement—its ideals and the course of its development—I believe we can arrive at a deeper sense of its significance for the way we live now.

Beginning with the poem "Harmonie du soir," I attempt to show how all the elements of a nascent aestheticism can be found in the work of Charles Baudelaire. Here consciousness dissolves the external world into impressionistic motifs, producing an initial chaos. Beneath the chaos, however, a formative impulse progressively manifests itself in the arrangement of the motifs. Impression passes over into emotion, which in turn is embodied in symbolism. At this stage, as if having reached its ultimate phase, the poem turns back upon itself through memory to recover an other consecrated through the self's affections. The whole sequence of the poem's emotions reveals the inherent form of a work of art. A similar preoccupation with the symbolic expression of emotion through color pervades Baudelaire's *Salon de 1846*. But now color creates form through chromatic harmony.

With Jacob Burckhardt's *Kultur der Renaissance in Italien* the form of a period itself becomes analogous to that of a work of art as aspects of Renaissance life are related to each other in "spatial" rather than temporal fashion, producing the effect of a composition. In contrast Walter Pater's *The Renaissance* transforms this feeling of life as art into a sense of "music"—the intuition of life's moments as forming some-how a symbolically expressive sequence. Oscar Wilde's *De Profundis* at first appears even to repudiate the aesthetic quest. Ultimately, how-ever, it discovers an intrinsic beauty in the dramatic form that an entire life (Wilde's own) assumes.

Henry James's *Ambassadors* and *The Golden Bowl* mark a crisis re-sulting in a shift from an aestheticism of consciousness to an aesthet-icism of form. *The Ambassadors* equates beauty with the intensity of an impression. Thus Lambert Strether's whole experience in Paris is one of progressive awakening to the aesthetic appeal of his own impressions. Yet such an appeal consists less of the sensation of a mo-ment than of associations that evoke the richness of accumulated depths of thought and emotion that in turn yield a finer, more complex awareness. Nevertheless, even the finest appreciation is defenseless against suffering. But if for this reason the moral consciousness finally emerges as supreme, that is only because it offers a medium for the richest, most complex impressions of all. The rejection of an aestheticism of consciousness in *The Ambassadors* leads James in *The Golden Bowl* to a religion of form. Here form consists of the deepest human relation-ships—of parent and child, of husband and wife. What such relation-ships seek to create is a meaning within human existence by subli-mating passion to form. Beginning with the symbolic descent into chaos that culminates in the consummation of the Prince's affair with Char-lotte at Matcham, I then trace Maggie's attempt to restore her mar-riage with the Prince as a quest for form whose ultimate triumph af-firms the possibility of assimilating life to art.

I conclude with Proust's *À la recherche du temps perdu*. For Proust the quest for happiness that attempts to preserve the sensation of a past moment ends in failure. Nevertheless, some of the narrator's ex-periences had seemed to possess a symbolic significance. The effort to elucidate these encompasses several stages, all of which are anticipated in three motifs from the very beginning of the "overture" to the *Re-cherche*. The process begins with the perception (in the "Martinville" episode) of an architectonic relation between various moments of the narrator's existence which transcends time. But that perception does not adequately reproduce the essence of existence, which consists of our experience of the passage of time. This is recaptured in Swann's hearing of the Vinteuil sonata. Yet the experience of time in music fails to recover the actual moments of one's past. Through his invol-untary remembrance of Venice in the courtyard of the Guermantes hôtel, the narrator re-experiences such a moment. In so doing he recognizes the essence of that moment as consisting of an emotion. But with this recognition he also realizes the recoverability (and hence permanence) of each moment of his past, their tacit formation of an ideal sequence. Thus he perceives his whole life as composing implicitly a work of art.

The history of Aestheticism, then, is in effect the history of a quest for specific impressions or experiences that are felt to possess an intrinsic significance—above all, the experience of beauty and the experience of form. Consequently, any attempt to elucidate that history must concern itself to some extent with the nature of those experiences. Each, however, is embodied in a particular moment, which is to say a particular apprehension that occurs in time. But if such apprehensions are subjective (and hence not entirely accessible to others), what remains most significant about them is the sequence they compose. It is both revealing and suggestive that the origins of Aestheticism should involve a preoccupation with the beauty of impressions, while the end of the movement attempts to give such impressions a form. What begins as a desire for something within an impression ends then as a quest for something beyond it: an ideal architectonics that would relate an impression to all the others in an individual's existence. By this means the apprehension of a theophanic aura within an impression itself yields ultimately to an intuition of form transcending the experience both of that impression and of consciousness in general.

The desire for something within an impression equates that impression with the meaning of a particular moment. But this implies that the meaning of a given moment is now being sought within experience itself. Under such circumstances, the nature of meaning necessarily differs from what it had been for a previous epoch. If the experience of a moment embodies no particular belief or faith, its meaning can only result from the effect it produces upon the individual who experiences it. Thus meaning becomes identified with intensity of impression. But if the meaning of an impression lies in its intensity, an impression can only be meaningful in a transitory sense at best. Hence the incessant quest for new sensations and impressions, and, ultimately, the failure of that quest. What results from this failure is not a renunciation of experience as meaningful but an attempt to discern a transcendent element within it. In shifting to the search for a transcendent element, however, Aestheticism raises an obvious question: is meaning intrinsically impossible within experience itself? And if so, must the quest for meaning necessarily become a quest for transcendence in one form or another? Whether the literature after Aestheticism really resolves this query must remain, I think, open to question. And if so, that in turn can suggest the particular significance a movement like Aestheticism possesses for us now.

In my presentation of a sequence of Aesthetic apprehensions, I often introduce a theme which is then taken up at a later point. Thus the equation of theater or drama with life, which appears first in Edmond de Goncourt's *La Faustin,* resurfaces later in Henry James's *Golden Bowl.* Similarly, the sense of all our past moments as forming an expressive or symbolic sequence like that of music occurs in Pater and subsequently in Wilde before achieving its final form with the music of Vinteuil in Proust's *Recherche.* What such recurrences of a theme make possible is something like a recognition of that theme. The experience of this recognition, in turn, gives this book its form. But that form is meant to correspond to an essential aspect of the Aesthetic movement itself: its own recognition of form both in life and in a work of art. And, just as that recognition had represented the culmination of Aestheticism as a movement, so my work, by reproducing it, seeks to recover in some fashion the history of Aestheticism by recapturing its consciousness of itself through form. Perhaps more than anything else, this consciousness of form is what defines Aestheticism. Hence the rationale for attempting to represent it.

Within the present interpretation, perception of form becomes one and the same with form itself. Form, in other words, consists simply of a recognition of form. But this recognition of form is based upon the actual experiences of individual moments; it emerges from relating these to each other. In this sense it is inseparable from experience itself. Thus even the recognition of a relation between different experiences becomes an experience. As such it too comprises a specific moment of existence. But if recognition of a relation between different experiences represents the experience of a given moment, it necessarily forms part of a particular individual's existence. Consequently it possesses its full significance only within that existence. Thus only by experiencing an individual's entire existence can we find the recognition of a relation between its different moments fully meaningful. For this reason we cannot really recover the actual recognitions that define the history of Aestheticism. What I have attempted to capture instead is something like the experience of recognition, through a sequence of Aesthetic "moments." Through that experience it becomes possible to arrive at a feeling of form, which is the final result of the Aesthetic quest for happiness.

But if in many individual instances the Aesthetic quest for happiness leads to a discovery of form, the nature of the Aesthetic movement as a whole also tends, on another level, toward an emphasis on form. This emphasis results not only from the fact that individual recognitions of form in existence often occur late in the movement (e.g., Henry Adams and Proust), but also from the recapitulation of certain themes (life as drama, life as music) arising from the Aesthetic quest. In its recapitulation of various themes the movement acquires something like a formal awareness of itself as a movement. To convey a sense of that awareness has been my objective in describing a sequence of Aesthetic "moments" governed by thematic recapitulation. The result, I hope, will be a progressively increasing formal awareness corresponding to the Aesthetic movement's own experience.

For that reason, I do not engage or make use of any of the contemporary modes of critical discourse. To do so would have made impossible all attempts at evoking the experience of the Aesthetic consciousness, and hence those recognitions that give form both to Aestheticism and to this book. Thus too the necessity for certain omissions or exclusions. It would have been possible, for instance, to offer a somewhat different interpretation of Baudelaire—one stressing his preoccupation with sin and the problem of evil, the struggle between "spleen" and "idéal," or the symbolism of his doctrine of "correspondances." Such concerns, however, fail to emphasize what is most crucial to any account of the aesthetic element in him. A similar point applies to the exclusion of other authors. With Mallarmé, a self-conscious symbolism leads to something like a metaphysics of the process of poetic creation that no longer takes into account individual moments or experiences. But Yeats too (especially the later Yeats) imparts to individual moments an archetypal symbolic quality such that their nature as sensations or experiences ceases to matter. With Hofmannsthal, moreover, apprehension of the archetypal significance of a moment becomes ultimately a sense of the allegorical quality of human existence. One might say the same (with significant qualifications) of both Stefan George and Rilke. For this and other reasons, German aestheticism is omitted almost entirely.

On the other hand, the relation of literature to both painting and music is touched upon in various places. Painting offers the possibility of exploring the symbolic significance of a particular sensation or impression, such as our experience of color. But in isolating such impressions it can also combine them into a timeless arrangement or harmony that transcends the evanescence of the moment in which they originally occur. If painting transcends time, music conversely embodies our experience of time. As a formal sequence, however, what it consists of is not so much the pure experience of an individual moment but rather the sense of an underlying pattern within our existence as a whole.

Perhaps a word about the illustrations may be appropriate here. For various reasons it was not possible to obtain adequate reproductions of many of the paintings discussed in the text. What I have chosen to present instead are examples from the work of three great photographers whose lives span the period covered by Aestheticism. Two of them were in fact associated with Aesthetic authors: Nadar with Baudelaire, and Coburn with Henry James. In both time and place, meanwhile, Atget's development corresponds in various respects to that of Proust. My hope, then, has been to convey something of the Aesthetic vision through the particular styles of these photographers, whose works form a complement to the text.

Finally, the "Prelude" attempts to treat various authors I do not discuss elsewhere. But the essential movement of the "Prelude," from a sacred symbolism to recognition of an intrinsic form in the relation between different moments of an individual's existence, remains the same as that of what follows. Thus it anticipates the larger sequence to come. And it is no accident that this larger sequence ends where the "Prelude" begins: with Venice.

Aestheticism

Abbreviations

In both text and notes, I make use of the following abbreviations:

OC = *Oeuvres complètes*
GW = *Gesammelte Werke*

PRELUDE

"And well may they fall back, for beyond those troops of ordered arches there rises a vision out of the earth, and all the great square seems to have opened from it in a kind of awe, that we may see it far away. . . ." Thus, according to Ruskin, the spectator in passing through the arcade of pillars at the end of the "Bocca di Piazza" emerges upon a great open space: beyond that space, the Basilica of St. Mark's in Venice, concrete expression not only of a faith but of a relation between the external, visible world and various spiritual presences that exemplifies Ruskin's own idea of the symbolism of human life.[1] Such symbolism transfigures our whole existence by endowing it with something of a sacred aura, a sense of the sacramental nature of both natural objects and the transactions that make up this existence. In so doing, it reveals the implicit aestheticism of our lives, the possibility of perceiving within them an element of beauty through a theophanic consciousness that illuminates the sacred quality of each of our moments. And perhaps for this perception what matters most is not so much the actual presence of the divine but simply our awareness of a sacramental element in our existence, which affects the way we perceive its various phenomena.[2]

In this respect it seems appropriate for Ruskin to describe what appears when the "ordered arches" fall back as a "vision." Combining what is seen with the process of perception, his description suggests how what we see is colored by the medium through which we perceive. At the same time, it also emphasizes the sacred quality of seeing, the sense in which it represents something like a religious rite: through it, we experience the beauty of what is seen as a celebration of the symbolic significance of the external world.[3] An object that possesses symbolic meaning is surrounded by an aura of mystery. We find this aura enhanced in seeing something at a distance. Thus Ruskin can speak of how, when the "vision" appears, "all the great square seems to have opened from it in a kind of awe," so that "we may see it far away." Here the "awe" conveys a religious sense informing the seeing of St. Mark's at a distance. Elsewhere, in *Modern Painters,* Ruskin attempts to show how the depiction of mountains at a distance in Turner's works creates a similar feeling of mystery (*Works* 6:89–90).

What the eye perceives at the end of St. Mark's Square according to *The Stones of Venice* is, first of all, "a multitude of pillars and white domes, clustered into a long low pyramid of coloured light" (*Works* 10:82). The apparent chaos of the "multitude" of pillars and white domes resolves itself into the formal order of a "pyramid." And "order, in its highest sense, is one of the necessities of art" (*Works* 10:205). Here order is symbolic of beauty: the object that exhibits order manifests a quality we ultimately appreciate for what it reveals of a higher idea, one expressive of the actual nature of God.[4] With this we arrive at Ruskin's theory of "Typical Beauty," the beauty of a graduated typological symbolism in nature itself.[5] In volume 2 of *Modern Painters* he asserts:

> Nevertheless, I think that the admission of different degrees of this glory and image of Himself upon creation, has the look of something meant especially for us; for although, in pursuance of the appointed system of Government by universal laws, these same degrees exist where we cannot witness them, yet the existence of degrees at all seems at first unlikely in Divine work; and I cannot see reason for it unless that palpable one of increasing in us the understanding of the sacred characters by showing us the results of their comparative absence. (*Works* 4:144)

For

> the fact of our deriving constant pleasure from whatever is a type or semblance of divine attributes, and from nothing but that which is so, is the most glorious of all that can be demonstrated of human nature . . . it seems a promise of a communion ultimately deep, close, and conscious, with the Being whose darkened manifestations we here feebly and unthinkingly delight in. Probably to every higher order of intelligence more of His image becomes palpable in all around them, and the glorified spirits and the angels have perceptions as much more full and rapturous than ours, as ours than those of beasts and creeping things. And . . . may we not see in these visionary pleasures, lightly as we too often regard them, cause for thankfulness, ground for hope, anchor for faith, more than in all the other manifold gifts and

guidances, wherewith God crowns the years, and hedges the paths of Men? (*Works* 4:144–45)

In contrast to the beauty of those things that induce us to share their consciousness, Typical Beauty offers only the "promise" of an ultimate communion with the divine consciousness. Nevertheless, the beauty of types possesses a special radiance, insofar as it consists of an apocalyptic recognition within the mind itself. To appreciate the beauty of vital things is to feel with their sensibility: to appreciate Typical Beauty, on the other hand, is to become aware of the beauty of mind, which makes possible a glimpse of the symbolic significance of things. But the experience of illumination that occurs in perceiving a type arises not only from recognition of the mind's own nature but from a feeling of divine effulgence, a spiritual brightness that issues from the type itself. The type reflects the splendor of its source even as it colors it: hence the "coloured light" that Ruskin speaks of, recalling the "translucence" Coleridge had ascribed to the symbol, or the "dome of many-coloured glass" that Shelley equates in *Adonais* with life, which "stains the white radiance of Eternity."[6] In perceiving an external object, we feel the energy of expression within it, the energeia of a divine essence that necessarily seeks to express itself out of its own abundance.[7]

The type then becomes a temporary form of stasis in an unceasing process of symbolic expression. Thus our feeling of the type as something constantly coming-to-be: in becoming a type the divine energeia achieves a form expressive of the whole movement by which that energy becomes manifest. The type, then, is something more than mere sign, more than a simple allegorical *figura*. But it also embodies more than the traditional scriptural or prophetic type. In absorbing the divine energy into itself, it takes on a sacramental quality: henceforth the natural object represents a divine presence. Consequently all our transactions with such objects become endowed with a kind of consecration, whose ultimate effect is to sanctify each moment of our existence with a natural rather than otherworldly grace.

On account of its clustering of pillars and white domes, the Basilica of St. Mark's suggests "a treasure-heap . . . partly of gold, and partly of opal and mother-of-pearl." But the church counts as "treasure" in a very special sense.[8] The first of Ruskin's lectures in *Sesame and Lilies* bears the title "Of Kings' Treasuries." Such treasuries consist not of gold and silver but of books. Together they constitute what we call tradition. Thus the most precious treasure of all is tradition, a transmission of the spiritual and cultural consciousness of past to present.

This transmission takes specific forms. In *Sesame and Lilies* we are told that reading forms our discourse with the dead. Tradition embodies this discourse, which implies a process of transmission: through our discourse with them, the thoughts and feelings of the dead assume the form of "living words" within our consciousness.[9]

But why do we seek to preserve our relation to the illustrious dead? "We come then to that great concourse of the Dead, not merely to know from them what is True, but chiefly to feel with them what is just" (*Works* 18:80). To feel with them, we must be like them, and being like them means "entering into their Hearts": "Having then faithfully listened to the great teachers, that you may enter into their Thoughts, you have yet this higher advance to make;—you have to enter into their Hearts. As you go to them first for clear sight, so you must stay with them, that you may share at last their just and mighty Passion" (*Works* 18:78). This passion Ruskin associates with "sensation," of which he then remarks: "I am not afraid of the word; still less of the thing. You have heard many outcries against sensation lately; but, I can tell you, it is not less sensation we want, but more. The ennobling difference between one man and another,—between one animal and another,—is precisely this, that one feels more than another. . . . we are only human in so far as we are sensitive, and our honour is precisely in proportion to our passion" (*Works* 18:78–79).[10]

The form of transmission we call tradition consists, then, of a transmission of feeling or passion. As such it corresponds to the process of symbolism. In its experience of Typical Beauty through the perception of a symbolic type, consciousness becomes consecrated by its sense of a divine presence within external things. But in a similar fashion, tradition too offers a form of consecration: in feeling the passions of the great Dead, we become sanctified by their aspirations and their consciousness. For the later Ruskin, human emotion is what consecrates. That something should have been an object of interest or desire, that it should have played a role in the hopes and actions of a past moment of human existence—this is what sanctifies it for us now. Emotion is not only the essence of human life but, above all, what affirms life, in a universe that opposes animate to inanimate without the government of a higher spiritual presence.

But even for the earlier Ruskin of *Stones of Venice*, it is possible to feel the consecrating influence of emotion or passion. In *The Seven Lamps of Architecture* he had written:

> For, indeed, the greatest glory of a building is not in its stones, nor in its gold. Its glory is in its Age, and in that deep sense of

voicefulness, of stern watching, of mysterious sympathy, nay, even of approval or condemnation, which we feel in walls that have long been washed by the passing waves of humanity. It is in their lasting witness against men, in their quiet contrast with the transitional character of all things, in the strength which, through the lapse of seasons and times, and the decline and birth of dynasties, and the changing of the face of the earth, and of the limits of the sea, maintains its sculptured shapeliness for a time insuperable, connects forgotten and following ages with each other, and half constitutes the identity, as it concentrates the sympathy, of nations: it is in that golden stain of time, that we are to look for the real light, and colour, and preciousness of architecture; and it is not until a building has assumed this character, till it has been entrusted with the fame, and hallowed by the deeds of men, till its walls have been witnesses of suffering, and its pillars rise out of the shadows of death, that its existence, more lasting as it is than that of the natural objects of the world around it, can be gifted with even so much as these possess, of language and of life. (*Works* 8:233–34)[11]

Thus age itself becomes the consecration of an edifice—not, however, merely on account of that edifice's silent testimony to the passage of time but because it becomes for us the visible embodiment of all the emotions it has witnessed. In this respect it becomes symbolically expressive. Through it we experience the consciousness of a past epoch or moment. What we experience, nevertheless, is not so much the actual emotions of a historical moment as a sense of the *presence* of these emotions. In seeing the edifice in which they occurred, we feel our nearness to them, without being able to recover the specific emotions. What remains is the consciousness of emotion itself as an affirmation of life. In the process, emotion assumes a sacred quality. As a feeling of the presence of something sacred, this consciousness of emotion corresponds to the experience of seeing natural objects symbolize a divine presence. Thus human edifices offer ultimately a secular form of sacred symbolism, presenting in effect another medium for the consecration of human life.

We are told that the colors of St. Mark's consist principally of gold, opal, and mother-of-pearl. Gold signifies, of course, treasure, wealth, abundance of riches, conceived of here, however, not merely as material splendor but in its highest sense as the wealth of tradition. Opal, on the other hand, with its milky whiteness, possesses no real color. Instead it suggests something like pure luminousness, that purity of

color which Ruskin elsewhere equates with the "purifying or sancti-
fying element of material beauty" (*Works* 7:417n).[12] Mother-of-pearl,
finally, recalls the symbolism of "coloured light" described earlier.
Through its iridescence it exemplifies the expression of light through
color, showing how light in assuming a specific tint becomes expressive. In a similar fashion, the luminous appearances of nature make
their impression upon the perceiving mind. Thus mother-of-pearl typifies the process by which natural phenomena acquire a symbolic significance.

The massed "treasure-heap" of pillars and domes composed of gold,
opal, and mother-of-pearl is "hollowed beneath into five great vaulted
porches, ceiled with fair mosaic, and beset with sculpture of alabaster,
clear as amber and delicate as ivory." The porch embodies our idea of
shelter—the fundamental principle of all edifices. Yet here we find this
idea elevated into something higher. Instead of being constructed simply of stones, the vault of these porches glitters with mosaic, transforming what had originally been conceived of merely as protection
from wind and rain into an ornament of human life. The ornament
culminates in sculptured alabaster, "clear as amber and delicate as ivory."
Amber we know as the material that miraculously preserves living things
within its deep rich golden texture, darkening as it consecrates with
age while allowing the form and nature of the object to be seen through
its transparent medium. In a similar sense, sculpture itself seeks to preserve and at the same time reveal the living emotions of its builders.
It becomes then an embodiment of tradition, the medium through
which those emotions achieve the consecration of time. But they in
turn are worthy of consecration only if they possess the purity of all
high art. It is this purity that ivory symbolizes. Thus what had been
constructed under the pressure of a necessity for shelter becomes a
means of beautifying our existence, expressive of the vision of a paradise on earth in which are contained the highest possibilities of both
material and spiritual fulfillment.

And what of the subjects of such sculpture? "Sculpture fantastic and
involved, of palm leaves and lilies, and grapes and pomegranates, and
birds clinging and fluttering among the branches, all twined together
into an endless network of buds and plumes; and in the midst of it,
the solemn forms of angels, sceptred, and robed to the feet, and leaning to each other across the gates, their figures indistinct among the
gleaming of the golden ground through the leaves beside them, interrupted and dim, like the morning light as it faded back among the
branches of Eden, when first its gates were angel-guarded long ago."
The profusion of vegetative and animal forms constitutes a sign of

life—of life seen as an expression of the "organic," which Ruskin defines in the final volume of *Modern Painters* in terms of a law of "help": "In substance which we call 'inanimate,'" as of clouds, or stones, their atoms may cohere to each other, or consist with each other, but they do not help each other. The removal of one part does not injure the rest. But in a plant, the taking away of any one part does injure the rest. Hurt or remove any portion of the sap, bark, or pith, the rest is injured. If any part enters into a state in which it no more assists the rest, and has thus become 'helpless,' we call it also 'dead.' The power which causes the several portions of the plant to help each other, we call life" (*Works* 7:205).[13]

When the various parts of a plant or animal "help" each other in this fashion, the plant or animal then assumes that "appearance of felicitous fulfilment of function in living things" (*Works* 4:64) which Ruskin calls Vital Beauty.[14] This Vital Beauty differs from the Typical Beauty described earlier insofar as it consists of a consciousness within the plant or animal rather than in the one who perceives them. Whereas Typical Beauty represents the external aspect, so to speak, of a plant or animal, its Vital Beauty is its internal aspect. Of course, we cannot know exactly what such a consciousness might be like. Yet ultimately its specific nature does not matter. Clearly, both plants and animals possess the capacity for feeling or sensation. Given that capacity, each can then feel the sense of a life within itself—the consciousness of its various parts contributing to create the rhythms of its existence—that forms the "felicitous fulfilment" Ruskin speaks of. Each then "can exult in its sense of life" (*Works* 4:7). Such exultation, however, will not be exactly like the human happiness that comes about through our response to external phenomena. The "happiness" of plants or animals is rather a consciousness of life itself, a sensation which affirms their own vital energy, their own life.

We do not know what such a consciousness consists of. But all we really need is the "appearance" of "felicitous fulfilment of function." In perceiving it, we recognize its analogy to human existence. As a result, we are brought to a consciousness of the life within ourselves, which is the ultimate objective of all depictions of vegetative or animal forms. In becoming conscious of our own life, we realize that it too is self-affirming. But our life represents something more than mere physical sensation. As thought and emotion, it attains a higher, spiritual nature, no longer subject to the vicissitudes of change and decay that affect physical things. Hence it approaches in its "felicitous fulfilment" something of the nature of the divine essence, for which Ruskin could claim, following Aristotle, that "perfect happiness is some sort of energy of Contemplation" (*Works* 4:7). At its highest, then, human life becomes like divine life, thereby assuming something of its sanctity as well.

Thus the "solemn forms of angels" appear "in the midst of" the profusion of vegetative and animal life, as an indication of the implicit sanctity of human life when it ascends from the physical or material to the realm of emotion and thought. In "leaning to each other across the gates," the angels too exemplify the "law of help" which is the principle of all life, showing that the higher reaches of human existence belong no less than the lower to the sphere of life. Indistinct from the golden background, dimly perceived, fading into an air from which they seem barely to emerge, these angels symbolize an apprehension of higher spiritual presences filling the moments of our daily existence, dim not from lack of power but because they form part of the very atmosphere in which we dwell. Depicted in this fashion, they are not to be understood as miraculous but rather as part of everyday life, which thereby approaches the state of an earthly paradise. Hence the dimness of their apparition: like the "morning light as it faded back among the branches of Eden," their luminous presence unobtrusively fills the atmosphere.[15] What the mind experiences, then, is the pervasive consciousness of a divine consecration of earthly things, like some rich and mysterious fragrance perfuming the air.

> And round the walls of the porches there are set pillars of variegated stones . . . their capitals rich with interwoven tracery, rooted knots of herbage, and drifting leaves of acanthus and vine, and mystical signs, all beginning and ending in the Cross; and above them, in the broad archivolts, a continuous chain of language and of life—angels, and the signs of heaven, and the labours of men, each in its appointed season upon the earth; and above these, another range of glittering pinnacles, mixed with white arches edged with scarlet flowers,—a confusion of delight, amidst which the breasts of the Greek horses are seen blazing in their breadth of golden strength, and the St. Mark's lion, lifted on a blue field covered with stars, until at last, as if in ecstasy, the crests of the arches break into a marble foam, and toss themselves far into the blue sky in flashes and wreaths of sculptured spray, as if the breakers on the Lido shore had been frost-bound before they fell, and the sea-nymphs had inlaid them with coral and amethyst.

An upward or ascending movement governs all of creation. From the lowest level of inanimate nature exemplified by "pillars of variegated stones" to the vegetative sphere symbolized by "rooted knots of herbage, and drifting leaves of acanthus and vine," the façade rises upward to humanity and the angels, forming throughout a "continuous chain" of life.[16] But if this chain manifests an ascending hierarchy, it admits simultaneously the possibility of imperfection at each level. Yet for Ruskin

> imperfection is in some sort essential to all that we know of life. It is the sign of life in a mortal body, that is to say, of a state of progress and change. Nothing that lives is, or can be, rigidly perfect; part of it is decaying, part nascent. . . . And in all things that live there are certain irregularities and deficiencies which are not only signs of life, but sources of beauty. No human face is exactly the same in its lines on each side, no leaf perfect in its lobes, no branch in its symmetry. All admit irregularity as they imply change; and to banish imperfection is to destroy expression, to check exertion, to paralyze vitality. All things are literally better, lovelier, and more beloved for the imperfections which have been divinely appointed, that the law of human life may be Effort, and the law of human judgment, Mercy. (*Works* 10:203–4)

Imperfections imply the existence of grades or degrees of perfection. Such degrees, in turn, make us capable of discerning differences of rank among different classes and of quality between those of the same class. Through such discriminations we obtain pleasure from those that are highest or best. Thus Ruskin observes: "For I know not that if all things had been equally beautiful, we could have received the idea of beauty at all; or, if we had, certainly it had become a matter of indifference to us, and of little thought; whereas, through the beneficent ordering of degrees in its manifestation, the hearts of men are stirred by its occasional occurrence in its noblest form, and all their energies are awakened in pursuit of it, and endeavour to arrest or recreate it, for themselves" (*Works* 4:144).

The existence of gradations in Nature makes symbolism possible: by noticing differences of degree between one object or creature and another, we come to recognize certain ideal forms. But at the moment we perceive these we experience an apprehension of the beautiful, which is the perception of nature as expressive of those ideal forms that we know to exist in their pure state within the mind alone. In exemplifying them, nature becomes suggestive of a higher revelation than any it actually offers in itself.[17] In this fashion, the depiction of nature becomes a "continuous chain" of language as well as life. And indeed

it seems appropriate that, intermixed with the "rooted knots of herbage" and the "drifting leaves of acanthus and vine," there should be
"mystical signs, all beginning and ending in the Cross." Because finally
all of nature consists of such mystical or spiritual signs, all pointing
ultimately to some higher or sacred significance.

Above nature, however, there is the human sphere, represented in
the golden horses brought from Byzantium during the Fourth
Crusade and in the St. Mark's lion. These are the symbols of Venice,
of its long and passionate history, consecrated by time and preserved
as a supreme embodiment of tradition.[18] Above even these, at the highest
level of the façade, form dissolves into movement, and the eye perceives at last only light and color. In a similar fashion, Ruskin's whole
conception of symbolism culminates in a theory of color.[19] Thus he
can speak elsewhere in *The Stones of Venice* of the "nobleness" and "sacredness" of color (*Works* 10:172). And, further: "Of all God's gifts
to the sight of man, colour is the holiest, the most divine, the most
solemn. . . . All good colour is in some degree pensive, the loveliest
is melancholy, and the purest and most thoughtful minds are those
which love colour the most" (*Works* 10:173). For Ruskin the symbolic
quality of natural objects finds its highest expression in color. Color
is intrinsically expressive: it is the visible medium of emotion, of those
"just and mighty Passions" to which it imparts its own intensity. Nothing else can have such immediate meaning. Hence his claim that all
painting is for the sake of color (*Works* 11:218–19; 7:412), as well
as his elevation of Turner to a supreme rank among painters.[20]

Perhaps one of the most moving passages in *Modern Painters* occurs
near the end of the final volume, where, after discussing Turner's predecessors and their attempts at rendering light, Ruskin then sums up
Turner's own achievement: "He becomes, separately and without rival,
the painter of the loveliness and light of the creation." Which is to
say: "Of its loveliness: that which may be beloved in it, the tenderest,
kindest, most feminine of its aspects. Of its light: light not merely
diffused, but interpreted; light seen pre-eminently in colour" (*Works*
7:410). Claude and Cuyp had painted the sunshine; Turner alone, the
sun *color*.[21] One thinks of the symbolic resonances of this: all the meaning contained in color, now illuminated by pure light. Nothing more
is possible to the art of visual expression: it is as if the luminousness
had been absorbed into something transcending even color—the source
of all color, and hence of all significance. At this point the process of
symbolism achieves in Ruskin its ultimate fulfillment.

With the poetical works of Dante Gabriel Rossetti, we encounter another form of symbolism, one that transforms the nature of symbolism by employing material objects to intensify an emotion.[22] To be sure, the concrete embodiment of emotion in an image had been made use of many times before (notably by Keats in poems such as his Ode to Autumn—to take but one among innumerable instances). With Rossetti, however, the deliberate *excess* of the external real actually absorbs all poetic emotion. As a result, the external real ceases to express that emotion. Instead, the process of symbolism becomes conscious of itself. In so doing it brings about an "aestheticization" of emotion, in which the real subject of the poem becomes not the emotion but its embodiment in a material image that has now become even more real (i.e., more intense) than the emotion.

For Rossetti, however, the ultimate object of this aestheticization is not the creation of a self-conscious poetry about symbolism or its sources. What he seeks to express is rather a sense of life itself as capable of assimilation into art. In *The House of Life,* the emotions of the speaker are susceptible of arrangement into a sequence and thus of assuming a poetic form. We witness an instance of this in sonnet 2:

> As when desire, long darkling, dawns, and first
>   The mother looks upon the newborn child,
>   Even so my Lady stood at gaze and smiled
> When her soul knew at length the Love it nurs'd.
> Born with her life, creature of poignant thirst
>   And exquisite hunger, at her heart Love lay
>   Quickening in darkness, till a voice that day
> Cried on him, and the bonds of birth were burst.
>
> (*Works,* p. 75)

Here the process of physical birth subsumes the emotion it is meant to express through its own excessive realism: "The mother looks upon the newborn child" is indistinguishable from the scene of an actual birth, "creature of poignant thirst / And exquisite hunger" describes the moment of sexual passion that results in pregnancy, and "till a voice that day / Cried on him, and the bonds of birth were burst" conveys literally the agonies of childbirth. In all these lines, moreover, certain delicate ambiguities make it impossible to distinguish what is being talked about—the actual process of birth or the love such a birth embodies. Thus when "desire, long darkling, dawns," it is difficult to say whether this passage from darkness to light refers primarily to desire or to the process of birth by which a child passes from the darkness of the womb into the light. Even more ambiguous, perhaps, the voice which "that day / Cried on him"—whose voice? The mother's (either from the pain of childbirth or desire that her child be born), that of a divine or angelic presence (commanding the child's birth to take place, or signalizing that the time for birth has come), or perhaps, in some reflexive fashion, that of the child itself (the dawning of consciousness: the child screams, but remains objectively detached from its scream, not being yet fully self-conscious)? Such ambiguities color the emotion expressed: the predominant feeling of the opening lines of sonnet 2 is less that of the woman's love than of the suffering through which that love is finally realized.

But this embodiment of the poem's emotions within a physical process points to the emergence of a new form of symbolism.[23] Here we might consider, for instance, the moment in Flaubert's *L'Éducation sentimentale* when Deslauriers brutally announces Frédéric's anticipated marriage with Mlle Roque to Mme Arnoux. She rings her bell to have him thrown out; then, suffering from the shock of what she has just heard, rushes to the window for air. On the other side of the street she sees a workman in shirtsleeves nailing shut a crate. She closes the window and sits down again, but high adjacent buildings intercept the sunlight, and a chill air falls upon the apartment. Here her emotion finds complete embodiment in the visible scene: as if the crate (*caisse*) were a coffin or casket, and the somber light and coldness of the apartment, perfectly natural in themselves, become luminously expressive of a subjective mood. But if Mme Arnoux's emotion finds complete realization in an external scene, that realization implies in turn a new consecration of the visible world, as if, having become the medium of her emotion, it is thereby endowed with a sacred aura. With Flaubert, this process manifests itself fully only in the late *Trois contes,* especially "Un Coeur simple" and "La Légende de Saint Julien l'Hospitalier." With Rossetti, the same phenomenon appears in a relatively little-known sonnet, "For an Annunciation: Early German":

> The lilies stand before her like a screen
>   Through which, upon this warm and solemn day,
>   God surely hears. For there she kneels to pray
> Who wafts our prayers to God—Mary the Queen.
>
> She was Faith's Present, parting what had been
>   From what began with her, and is for aye.
>   On either hand, God's twofold system lay:
> With meek bowed face a Virgin prayed between.

> So prays she, and the Dove flies in to her,
>   And she has turned. At the low porch is one
>   Who looks as though deep awe made him to smile.
> Heavy with heat, the plants yield shadow there;
>   The loud flies cross each other in the sun;
>   And the aisled pillars meet the poplar-aisle.
>
> <div align="right">(<i>Works</i>, p. 166)</div>

The consciousness of a crucial moment fills the air: the Virgin stands at a parting of the ways, upon the threshold of an event that is about to change the course of historical time. "With meek bowed face" she "prayed between." But if the Virgin stands poised between two moments, one past, the other about to be, in another sense the lilies fulfill a similar function, standing "before her like a screen" between herself and God. By means of this similitude, it becomes possible to equate the two, seeing the lilies as a symbolic embodiment of the Virgin. What seems most striking about these lilies is the sense of their physical presence: by standing "like a screen" between God and the Virgin, they seem literally to separate an immaterial from a material presence. The "warm and solemn day," moreover, fills the air with a latent sensuousness, offset by the purity of the lilies. By being able to separate God and the Virgin, however, the lilies impart to God a physical presence, the effect of which is an intensified consciousness of nearness to divine being.

In the second stanza, the introduction of a bystander adds realism to the scene. But the climax of the episode occurs as the poem turns to what is visible outside the Virgin's house. We know the Dove has already flown in to her but are not vouchsafed a glimpse of what then takes place. All we now know is embodied in what we perceive: the languor of the air, which the heat has made heavy; the shadows of the plants, the flies that make the entire scene natural and real; and, finally, a formal motif—a row of pillars meeting a row of poplars.[24] All the emotion of the moment is concentrated and embodied in this vision. The stillness suggests serenity and peace, as of a quiet contentment with what must be; the formal motif, a perfect harmony, purposefulness of arrangement, the presence of a divine scheme. As with Flaubert's *L'Éducation sentimentale,* the visible scene becomes symbolically expressive of emotion.[25] Through the nature of that emotion, however, the visible world now becomes endowed with a sacred aura which is as a consecration of the material sphere through the transforming influence of the inspired consciousness that perceives it.[26]

The consecration of the visible: so we might also describe the feeling that was to lead the young Ernest Renan away from the Church he had been destined for in childhood, on to a lifelong quest for the historical sources of early Christianity and the religions of classical antiquity.[27] In his *Souvenirs d'Enfance et de Jeunesse* he recalls one of the turning points of his life, his years at the seminary of Issy. Of his reminiscences of this school perhaps none is more luminous than that of the park, "ce beau parc mystique d'Issy," in which he was to take some of the crucial steps leading to renunciation of the religious life:

> Je passais des heures sous ces longues allées de charmes, assis sur un banc de pierre et lisant. C'est là que j'ai pris (avec bien des rhumatismes peut-être) un goût extrême de notre nature humide, automnale, du nord de la France. . . . Mon premier idéal est une froide charmille janséniste du XVIIe siècle, en octobre, avec l'impression vive de l'air et l'odeur pénétrante des feuilles tombées. Je ne vois jamais une vieille maison française de Seine-et-Oise ou de Seine-et-Marne, avec son jardin aux palissades taillées, sans que mon imagination me représente les livres austères qu'on a lus jadis sous ces allées. Malheur à qui n'a senti ces mélancolies et ne sait combien de soupirs ont dû précéder les joies actuelles de nos coeurs! (*OC* 2:835)

> [I passed hours under these long walks of elms, sitting upon a stone bench and reading. It was there that I developed (with much rheumatism perhaps) an extreme taste for our humid, autumnal nature of northern France. . . . My first ideal was a cool Jansenist arbor of the seventeenth century, in October, with a vivid impression of the air and of the penetrating odor of fallen leaves. I never see an old French house of Seine-et-Oise or of Seine-et-Marne, with its garden of well-fashioned palisades, without picturing in my imagination the austere works one had once read under these walks. Unfortunate, those who have not felt these melancholy moods, and do not know how many sighs must have preceded the present joys of our hearts!]

There is a delicate sensuousness in autumn, that blends color and sunlight with the fragrance of dying leaves, a feeling of ripeness and the imminence of decay that make life all the sweeter. "Season of mists and mellow fruitfulness," Keats had exclaimed. More discreet than the overblown sensuality of summer, the sere air of autumn brings with it those finer pleasures in which the mind comes to share the exhilaration of the senses, where thought and emotion become fused with autumnal color and the vividness of an air that just perceptibly lingers on long declining afternoons. But precisely because in this temperate air thought merges with sensation, the reflections of Jansenist theology cease to appear merely as theological argument and assume the color of our moods at a particular moment. Thought becomes emotion: the feeling of restraint or renunciation carries (as Pascal might have observed) its own voluptuousness, one we appreciate especially in autumn in noticing how such restraint belongs to the very life of nature—in the receding of the vital tide from plants and trees, their preparation for decay and death. Fraught with these associations, renunciation ceases to seem harsh: its emotional accompaniment is a pensive melancholy that, as Ruskin remarks, is perhaps the finest mood of all.

From this standpoint, it is no longer necessary to experience abstract thinking abstractly. The rationalism that had dominated the religious speculation of Port-Royal ceases to exercise its force over Renan: abstract thought becomes but one means of apprehending the world.[28] For it is equally possible to experience the world through emotion. Thus the pleasure he receives in being introduced to secular literature at Saint-Nicolas du Chardonnet under M. Dupanloup after the ascetic discipline of his earlier studies is reproduced, in a sense, through his experience in the park of Issy. This same opposition, between a bright, attractive secularism and the monastic rigidity of abstract dogma runs through the *Souvenirs* like a leitmotiv. As Renan himself recognizes, secularism can often be shallower than the more austere forms of religion it seeks to deny. But the charm of this secularism lies in its appreciation of the beauty and sacredness of the visible world, the radiance that surrounds all the moments of our present existence when we experience the emotions of the present for what they are in themselves.

That is the theme, in part, of Renan's *Vie de Jésus,* which had sought to present in effect a secular Savior, affirming the beauty of the present moment and the profound joy of existence. We must be capable of responding to the appeal of the world, of the here and now, not for the sake of material gratification but for the enrichment of the mind through those higher emotions that come to all those who open themselves to the beauty of the present. For Renan, emotion *is* pleasure, and there is no other form of true pleasure. In this equation of emotion with pleasure we encounter the aesthetic impulse in him. The experience of the world in all its fullness comes about through emotion, which is finally nothing other than pleasure. But if emotion for Renan is the immediate source of pleasure, such emotion cannot be

Nadar, *Théophile Gautier* (1856).

pursued as an end in itself. It arises, rather, through a particular relation between the self and the external world, a relation that consists
of preserving one's openness to those impressions that come to us of
themselves.

With Ruskin, color had assumed a symbolic role through the emotions
it inspires. It yields for him an immediate impression not translatable
except through emotion—which is to say, through the subjective *experience* of meaning. It remains for Théophile Gautier to have discov-
ered the "secret affinities" (*affinités secrètes*) between color and other
symbolic phenomena like music. The poem "Variations sur le Carnaval
de Venise" contains a tribute to Paganini as one who—through the
magnificent virtuosity of his performances—makes it possible to perceive these affinities:

> Paganini, le fantastique,
> Un soir, comme avec un crochet,
> A ramassé le thème antique
> Du bout de son divin archet,
>
> Et, brodant la gaze fanée
> Que l'oripeau rougit encor,
> Fait sur la phrase dédaignée
> Courir ses arabesques d'or.
>
> (*Émaux et Camées*, p. 37)

> [Paganini, the fantastic,
> One night, as if with a hook,
> Brought back the antique theme
> With the end of his divine bow,
>
> And, embroidering the faded veil
> That finery still reddens,
> Made to run upon the disdained phrase
> His arabesques of gold.]

The "Carnaval de Venise," a popular Venetian song, is merely a "faded
veil," to which only a bit of finery (its charming theme) still lends
color and emotion. Upon this small touch of red, Paganini weaves his
magical variations or "arabesques of gold." Here the poem does not
simply *represent* an aesthetic effect (the impression of Paganini's performance upon the listener) but actually *creates* one: the juxtaposition
of red and gold transposes an aesthetic experience from the realm of
sound to that of color.[29]

That transposition is possible only by assuming affinities between

the different impressions we receive. But this assumption, and
Gautier's consequent "transposition," indicates a shift in the nature of
symbolism. For Ruskin, color means something intrinsically—we cannot express what it means in any other form because that meaning
corresponds to an attribute of color rather than to anything in our
impressions. With Gautier, on the other hand, the possibility of translating musical symbolism into color implies that the essence of either
inheres less in its medium than in our impression of it. Hence the
creative possibilities of symbolism. From this standpoint, symbolism
ceases to reflect (as it had earlier for the Romantics) an aspect of nature.[30] Instead it becomes a means of artistic expressiveness. By not
revealing the essence of nature or some higher presence, it becomes a
medium for transmuting impressions the artist receives into personal
expressions of mood or emotion. And perhaps this is, in part, the rationale for Gautier's transformation of symbolism. It becomes yet another argument in his crusade for the independence of art, of art for
art's sake, a doctrine he had advanced nearly two decades earlier in his
preface to *Mademoiselle de Maupin*.[31]

Of the aesthetic possibilities opened up by the idea of affinities,
there is perhaps no finer instance in Gautier's own work than the poem
"Symphonie en blanc majeur."[32] As Whistler was later to point out
concerning his own Nocturnes, a "harmony," or arrangement in a particular color, need not consist only of that color. Nevertheless, there
is a special intensity in the effect of white upon white, of one shade
of whiteness contrasted with another.[33] This becomes especially intense when one layer of whiteness is uncovered to reveal a greater,
more brilliant whiteness. Thus the "femmes-cygnes" (women-swans,
precursors of the swans of Mallarmé), singing and swimming near the
shores of the Rhine,

> Ou, suspendant à quelque branche
> Le plumage qui les revêt,
> Faire luire leur peau plus blanche
> Que la neige de leur duvet.
>
> (*Émaux et Camées*, p. 42)

> [Or, hanging upon some branch
> The plumage that clothes them,
> Display [lit., "make gleam"] their skin which is whiter
> Than the snow of their down.]

A similar effect occurs in Gautier's description of the body and dress
of one woman-swan in particular:

Son sein, neige moulée en globe,
Contre les camélias blancs
Et le blanc satin de sa robe
Soutient des combats insolents.

[Her breast, snow shaped as a globe,
Against the white camellias
And the white satin of her dress
Sustains provocative conflicts.]

Such intense whiteness is more than just a coloristic impression. Ultimately, it transforms itself into something like a "white" consciousness,

Conviant la vue enivrée
De sa boréale fraîcheur
A des régals de chair nacrée,
A des débauches de blancheur!

[Inviting the view intoxicated
With her boreal freshness
To feasts with flesh of mother-of-pearl,
To debauches of whiteness!]

This immersion in whiteness no longer affects the eye alone but rather the viewer's whole consciousness. In its debauches the mind loses itself in the splendor (sexual or aesthetic) embodied in the woman's fleshy whiteness. But perhaps the most remarkable tonal variation on whiteness occurs at the very end of the poem:

Sous la glace où calme il repose,
Oh! qui pourra fondre ce coeur!
Oh! qui pourra mettre un ton rose
Dans cette implacable blancheur!

[Under the ice where calmly it reposes,
Oh! who can melt that heart!
Oh! who can place a tint of rose
In this implacable whiteness!]

Previously the poem had developed an "aesthetic" of whiteness by evoking objects displaying this color. One might even go so far as to ask whether the contrast between these objects does not in fact create differing intensities of whiteness (a contrast made explicit in the above passages), and whether the poem, while seeming to concern itself only with whiteness (as absence of color) has not actually had color as its real subject—defined in terms of differing intensities of impression. Although the color of each object is white (and presumably there are no degrees of pure whiteness), the impression caused by each object possesses a unique intensity, distinguishing it from all others. Hence Gautier's idea of color depends specifically upon the subjective *impression* caused by an object rather than its actual color. What emerges is an apologia for impressionism, insofar as the poem manages to evoke a sense of differing intensities of whiteness in various objects, where there should be (strictly speaking) no difference at all. Which is to say: an apologia for the primacy of our impression of color over color itself.

But in reaching its conclusion the poem ironically reverses itself. What had previously seemed to constitute color, i.e., differing intensities of whiteness, now becomes absence of color—"this implacable whiteness." The reversal only indicates that, objectively, none of the various forms of white appearing earlier in the poem counts as color. Yet, in light of the poem's differing intensities of whiteness, this objective absence of color can only imply that color is essentially subjective. But if the phenomenon of color originates in the mind rather than in nature, color becomes a medium for the subjective art Gautier had sought to advocate. Whereas for Ruskin emotion expresses an impression of the external world, for Gautier emotion becomes purely aesthetic, i.e., a lyrical feeling not necessarily associated with any particular object. This is not to deny the link between the feeling embodied in color and a particular object. But for Gautier the lyricism of color lies in emotions rather than in the objects associated with them. It is a lyricism of "aesthetic" emotions that have themselves become as formal as elements in a work of art.

Perhaps nowhere is this more apparent than in the celebrated controversy between the painter J.A.M. Whistler and Ruskin, immortalized in Whistler's *The Gentle Art of Making Enemies*. Here the battle lines are distinctly drawn, between an art that sees colors as formally expressive and a criticism that regards them only as impressions of nature. And what of the object of this controversy? In his trial, Whistler had referred to his *Nocturne in Black and Gold* as an "artistic arrangement" (*The Gentle Art*, p. 3). Later, in an attack on literal representation in painting, he explains: "As music is the poetry of sound, so is painting the poetry of sight, and the subject-matter has nothing to do with harmony of sound or of colour" (*The Gentle Art*, p. 127). And subsequently: "Art should be independent of clap-trap—should stand alone, and appeal to the artistic sense of eye or ear, without confounding this with emotions entirely foreign to it, as devotion, pity, love, patriotism, and the like. All these have no kind of concern with it; and that is why I insist on calling my works 'arrangements' and 'harmonies'" (ibid., pp. 127–28).

Equally revealing is Whistler's trial testimony concerning his beautiful *Nocturne in Blue and Gold: Old Battersea Bridge*. Asked whether his painting is a correct representation of Battersea Bridge, the artist replies: "I did not intend it to be a 'correct' portrait of the bridge. It is only a moonlight scene and the pier in the centre of the bridge may not be like the piers at Battersea Bridge as you know them in broad daylight. As to what the picture represents that depends upon who looks at it. To some persons it may represent all that is intended; to others it may represent nothing" (ibid., p. 8). Even the subject of the work now becomes a matter of subjective interpretation. Nor is it possible to specify its prevailing color. "Perhaps" blue—but this too might be a subjective impression. If one considers the silhouette of the bridge as the dominant motif, that silhouette, examined under different lights, might easily seem more gray than blue. Likewise, the figures on top of the bridge may or may not be people, and—as Whistler concludes—his "whole scheme was to bring about a certain harmony of colour" (ibid.).

The culmination of these scattered assertions occurs in Whistler's famous "Ten O'Clock" lecture, where he defines the relation of art to nature:

> Nature contains the elements, in colour and form, of all pictures, as the keyboard contains the notes of all music.
>
> But the artist is born to pick, and choose, and group with science, these elements, that the result may be beautiful—as the musician gathers his notes, and forms his chords, until he bring forth from chaos glorious harmony. (*The Gentle Art*, pp. 142–43)

For Whistler, as for Gautier, colors assume a formal role within a composition.[34] And as with Gautier art employs color expressively rather than mimetically. With Whistler, however, the idea of harmony in a work suggests even richer possibilities. We recall his remark that a "harmony" need not consist solely of one color. In fact, his own Nocturnes offer instances of dynamic harmony based upon several colors of differing intensity. In the *Nocturne in Black and Gold*, a gleaming shower of gold falls from the sky while a brilliant yellow impasto illuminates the waterline. Flaring upward from the ship, swirls of fiery smoke glow with a foggy light. All the rest appears plunged in a bluish-black darkness that—in contrast to the gemlike clarity of a few luminous spots—displays a vague, diffuse quality like that of stains. Between these opposing motifs of light and darkness, a series of blue-gray washes imparts a soft glow to the night, harmonizing the light and color scheme of the composition.

In the *Nocturne in Blue and Gold,* Whistler develops a different kind of harmony. Here the entire painting seems to consist of a single color, its only contrast one of light and darkness that sets the bridge's dark silhouette against a luminous space of night and water. As if to heighten the nocturnal brightness, Whistler drops a soft shower of gold through the sky; on the shoreline, a few sharp gleams of reflected light intensify the radiance of a shimmering sea. The whole composition explores various tonal harmonies, establishing a gradual progression from darkness to light (rather than the dynamic opposition of the *Nocturne in Black and Gold*). Here, however, virtually all the colors are soft, the few sharp effects from fireworks and shorelights being muted and distant. Hence the emphasis upon tonal variations, while simultaneously preserving the work's overall harmony. Like the *Nocturne in Black and Gold,* then, if in a different sense, this Nocturne constitutes a triumphant demonstration of the possibilities of chromatic harmony.

One of the favorite arts of Aestheticism, besides painting, is theater. It figures in Henry James's *Tragic Muse,* in addition to being the principal object of his efforts during the decade 1890–1900; it enters into Oscar Wilde's *Picture of Dorian Gray* and forms the medium of most of his works.[35] Of the various works devoted to theatrical life, a special place belongs to Edmond de Goncourt's *La Faustin.* Proust alludes to it in *Le Temps retrouvé* (*À la recherche du temps perdu* 3:711), and Huysmans makes it the subject of an extravagant eulogy in *À Rebours* (*OC* 7:275–76). (For Huysmans, one may surmise, the theater offers a source of pleasure inasmuch as it constitutes the most *artificial* form of existence.) More than any of the other arts, theater brings to the forefront the whole problem of the relationship between art and life. The actor or actress embodies this problem: is the life enacted upon the stage a reproduction of actual life, the highest possible creation of realism insofar as it involves performance by a living individual, or is the performer's actual life but a shadow, finally, of his or her existence upon the stage?

In *La Faustin,* Edmond de Goncourt attempts to resolve this question. The novel focuses upon a celebrated French actress, Juliette Faustin, as she prepares to undertake the greatest of all French tragic roles: Racine's Phèdre. As she studies her part, she feels herself entering into the mood of Theseus' wife—a heightened consciousness of

sensual pleasure, of vivid impressions received from a flower's pene-
trating fragrance or the soft whisper of a seashell placed against one's
ear, ardent reveries merging with a furious desire to love. She wonders
if it is not necessary to fall in love again in order to impart to her role
the proper tenderness and fire. Thus the exigencies of art dictate to
life, shaping it to meet the demands of a higher, more intense form
of existence. When by accident La Faustin encounters her former
youthful lover, Lord Annandale, all her earlier passion is rekindled.
After a mediocre first-night performance, she vows on the second night
to play the role of Phèdre *for him*—as an expression of her own passion. Her performance is electrifying: the words of Racine no longer
speak to the public of Phèdre's love for Hippolytus but of Juliette's
for William, while all the audience struggles for a glimpse of the unknown figure concealed in the darkness of one of the boxes who is
the object of a grand actress's passion. In the second act, during Phèdre's
famous declaration of love, La Faustin's voice fails her. But the audience sees this only as the result of a soul's exhaustion by passion.
"Perhaps never," writes the author, "had the famous tirade produced
upon the spectators so powerful an impression." The climax of La
Faustin's whole illustrious career, it symbolizes the moment in which
art, through life, achieves its highest possible fulfillment.

The idea that art does more than reproduce life—indeed, it enhances, puri-
fies, transforms it. At the same time, without life, art alone is meaningless—a suave, polished performance, nothing more. In assimilating
real passion, it becomes expressive. But it also gives a *form* to La Faustin's
existence, by defining the form of her deepest affections. Thus the role
of Phèdre defines the relationship of La Faustin and Lord Annandale.
From this standpoint, his ultimate rejection of her as an actress even
in love is but ironic testimony to art's triumphant power to shape the
fundamental relations of human existence.

The idea that art should not only represent but transform life becomes the dominant theme of the work Arthur Symons would later
call "the breviary of the decadence": J.-K. Huysmans's *À Rebours*.[36] Its
subject: an aesthete's pursuit of the most refined and exquisite sensations. But these can come only from art. Indeed, for des Esseintes,
the protagonist of *À Rebours*, art consists of nothing more than this—
a source of the most exquisite sensations. The words of the Chimera
sum up perfectly his objective: "Je cherche des parfums nouveaux, des
fleurs plus larges, des plaisirs inéprouvés" (*OC* 7:163). [I seek new
perfumes, larger flowers, untasted pleasures.] We recall Wilde's Lord
Henry Wotton: "Be always searching for new sensations" (*The Picture
of Dorian Gray*, p. 23). For des Esseintes, as well as for Huysmans

himself at the time of *À Rebours,* only hitherto unfelt sensations can yield pleasure. What has already been experienced no longer excites.[37] And excitement, especially that which comes from subtle sensations, is essential to pleasure. Pleasure results simply from whatever stimulates consciousness.[38] What ceases to stimulate no longer affords pleasure. Hence the praise of decadent, sophisticated Latin authors such as Petronius or those who write in the declining twilight of Rome— Ausonius, Rutilius, Claudian. Through their somber, contorted style, their rejection of the ordinary senses of words or phrases, they offer more rarefied allurements, which a sensibility tired of the blandishments of simple pastoral existence or the virtues of *pietas* can appreciate—above all, the fascination of a poetry full of self-conscious artifice, one more concerned with its own art than with the things it ostensibly speaks of.[39]

Decadent literature, however, is but one of the sources of pleasure sought out by des Esseintes. Flowers, gems, art, music, even the solemn and soothing sensations afforded by witnessing religious ceremonies, all conspire to yield various forms of gratification.[40] What is necessary to all these is an emphasis upon the esoteric (whether in nature or in art), the *artificial,* that which manifests a complexity resulting from transformation of earlier, simpler forms.[41] Thus the narrator observes that almost never do perfumes derive from the flowers whose names they assume; the artist who would dare to create a perfume from natural sources alone would produce but a poor imitation, considering that the essence obtained by a distillation of flowers offers but a remote analogy to an actual flower's intense fragrance (*OC* 7:170– 71). Hence the impossibility of mirroring nature in art; instead, art should strive for the most artificial, that which reflects its own essence. For des Esseintes, "le tout est . . . de savoir s'abstraire suffisamment pour amener l'hallucination et pouvoir substituer le rêve de la réalité à la réalité même" (*OC* 7:34–35). [The main thing is . . . to know how to abstract oneself sufficiently in order to elicit the hallucination and substitute the dream of reality for reality itself.] Thus "artifice appeared to des Esseintes the distinctive mark of genius in man" (*OC* 7:35). His ideal: not even artificial flowers that imitate the actual, but rather actual ones that imitate the artificial (*OC* 7:134).[42]

The pursuit of new sensations and impressions rapidly assumes the nature of a quest, since what has previously been experienced no longer satisfies.[43] At the same time, memory cannot retain earlier sensations or impressions in their original freshness. Hence the constant desire for new sensations, without which the self loses its animation. In effect we become intensely conscious only in experiencing something distinctly different from what we already know: only then do we feel the excitement of actual experience. In his quest for new sensations, however, what attracts des Esseintes is not so much a sensation but rather the *idea* embodied in it.[44] Which is to say: the idea of a particular fragrance rather than the physical sensation it produces. But ultimately, not even the idea is worth pursuing, since, once known, it ceases to satisfy. *Only the sensation of experience caused by the introduction of a new idea* yields pleasure. In this sense, the ultimate object of Huysmans's aestheticism is the sensation of consciousness itself.

The pursuit of an aestheticism of consciousness necessarily creates a void that must be filled: as soon as an idea has been "experienced," the sensation it inspires disappears, without the possibility of our ever fully recapturing it. Hence the need for new "ideas"—i.e., new sensations. But given the limits of human existence, the quest for new sensations becomes increasingly difficult. At the same time, the desire for them intensifies. Since the objective of his quest is not the idea of a thing but simply an intensification of his own consciousness, it is only natural for des Esseintes to ask himself whether another means might not achieve the same effect. He then considers religion, especially Catholicism. Earlier, he had already noticed that his own mode of existence was strikingly similar to that of a monk (*OC* 7:101–2). On closer examination he finds that

> la sympathie qu'il conservait pour ses anciens maîtres arrivait à le faire s'intéresser à leurs travaux, à leurs doctrines; ces accents inimitables de la conviction, ces voix ardentes d'hommes d'une intelligence supérieure lui revenaient, l'amenaient à douter de son esprit et de ses forces. (*OC* 7:117)

> [the sympathy he preserved for his old masters caused him to interest himself in their work, in their doctrines; those inimitable accents of conviction, those ardent voices of men of a superior intelligence came back to him, brought him to doubt his own mind and his strengths.]

He finds himself attracted to the rituals and ceremonies of the Church, with all their weight of tradition and the infinite vastness of music that accompanies them, "lamentable et tendre." Thus the road that was to lead to Huysmans's conversion to Catholicism becomes clear.[45] Indeed, in *À Rebours,* even sadism is perceived merely as an inverted form of Catholicism, "l'inobservance des préceptes catholiques qu'on suit même à rebours" [the nonobservance of Catholic precepts that one nevertheless follows in a contrary or reverse fashion].[46] From such a standpoint, it is entirely appropriate that the novel should end with a prayer: "Seigneur, prenez pitié du chrétien qui doute, de l'incrédule qui voudrait croire, du forçat de la vie qui s'embarque seul, dans la nuit, sous un firmament que n'éclairent plus les consolants fanaux du vieil espoir!" (*OC* 7:337). [Lord, take pity upon a Christian who doubts, upon a sceptic who wants to believe, upon a convict of life who embarks alone, in the night, under a firmament no longer illuminated by the consoling beacons of the old hope!][47]

In a chapter of *À Rebours* devoted to criticism of contemporary French authors, we are told that "despite their magnificent form, despite the imposing allure of his verses which drew themselves up with such brilliance that even the hexameters of Hugo seemed, in comparison, dismal and dull," the poetry of Leconte de Lisle had ceased to satisfy des Esseintes (*OC* 7:286). And, from our perspective, it can indeed seem that there is little in Leconte de Lisle or the "École parnassienne" of any importance for Aestheticism. His evocation of the heartless immensities of space and the purposeless motions of atoms, the puerile conversations between a rising yet barbaric Christianity and an elegant, cultured paganism in decline no longer move us.[48]

   But there is one poem which stands out from the mass of his *oeuvre*. Grouped among the "Poésies diverses" of the *Poèmes Antiques,* "Midi" possesses a sensuousness and a fullness of color difficult to find elsewhere in Leconte de Lisle:

> Midi, Roi des étés, épandu sur la plaine,
> Tombe en nappes d'argent des hauteurs du ciel bleu.
> Tout se tait. L'air flamboie et brûle sans haleine;
> La Terre est assoupie en sa robe de feu.

> *(Oeuvres* 1:290)

> [Noon, King of summers, poured out upon the plain,
> Falls in sheets of silver from the heights of a blue sky.
> Everything is hushed. The air flames and burns without breath;
> The Earth is drowsy in its robe of fire.]

A moment of stillness reigns. But it is a stillness of intense consciousness: an immense expanse of fields of ripened grain, like an "ocean of gold," "fearlessly drink the cup of the Sun." In this landscape of brilliant light, there are no shadows offering relief to the few creatures that inhabit the scene. This moment of intensest consciousness is one of supreme clarity, in which everything strikes the eye or affects the senses with a vividness of impression resulting from an absence of external associations or subjective emotions.[49] To those disillusioned with tears or laughter, affected by the forgetfulness of a feverish world, who long only to taste a supreme and melancholy voluptuousness, the poem replies:

> Viens! Le soleil te parle en paroles sublimes;
> Dans sa flamme implacable absorbe-toi sans fin;
> Et retourne à pas lents vers les cités infimes,
> Le coeur trempé sept fois dans le Néant divin.

(Oeuvres 1:291)

> [Come! The sun speaks to you in sublime words;
> In its implacable flame absorb yourself endlessly;
> Return slowly to mean or lowly cities,
> Your heart steeped seven times in the divine Nothingness.]

For Leconte de Lisle, the implacable sunlight symbolizes intensity of vision. Like Pater, he could say that intensity was everything: a light of consciousness that illuminates all objects in its clear brilliance until things themselves become but reflecting surfaces for a moment of pure transparence. In this vision there is no appeal to the soft harmonies of color, the falling mist of twilight, or whatever else composes the charm of the world. Only in the intensity of consciousness that it brings to its perception do we receive glimpses of a possible aestheticism in Leconte de Lisle.

What Huysmans had said of Leconte de Lisle in *À Rebours* might also, with some justice, be applied to the French Parnassian's English counterpart: Algernon Swinburne. In his *Education,* Henry Adams recalls the extraordinary impression made upon him by his first meeting with Swinburne at the country house of Richard Monckton Milnes: "Then, at last, if never before, Adams acquired education. What he had sought so long, he found; but he was none the wiser; only the more astonished. For once, too, he felt at ease, for the others were no less astonished than himself, and their astonishment grew apace. For the rest of the evening Swinburne figured alone . . . after dinner, all sat . . . till far into the night, listening to the rush of Swinburne's talk. In a long experience, before or after, no one ever approached it. . . . They could not believe his incredible memory and knowledge of literature, classic, mediaeval, and modern; his faculty of reciting a play of Sophocles or a play of Shakespeare, forward or backward, from end to beginning; or Dante, or Villon, or Victor Hugo" (*The Education,* p. 140).

Of this brilliant promise, the written works represent but a meager fulfillment. One feels that—like Leconte de Lisle—Swinburne has been seduced into worship of a chaste and pure *beau idéal* burdened with classical erudition and transformed finally into something quite dull. All the attempts at color, the contorted, difficult style, the straining for extravagant effects, seem like excrescences upon what is essentially a futile scheme for renewing classicism—a classicism which is, to be sure, more influenced by Homeric archaicism and the Greek tragic style than by an earlier neoclassicism, but one in which all efforts at transposing the consciousness of that antique world come to seem quite artificial.[50] One might well ask why, with such splendid resources and aspirations, Swinburne fails to achieve more—in particular, why one does not encounter in him either an aestheticism of consciousness (Rossetti, Renan, Huysmans) or an aestheticism of form (Ruskin, Gautier, Whistler). Apart from the melodrama of poems like "Faustine," the problem with Swinburne lies precisely in the straining of each line for effect (in reading him, one feels instinctively what Adams must have felt in listening to his "rhetorical recitation" of his ballads, which he "declaimed as though they were books of the Iliad"); hence the presence of much sensuousness and even beauty in individual lines, without any of the deeper aesthetic tendencies.[51] The overall impression: a lack of vision. From this we see that aestheticism consists of something more than mere sensuousness. It can be receptive and subjective (consciousness) or it can be in some sense objective (form), but in either case it presupposes an assimilation of life into literature, the transformation of our existence into something like a work of art.[52]

In his Nocturnes, Whistler had sought to create harmonies of color with an effect similar to that of music. Here the "musical" effect, as we have seen, involves a dissociation of color from the object it modifies. It thus becomes expressive like a musical motif, capable of formal relation to others. In his *Appreciations*, Pater had declared that all the arts aspire to the condition of music. From this standpoint, it seems strange to see the French poet Paul Verlaine actually *opposing* music to color, as he does in his celebrated "Art poétique." He begins with an affirmation of music:

> De la musique avant toute chose,
> Et pour cela préfère l'Impair
> Plus vague et plus soluble dans l'air,
> Sans rien en lui qui pèse ou qui pose.

> (*Oeuvres poétiques complètes,* p. 326)

[Music above all else,
And for this prefer the Uneven
More vague and more soluble in air,
Without anything in it which weighs or which poses.]

The "Uneven" (*l'Impair*) violates symmetry and proportion—hence
sins against neoclassical canons. "The Uneven" might refer to a poem's
metrical scheme or a more general absence of form. That formal imperfection should be associated with music is significant. It implies
that, for Verlaine, music consists of movement, rhythmic *élan*—above
all, whatever is more expressive. Hence it should be "more vague."
Here we perceive something like Ruskin's praise of Turner's indis-
tinctness, what he had termed "Turnerian Mystery." Such music should
be "soluble in air," like a mist that evaporates without leaving a trace
of itself.

The form of this music, then, is self-effacing; once past, it leaves
nothing but an impression of movement and lightness. Above all,
lightness! "Sans rien en lui qui pèse ou qui pose." Because that which
poses, that which gestures or declaims, is heavy and dull—nothing but
poetic rhetoric. But the absence of weight? Doesn't this also imply
absence of substance? Yet the music Verlaine speaks of should be capable of dissolving in air: its essence, then, consists of an *impression,*
but—unlike the color-impressions of Gautier or Whistler—one whose
expression disappears, leaving only a feeling, an impression of indescribable fineness. Hence Verlaine's opposition to color, which retains
a certain definiteness:

> Car nous voulons la Nuance encor,
> Pas la Couleur, rien que la nuance!
> Oh! la nuance seule fiance
> Le rêve au rêve et la flûte au cor!
>
> (*Oeuvres poétiques complètes*, p. 327)

[Because we want yet more Nuance,
No color, nothing but nuance!
Oh! nuance alone betroths
Dream to dream and the flute to the horn!]

A nuance is not a thing in itself: it is only a shade, a tone, a modulation of sound or color. It consists of what softens an outline, the
shadow of a contour, a transition from one note to the next. It contains nothing definite, depending for its perception upon what it modifies. Color opposes nuance insofar as it (color) possesses a definite

quality or attribute. In a spectrum composed solely of nuances, one
could no longer distinguish one tint from another. Each would possess
something of the rest, and the whole might be equated with any of
its individual shades. Whistler, of course, had employed tints of this
kind in his Nocturnes but set against or contrasted with solid colors:
the brilliant gold of the fireworks, the deep bluish blackness of night.
For Verlaine, a nuance "harmonizes" in a similar sense, forming a transition between disparate objects (one dream and another, or the soft
tones of a flute and the mellow, brassy richness of a horn). But he
seeks to create a kind of poem in which these disparate elements disappear, dissolving into a modulation that blends them together so that
we are conscious, finally, only of this modulation and the splendid
harmony it achieves. As a result, the movement of harmonization becomes the poem's real theme. The poem "Chanson d'automne" (from
Poèmes saturniens) exemplifies such a movement precisely:

> Les sanglots longs
> Des violons
>   De l'automne
> Blessent mon coeur
> D'une langueur
>   Monotone.
>
> (*Oeuvres poétiques complètes*, p. 72)
>
> [The long sobbings
> Of the violins
>   Of autumn
> Wound my heart
> With a languor
>   Monotonic.]

The breaking-up of normally longer lines emphasizes the disparity
between different elements introduced by the opening stanza: music,
languor or sadness, autumn.[53] The effect of such abrupt line divisions
is, however, to manifest the poetic harmony that blends such disparate
"notes" together. In reading these lines, one ceases to be conscious of
disparities: instead, through an imperceptible series of modulations,
reading passes from one motif to the next, noticing only the "coloring"
each imparts to the poem's progression.

Like the "violin which shudders like a heart that one afflicts" of
Baudelaire's "Harmonie du soir," the "long sobbings" of the violins
in "Chanson d'automne" depict an outpouring of passion. These "long
sobbings" cannot be musical in the ordinary sense—they are too dis-

cordant, too harsh and piercing, like a prolonged scream. As such they express merely emotion rather than harmony. But the addition "of autumn" produces a curious effect. The "violins of autumn" have no sound: autumn, with its gradual, almost imperceptible changes, is silent. Thus the "long sobbings of the violins of autumn" offer only a soundless threnody for life which passes away with autumn's decline.[54] And because autumn evokes in this fashion the transience of things, it can also inspire nostalgia for the past, for the brightness of moments now irretrievably lost. Perhaps this is why such silent sobbings "wound" the heart of the speaker. Their effect, however, is curiously one of "languor monotonic." One wonders how the expression of so much passion can result in such a subdued response. Perhaps it is because the nostalgia of autumn recalls something felt many times before—so often that the heart is now insensible to its pain, feeling only a heavy dullness in its place. For that heart, nostalgia always strikes the same note—hence its "monotonic" quality. The "long sobbings" of violins end, then, in a monotone.

Here there can be no question of audible harmony: the only "music" consists of the falling cadences of the lines, corresponding thematically to a declining intensity in the emotion from its passionate outbreak into indifferent acceptance. Such "music" leaves no trace except an impression of graceful movement through a series of motifs expressive of emotional "nuances." Thus the poem manifests a quintessential lightness, the faintest, most delicate suggestion of all.

A later poem ("Mandoline") attempts an even subtler effect—to create a feeling of music through a series of visual motifs where the only explicit musical allusion comes from the description of a Watteau painting that depicts lovers in a pastoral scene listening to the playing of a mandolin:

> Les donneurs de sérénades
> Et les belles écouteuses
> Échangent des propos fades
> Sous les ramures chanteuses.
>
> (*Oeuvres poétiques complètes*, p. 115)
>
> [The givers of serenades
> And the beautiful listeners
> Exchange some pale remarks
> Under the singing branches.]

Only the branches are "singing"; the lovers merely engage in dull talk. Their remarks are "pale" in more than one sense: the term "fade" ("des propos fades") can also refer to the faded quality of the painting. Yet if the conversation seems dull, the listeners are nevertheless beautiful, and in the poem's conclusion their beauty achieves its apotheosis:

> Leurs courtes vestes de soie,
> Leurs longues robes à queues,
> Leur élégance, leur joie
> Et leurs molles ombres bleues
>
> Tourbillonnent dans l'extase
> D'une lune rose et grise,
> Et la mandoline jase
> Parmi les frissons de brise.
>
> (*Oeuvres poétiques complètes*, p. 116

[Their short jackets of silk,
Their long gowns with trains,
Their elegance, their joy
And their soft blue shadows

Whirl round in the ecstasy
Of a moon in rose and gray
And the mandolin gossips
Amid the shivers of a breeze.]

One can only imagine the brilliance of these jackets (*vestes*) as they absorb the light in their cool silken folds; painting alone can render their smooth, sensuous surface and soft colors. And then the long gowns with trains form a visual counterpoint to the jackets' shortness, creating a vivid contrast with the greenness of the grass. This is elegance, which gives joy to those who create it.[55] One can almost feel how the verses' alternating cadence reflects the movement of these figures—the grace of their walk, the sparkle in their glances.

At this point the movement of the verse slows down, as if to mirror the lengthening of the shadows, those "soft blue shadows" that produce enchanting harmonies of color. But these shadows are lifted up into a chaos of color, mingling with rose and gray, in a kaleidoscopic motion that recalls Baudelaire's "Harmonie du soir":

> Les sons et les parfums tournent dans l'air du soir;
> Valse mélancolique et langoureux vertige!
>
> [Sounds and fragrances whirl about in the evening air;
> Melancholy waltz and languorous vertigo!]

Here the soft vocables of "leurs molles ombres bleues" ignite a dazzling resonance of consonants that in turn evokes a vision of pure
colors. The moon could not possibly be rose and gray, but that no
longer matters: all that matters now is the uplifting motion that meta-
morphoses this painted scene into a scintillating play of light and color.
The mandolin itself ceases to matter: it merely "gossips" amid the shiv-
erings of a breeze. The real "music" of the scene consists of something
else: a "tourbillonnement" that transforms color into iridescent motifs.
We recall how in his "Art poétique" Verlaine had insisted, "Pas la
Couleur, rien que la nuance!" Here the value of color lies not in its
precise chromatic qualities but rather in its being suggestive. Above
all, there is a progression through various experiences, culminating finally in one supreme apprehension: a feeling of acceding to the rhythm
of the verse and the beautiful world it depicts, which in turn offers
glimpses of a higher harmony, a concurrence of light, sound, and
movement in expressive arrangement that gives us a sense of our whole
existence as assimilated into a formal sequence of time, transforming
that existence into something luminously beautiful.

> Of all this that was being done to complicate his education, he
> knew only the color of yellow. He first found himself sitting on
> a yellow kitchen floor in strong sunlight. He was three years old
> when he took this earliest step in education; a lesson of color.
> The second followed soon; a lesson of taste. On December 3,
> 1841, he developed scarlet fever. For several days he was as good
> as dead, reviving only under the careful nursing of his family.
> When he began to recover strength, about January 1, 1842, his
> hunger must have been stronger than any other pleasure or pain,
> for while in after life he retained not the faintest recollection of
> his illness, he remembered quite clearly his aunt entering the sick-
> room bearing in her hand a saucer with a baked apple. (*The Ed-
> ucation,* p. 5)

Such are, for Henry Adams, the beginnings of education. Earlier
we have seen how color possesses for someone like Ruskin an immediate symbolic significance. A symbolism of colors emerges in which
each tint in nature inspires a particular emotion. For Gautier and
Whistler, this symbolism belongs to the realm of art; color becomes
a formal motif, capable of yielding aesthetic harmonies when combined with others. At a still later period, color even becomes expressive
of the drama of human situations, as in the works of Alphonse Daudet.

With Adams, however, all traces of such symbolism disappear. If color evokes any emotion, that emotion is only a measure of our subjective response to external appearances. Nevertheless, that Adams's first lesson should be a "lesson of color" seems revealing: it could have been a "lesson in light," since the child finds himself sitting on a kitchen floor illuminated by "strong sunlight." But the sunlight would have imparted a sensation not only of brightness but also of warmth. The effect of the whole, the light intensifying the color of the floor and flooding the room with a warm radiance, would have produced a certain sensuousness. And perhaps this has something to do with why the impression was registered as a "lesson of color." The color yellow, intensified by the sunlight, preserves the memory of warmth and hence of the sensuous pleasure of basking in its brilliance. A similar phenomenon might be said to occur with the child's second lesson, a "lesson of taste." Of the sensations of his illness Adams professes to have no recollection. Yet the experience of these at the time must have sharpened his desire for the apple, heightening the pleasure of actually eating it. His image of the baked apple being brought in preserves a remembrance of this pleasure. In both instances, what is retained is the memory of a moment of sensuousness, the pleasurable feeling that comes from the mind's response to particular sensations caused by external phenomena at a given point in its existence. Here the ultimate cause of that pleasure remains unknown. Perhaps even the actual feeling of pleasure is hardly recognized as such. Nevertheless, the remembrance of the moment attests to its importance.

The experience of sensuousness at a fleeting moment of existence elicits a desire to prolong that moment, so as to be able to taste its emotion more fully. Were it possible to immerse oneself in it completely, the result would be an obliteration of time, a transcendence of that process by which we experience all sensations as evanescent. This transcendence would, however, be lacking in form: in identifying completely with the emotion of a moment, what one loses is ultimately a sense of the relation of that moment to all the others in one's life, hence the perception of that moment's meaning. But if this sense can come only from perceiving a moment's relation to others, our apprehension of meaning must become in effect an apprehension of form. This apprehension of form appears for the first time in Adams's chance recognition of the movement of a Beethoven symphony during his stay in Berlin:

> Sitting thus at his beer-table, mentally impassive, he was one day surprised to notice that his mind followed the movement of a

Sinfonie. He could not have been more astonished had he suddenly read a new language. Among the marvels of education, this
was the most marvellous. A prison-wall that barred his senses on
one great side of life, suddenly fell, of its own accord, without
so much as his knowing when it happened. Amid the fumes of
coarse tobacco and poor beer, surrounded by the commonest of
German Haus-frauen, a new sense burst out like a flower in his
life, so superior to the old senses, so bewildering, so astonished
at its own existence, that he could not credit it, and watched it
as something apart, accidental, and not to be trusted. (*The Education*, pp. 80–81)

The surprise of this discovery is amplified by its having come without effort on his part. "Mentally impassive," not knowing how or when
it happened, the narrator might indeed wonder if such a perception
can count as a genuine intellectual apprehension of form. Arising,
moreover, out of the coarsest circumstances, it necessarily signifies
something quite different from those moments of sensuousness he had
experienced before: the sense of an inner coherence, an underlying
theme running through all the confused mass of sounds and imparting
to them a hidden significance that becomes clear only when one can
discern their implicit relation to each other. Whereas moments of sensuousness evoke a longing to transcend time, however, the perception
of form in music emerges precisely in and through the experience of
a temporal sequence. On account of its nature such a perception might
for Adams aptly symbolize another: that in which one sees the hidden
relation or "theme" unifying all the disparate moments of an individual's existence.[56]

But if this first, accidental apprehension of form is meant as a kind
of leitmotiv for subsequent experiences, it remains without echo
throughout the first half of the narrative. In part it seems necessary
for the narrator to undergo certain other experiences first: the encounter with Swinburne, the exposure to Lyell and uniformitarianism,
the aporia that results from his father's dealings as minister with Pal-
merston, Gladstone, and Russell. Above all there is the horror of his
sister's death from tetanus, the consequence of a cab accident at the
Bagni di Lucca:

The hot Italian summer brooded outside, over the market-place
and the picturesque peasants, and, in the singular color of the
Tuscan atmosphere, the hills and vineyards of the Apennines
seemed bursting with midsummer blood. The sickroom itself
glowed with the Italian joy of life; friends filled it; no harsh

northern lights pierced the soft shadows; even the dying woman shared the sense of the Italian summer, the soft, velvet air, the humor, the courage, the sensual fulness of Nature and man. She faced death, as women mostly do, bravely and even gaily, racked slowly to unconsciousness, but yielding only to violence, as a soldier sabred in battle. For many thousands of years, on these hills and plains, Nature had gone on sabring men and women with the same air of sensual pleasure. (*The Education*, p. 288)

An irrational conjunction of circumstances mixes the sensuousness that had given a mysterious allure to past moments of his life with the unspeakable ordeal of watching his sister die in convulsions after ten days of hellish suffering. The sensuous fullness of summer still yields pleasure, but one can no longer desire to prolong it or the moment: even the desire ceases to make sense. At this point all reasoning, all understanding breaks down: "For the first time, the stage-scenery of the senses collapsed; the human mind felt itself stripped naked, vibrating in a void of shapeless energies, with resistless mass, colliding, crushing, wasting, and destroying what these same energies had created and labored from eternity to perfect" (*The Education*, p. 288).

The lacuna that ensues after the following year covers a span of two decades. In one respect at least, it seems inevitable, since with the death of Adams's sister "the last lesson," the "sum and term of education," had been reached. But this is education only in a passive sense, the sense in which one submits to external events.[57] What remains to be acquired is the education which consists of an explicit recognition of that process: "The sum of force attracts; the feeble atom or molecule called man is attracted; he suffers education or growth; he is the sum of the forces that attract him; his body and his thought are alike their product; the movement of the forces controls the progress of his mind, since he can know nothing but the motions which impinge on his senses, whose sum makes education" (*The Education*, p. 474). The sum of force attracts, and the feeble atom or molecule called man is attracted, but he ceases simply to suffer education or growth at the moment he perceives forces as such and defines them in terms of their attractive power upon the mind. He thus transforms them from something completely external to the mind into something apprehensible as thought.[58] By defining force as that which attracts, he translates its nature into one of mind, which can feel an attraction only to what acts within the same medium as itself—the medium of thought. In transforming forces into something apprehensible as thought, however, the mind ultimately makes possible its own assimilation of them.

For this reason Adams can seek to persuade concerning the virtues of Lord Bacon's approach: "He urged society to lay aside the idea of evolving the universe from a thought, and to try evolving thought from the universe. The mind should observe and register forces—take them apart and put them together—without assuming unity at all" (*The Education*, p. 484).

Here, observing and registering forces consists of measuring the attraction they exert upon the mind. In the process, what the mind ultimately discovers is its own development. As the record of movements of force, consciousness necessarily attains a definite form. By being apprehended within the medium of thought, all such movements inherently possess a specifiable relation to each other. Perception of this relation leads to the crowning recognition: "Thought alone was Form. Mind and Unity flourished or perished together" (*The Education*, p. 429). Thought alone is Form because it alone offers a medium through which to apprehend forces and hence their relation to each other.[59] Here the apprehension of forces necessarily implies apprehending their relation, since it is by means of relation that the mind ultimately grasps them.[60] But this perception of relation is in effect nothing other than what had come to Adams years earlier in the Berlin café while following the movement of a Beethoven Sinfonie. Like his earlier perception, the present one discerns the existence of a sequence in the expression of forces comparable to the sequence of notes that constitutes a phrase or a movement. As with music, moreover, the perception of an intrinsic pattern in events makes possible the recognition of sequence. But whereas the apprehension of form in music can possess at best only a symbolic significance, the present recognition touches directly upon the narrator's whole existence. If that existence consists of his attraction by various forces, the perception of a sequence within the series of these attractions suffices to assimilate them to the nature of mind, thus transforming life into the intellectual element of form.

In his recognition of thought as form, the narrator asserts that "Mind and Unity flourished or perished together." Yet subsequently he can feel impelled to ask: "What was Unity? Why was one to be forced to affirm it?" (*The Education*, p. 431). If mind and unity can be said to flourish or perish together, their common course suggests that unity must partake in some sense of the nature of mind, which is to say that it belongs to mind rather than to the realm of external phenomena. But mind consists, as we have seen, of that which "suffers education or growth," the attraction of forces whose movement governs its development, since it can know nothing but the motions that impinge on the senses, whose sum is said to make education. Hence the history of an individual mind must be that of the attractions exerted upon it by various forces. If such attractions express themselves as thought, however, to compel thought to assume the shape of unity would imply exercising a control over those forces. Since unity does not exist in nature, to create it in thought means nothing less than subsuming force to mind. For Adams, then, the affirmation of unity in no way implies belief in its intrinsic existence in nature. On the contrary, unity manifests simply the constructive will of the mind. If thought begins merely as the passive reception of impressions caused by external forces, the ordering of thought into unity is an active assertion of the mind, attesting to its dominance over nature. But in exerting control over the attractive forces that influence it, the self acquires simultaneously the possibility of shaping the whole of its past existence, insofar as that existence is summed up in the history of its thoughts. To order or define the relation of its thoughts to each other, then, becomes for the self a means of transforming all the moments of lived experience, of past pleasure or of past suffering, into the permanent coherence of form.

Hence the necessity for something like a dynamic theory of history, which concerns itself with "the development and economy of Forces" (*The Education,* p. 474). In order to control external forces, one must first understand the economy that governs their expression.[61] Yet even the dynamic theory which describes this economy is merely a means of achieving that unity of thought which is the mind's ultimate objective.[62] To understand the economy of force leads to the possibility of giving form to that economy as thought. But to express this economy as theory exemplifies the possibility of subsuming force to the element of mind. If a theory of the economy of force encompasses a knowledge of all of force's past expressions, the theory of force's economy becomes tantamount to subsuming history itself to mind. At the same time, however, the mind does not simply recapitulate the lived experience of past moments. Instead, by defining these moments as expressions not only of force but of an economy of force, it imposes an intellectual form upon them. But this imposition of form is, in the last analysis, nothing else than a recapitulation on the collective scale of what the narrator of *The Education* has done for his individual life: not merely to re-create it as the sum of all the past moments of his existence but rather to give to those moments a permanent and meaningful form.

Color intensified by light: with this impression consciousness begins in *The Education.* Hence it seems only appropriate that a similar impression should crown the vision of Chartres which forms the centerpiece of *Mont Saint Michel and Chartres*. The glory of Chartres lies in its windows, and the glory of those windows consists above all of their blue. On this subject Adams quotes Viollet-le-Duc (translating freely, as he says), and we, to appreciate the effect Adams himself seeks to achieve here, may quote him:

> The blue is the light in windows, and light has value only by opposition. . . . But it is also that luminous color which gives value to all others. . . . So the composition of blue glass singularly preoccupied the glass-workers of the twelfth and thirteenth centuries. If there is only one red, two yellows, two or three purples, and two or three greens at the most, there are infinite shades of blue, . . . and these blues are placed with a very delicate observation of the effects they should produce on other tones, and other tones on them. . . . The blue tone of the principal subject [i.e., the ground of the Tree of Jesse] has commanded the tonality of all the rest. This medium was necessary to enable the luminous splendor to display its energy. This primary condition has dictated the red ground for the prophets, and the return to the blue on reaching the outside semicircular band. To give full value both to the vigor of the red, and to the radiating transparency of the blue, the ground of the corners is put in emerald green; but then, in the corners themselves, the blue is recalled and is given an additional solidity of value by the delicate ornamentation of the squares. (*Novels*, pp. 461–62)[63]

With too intense direct sunlight the windows are said to suffer in effect. They become "a cluster of jewels—a delirium of colored light" (p. 468). The positive or negative value of these effects leads in turn to a discussion of the relative merits of line as opposed to color. Of this controversy, frequently renewed in the history of art, Adams remarks:

> we can leave Delacroix and his school to fight out the battle they began against Ingres and his school, in French art, nearly a hundred years ago, which turned in substance on the same point. Ingres held that the first motive in color-decoration was line, and that a picture which was well drawn was well enough colored. Society seemed, on the whole, to agree with him. Society in the twelfth century agreed with Delacroix. The French held then that the first point in color-decoration was color, and they never hesitated to put their color where they wanted it, or cared whether a green

camel or a pink lion looked like a dog or a donkey provided they got their harmony or value. (*Novels*, p. 468)[64]

Here even light is subordinated to color, its whole purpose being one of intensifying, increasing, glorifying color: "If the Tree of Jesse teaches anything at all, it is that the artist thought first of controlling his light, but he wanted to do it not in order to dim the colors; on the contrary, he toiled, like a jeweller setting diamonds and rubies, to increase their splendor" (ibid., p. 463). For the twelfth-century glass-worker, then, the jeweled effect of a "delirium of colored light" did not seem to pose a problem. On the contrary, the artist appears to have reveled in it. Similarly, we are told that "under the protection of the Empress Virgin, Saint Bernard himself could have afforded to sin even to drunkenness of color" (ibid., p. 467). Yet this extravagant display is not without purpose. Looked at more closely, the colors of the windows become more and more expressive, culminating finally in a specific appeal:

> With trifling expense of imagination one can still catch a glimpse of the crusades in the glory of the glass. The longer one looks into it, the more overpowering it becomes, until one begins almost to feel an echo of what our two hundred and fifty million arithmetical ancestors, drunk with the passion of youth and the splendor of the Virgin, have been calling to us from Mont Saint Michel and Chartres. No words and no wine could revive their emotions so vividly as they glow in the purity of the colors; the limpidity of the blues; the depth of the red; the intensity of the green; the complicated harmonies; the sparkle and splendor of the light; and the quiet and certain strength of the mass. (Ibid., p. 468)

We recall everything we have already seen concerning harmony in color; but there is nothing quite like this. No one else, first of all, has dealt with the effect of actual sunlight upon color. Sunlight both intensifies and transforms color. Thus the blue of the Chartres windows, when illuminated, does not merely appear more intense. Instead, color itself seems brilliant with the radiance of light. And this in turn intensifies the *impression* of that color. It is as if color itself possessed a luminous energy or force. We have seen how energy consists of an attraction upon mind. Here the force of that attraction fills consciousness. Since light intensifies the impression of blue upon the mind, the energy contained within light and expressed as color becomes one with the energy of consciousness as the mind's impression assimilates the energy of external phenomena to thought. Thus intensity of impression becomes intensity of consciousness, and the radiance of the glass appears as a measure of the vividness with which consciousness experiences the external world. Vividness and immediacy: the most vivid, most immediate moment for consciousness is that in which it most intensely feels itself, when it experiences not only the external world but its own sensation. At that moment the world assumes an ineffable splendor of which the light streaming through the blue of the windows offers a symbolic expression.

But the intense brilliance of the blue by itself is insufficient: its effect depends in part upon the harmony it produces with other colors— reds, yellows, purples, greens. The resulting harmony is one of both color and form. Thus the prophets are seen against a red ground for contrast, but the blue returns on the external semicircular band so as to surround the red with an intensity that sets off the red's deeper warmth. Finally, the corners of that band are enriched with an emerald green whose darkness makes the blue more transparent while at the same time vivifying the red, which now seems as a result of the juxtaposition brighter as well as warmer. The formal harmony these colors produce implies that color alone does not suffice to achieve the desired aesthetic effect. By intensifying color, by energizing that color, so to speak, light creates a formal pattern that assimilates the windows' luminous energies. Without this, the impressions of color created by illumination of the windows cannot achieve their proper expressiveness. Here form or the arrangement of colors orders these impressions so as to enable each to complement the effect of the other. Through form, individual impressions acquire a relation to each other, whose sum forms a pattern that in turn elevates color above the effect attainable through individual intensity alone. Insofar as each color motif now plays its part within a larger scheme, the whole becomes a dynamic composition of balances and oppositions whose collective harmony transcends all individual intensities through a visible idea, the sublimation of energies to a higher thought.

At the same time, there is no sense of color being sacrificed to form. Instead, through a series of infinite variations in shades of blue, the windows achieve a richness in their modulation of light comparable to the modulation of a harmony in music. By means of such variations it becomes possible to augment or diminish the intensity of light, and, as a result, to impart a slightly different effect to each occurrence of red, yellow, or green. Since in a color scheme the precise value of each color depends upon its relation to the rest, the impression of each occurrence of color in one of these windows will also depend upon the impressions produced by all the others. Thus no single impression can be independent of the rest; rather, each influences the others, and the effect of the whole differs in its nature from individual impressions in being permeated by a consciousness of composition. But the variation in shades of blue does more than just affect what we might describe as the "tonality" of each color: in each instance, it also intensifies it. We have seen that the light which passes through various shades of blue intensifies the impression of that color. But this same intensity of impression will also affect all the other colors, since, in intensifying our consciousness of color, the light in blue necessarily heightens our sense of all the colors composing our impression of a window. Thus, without acquiring the transparent quality of the blue, each of the other colors becomes luminous to both eye and mind, the source of its brilliance consisting ultimately not of material light but of the impression it makes upon the mind.

In calculating the effects of various shades of blue, the artist, we are told, had wanted to control his light "not in order to dim the colors" but, on the contrary, "like a jeweller setting diamonds and rubies, to increase their splendor." The comparison suggests that there is something innately precious about these colors themselves. Each makes an intense but fleeting impression upon the eye: the more intense, the shorter its duration. One feels a desire to hold onto that impression, similar to our desire to retain all the most intensely pleasurable moments of our existence. Inasmuch as color fills the mind, flooding it with something like a color consciousness, the experience of color becomes analogous to the experience of pure consciousness, in which we no longer perceive specific objects but rather the radiance of vision itself. For this reason, the color of the Chartres windows seems precious. By setting colored panes like diamonds or rubies, the artist seeks in some fashion to perpetuate their impression, hoping to eternize the intensity of their light by assimilating it to a formal pattern which can then be retained by the mind. Pure intensity of impression can never be retained: one would have to recover the original impression in order to experience that intensity again. But assimilated to form, an impression becomes a possession of the mind, and what remains of it is something more than merely the ornament of a formal configuration. Rather, in the case of these windows, a pattern becomes ultimately but the visible form that radiance assumes.

We may perhaps wonder a little at the purpose of Adams's discussion of Ingres and Delacroix. What is at stake here, however, is something more than the question of whether color or line deserves precedence in painting. From another perspective, one may see in it nothing

less than the opposition between two fundamental forms of aestheticism: the aestheticism of consciousness and the aestheticism of form.[65]
We have seen how the aestheticism of consciousness finds its fulfillment in intensity of impression. To experience a moment with such
heightened awareness that one then feels the actual process of sensation offers the ultimate embodiment of sensuousness. By their very
nature, however, impressions of this kind cannot be preserved: hence
the necessity for form. Through form it becomes possible to eternize
an aesthetic impression, insofar as that impression depends not upon
intensity of consciousness but rather upon a formal harmony of various motifs. In reality the solution of the twelfth century consists,
however, of something that transcends either of these forms of aestheticism. Its insight is that it is possible to create formal harmonies
from pure color alone, and thus that the intensity of color and impression need not be sacrificed to form. Instead, form exists only for the
sake of color, to achieve the dynamic balances and oppositions that
will give color its maximum intensity of light and expression. One
might almost compare this process to composing with pure impressions, in which the light that streams through the glass imparts to its
colors the intensified radiance of consciousness. From that standpoint
it should also be possible to compose with other impressions, consisting of all the moments of an individual's existence, arranged in a
formal sequence that assimilates the sensuousness of each moment to
the recognition of a higher scheme that gives each moment a luminous
aura. If the windows of Chartres afford a glimpse of such possibilities,
they also express, through the energy of their colors, the formula that
haunts the consciousness of *Mont Saint Michel and Chartres,* that energy "is the inherent effort of every multiplicity to become unity." For
Aestheticism one might say, in a similar fashion, that art is the inherent
effort of every multiplicity to become unity while preserving all its
color and all its light.

1

"HARMONIE DU SOIR"

Voici venir les temps où vibrant sur sa tige
Chaque fleur s'évapore ainsi qu'un encensoir;
Les sons et les parfums tournent dans l'air du soir;
Valse mélancolique et langoureux vertige!

Chaque fleur s'évapore ainsi qu'un encensoir;
Le violon frémit comme un coeur qu'on afflige;
Valse mélancolique et langoureux vertige!
Le ciel est triste et beau comme un grand reposoir.

Le violon frémit comme un coeur qu'on afflige,
Un coeur tendre, qui hait le néant vaste et noir!
Le ciel est triste et beau comme un grand reposoir;
Le soleil s'est noyé dans son sang qui se fige.

Un coeur tendre, qui hait le néant vaste et noir,
Du passé lumineux recueille tout vestige!
Le soleil s'est noyé dans son sang qui se fige. . . .
Ton souvenir en moi luit comme un ostensoir!

—(Baudelaire, *OC* 1:47)

[Now come the moments when vibrating upon its stem
Each flower evaporates like a censer;
Sounds and fragrances revolve in the evening air;
Melancholy waltz and languorous vertigo!

Each flower evaporates like a censer;
The violin shudders like a heart one afflicts;
Melancholy waltz and languorous vertigo!
The sky is sad and beautiful like a grand altar.

The violin shudders like a heart one afflicts,
A tender heart, that hates the vast and black void!

The sky is sad and beautiful like a grand altar;
The sun drowns itself in its blood which congeals.

A tender heart, that hates the vast and black void,
From the luminous past collects every vestige!
The sun drowns itself in its blood which congeals. . . .
The memory of you in me gleams like a monstrance!

The poem opens with a curious image: "vibrating upon its stem, /
Each flower evaporates like a censer."[1] We know that the word
"s'évaporer" carries the figurative meaning "to vanish, to disappear"
when speaking of dreams or hopes. Perhaps these flowers are meant
to suggest the well-known Baudelairean "rêve," a dream or reverie.[2]
If so, it is a little odd that the advent of evening, a time most con-
ducive to reverie, should bring about their dissipation. But do they
actually disappear? Or do they not, on the contrary, become diffused
like a fine mist through the evening air? And, as a result, isn't twilight
itself now the medium of Baudelairean reverie? In this fashion the imaginative faculty expands to suffuse the whole nighttime of the great
metropolis, embracing the moment that brings about a cessation of
the day's frenetic activity and invites the coming of dreams.[3]

The vibration of these flowers upon their stems suggests a kind of
nervous vitality—a movement indicative of emotion perhaps, or even
of something like desire, if in so phrasing it we are not succumbing
to a tendency to personify the flowers. The significance of that desire,
however, remains for the moment unknown. At the same time the
advent of twilight announces a change in the nature of poetic perception. To a large extent this will be the subject of Baudelaire's poem:
not the meaning of specific images but rather of perception itself. The
very title of the poem, "Harmonie du soir," suggests its new aesthetic
criteria. Like Whistler's "harmonies," Baudelaire's combines color,
emotion, and sensation to create a formal arrangement whose effect
seeks to approximate that of a painting or music.[4]

This transformed aesthetic begins with a new attitude toward perception itself. The flowers are said to evaporate "like a censer." The
religious aura (a characteristically Baudelairean notion) that associates
itself with this simile is significant.[5] Here Baudelaire refers, of course,
not to the censer itself but to the incense-smoke given off by it. The
use of a censer only at High Mass deserves notice, as does the implied
allusion to its distinctive fragrance. Whoever has even once witnessed
this ceremony will undoubtedly recall it, as well as its effect upon one's
memory of the mass itself. Like Proust, Baudelaire is aware of the role

Nadar, *Charles Baudelaire* (1862).

of sensory impressions in stimulating memory. By associating these
with the ritual of the mass, he imparts to them a specifically religious
coloring. The flowers evaporate like the incense-fragrance given off by
a censer: thus a hint of the sacred attaches itself to the perception of
beauty (the sight and smell of flowers). Romanticism had conferred a
sanctified aura upon the moment of apocalyptic consciousness that
vouchsafes a revelation of divine presence to the self. Never, however,
had it accorded mere sensory impressions a sacred quality. In so doing
Baudelaire elevates the senses to a new role, as a medium of our initiation into a new form of religious experience.

A first hint of this new role of the senses emerges in the evocation
of "sounds and fragrances revolving in the evening air." Here the word
"parfums" conveys a suggestion both of the religious (the incense-fragrance of the censer) and the aesthetic (perfume).[6] The "revolving" of
sounds and fragrances implies a detachment of sensory impressions
from the objects that produce them. Like colors of a kaleidoscope or
scraps of paper blown about by the wind, these impressions now begin
to float in a process of free association that results in phenomena like
synesthesia.[7] We know of Baudelaire's preoccupation with this particular state, which lies poised on the threshold of imaginative creation.
Peculiarly appropriate to reverie, it is for Baudelaire (as for Rousseau)
the "volupté" par excellence. For Baudelaire, however, synesthesia is
not only a subjective state; it also equates the external world with various impressions or motifs. The sonnet "Correspondances" declares that
nature consists of "des forêts de symboles" [forests of symbols] where
"les parfums, les couleurs et les sons se répondent" [fragrances, colors,
and sounds respond to each other]. Thus nature appears in synesthesia
as an expression of the imaginative faculty's creative ferment.

The "revolving" of sounds and fragrances in the evening air also
conveys the hint of a lilting motion, which the poem now amplifies
in "Melancholy waltz and languorous vertigo." Here the waltz replaces
the eighteenth-century minuet as the dance most appropriate for soul-
ful longing. But Baudelaire's waltz is melancholy, suggestive of a declining passion. Like twilight, however, melancholy makes possible a
state of heightened awareness, in which emotion is experienced as dissociated from its object. But this in turn allows one to regard such
emotions aesthetically. As a result they can assume an artistic form—
that of the "valse mélancolique." Thus melancholy offers a pleasure
comparable to that of reverie, in which the mind obtains delight from
the sensation of its own consciousness. The "languorous vertigo" Baudelaire associates with this waltz represents an intensification of mel-

ancholy. "Languor" describes the sensation induced by melancholy it-self. When melancholy is intensified, however, languor becomes vertiginous. It is as if one were to subject old passions or the expe-rience of past moments to sudden renewal. The result: a feeling of vertigo, arising from a glimpse of hitherto-unsuspected emotional pos-sibilities.

The second quatrain begins by repeating a line from the first: "Cha-que fleur s'évapore ainsi qu'un encensoir." Here repetition reveals the essentially musical nature of the poem, anticipating the explicit intro-duction of music: "The violin shudders like a heart one afflicts." These shuddering sounds produced by a violin recall Paganini's demonic vir-tuosity, and (for Baudelaire especially) Delacroix's famous portrait of the violinist. Beyond this, the evocation of music suggestive of a soul under torture conveys even more clearly the poem's expressive ideal. To push this expressiveness to its furthest extreme now seems to be the poem's objective. In its intensification of emotion lies the source of the violin's aesthetic pleasure. As an instrument it possesses the ca-pacity to intensify emotion further than normally possible within the limits of human sensibility, since for the violin such intensification is merely a *mechanical* rather than emotional process. Thus it renews the experience of "vertigo" described earlier: the psyche surrenders to emotion intensified to its furthest possible extreme and experiences once more the "volupté" of an abyss, in which excess of emotion makes possible a loss of self.

One might also wish to ask at this point: what precisely does the shuddering violin *represent*? Whose heart is being afflicted? And what is the relation of that heart to the poet or narrator, the "I" of the poem? Because of the dissociation between the new source of emotion (the violin) and the "I," the violin becomes a means of representing the self. If the sounds produced by the violin express an intensified emotion which the self identifies as its own, the violin (as the source of emotion) becomes equivalent to the self—in effect, its self-repre-sentation. Here the imaginative faculty that ultimately makes this self-representation possible by evoking the image of the violin experiences the pleasure of witnessing its own creative potency.

This image of the violin also imparts a new significance to the rep-etition of "Valse mélancolique et langoureux vertige!" For if the vi-olin's shuddering (like that of a heart in agony) is itself part of the music of the "melancholy waltz," it too is subject to a definite musical rhythm. But the expression of emotion in rhythmic form defines the essence of poetry, especially the lyric. Thus the presence of the violin's shudder within the movement of a waltz reveals even the most intense emotion as intrinsically aesthetic. This incorporation of the most extreme emotion into music affirms the assimilation of life to art.

Melancholy, intensified, leads to vertigo. But what follows solaces with a kind of calm: "Le ciel est triste et beau comme un grand reposoir." It is difficult here to offer an exact equivalent for "triste." Applied to the sky's appearance, one might be tempted to say "dreary," but the feeling of something like "sadness" is present as well. It suggests, moreover, a pensive sweetness, a kind of *Weltschmerz* not without emotional sensuousness. Both its dreariness and its sweetness contribute to the sky's other aspect: its beauty. The overall effect of the line is to temper drastically the frenetic emotion that precedes it. For this purpose the use of "reposoir," with its literal meaning of "altar" but implied sense of "repose," can hardly be accidental. Its tone of perfect tranquillity contrasts with the preceding mood of the stanza. The effect seems similar to that of a major-key resolution of tensions generated by a minor-key intrusion. An air of finality pervades the atmosphere. One envisions the clear and serene lines of the altar, conveying the repose implied in "reposoir." In this beautifully achieved harmony, only a stray note or two strikes one as discordant. A "reposoir" is only a temporary—rather than permanent—altar. Moreover, the image of an altar points to a sacrificial rite. But what is to be sacrificed? The hint that it would be the self is only silently adumbrated: to achieve the dreary but beautiful serenity of the sky, one must relinquish one's attachment to existence.[8]

The religious aspect of the "reposoir" (like that of the censer) endows the sky with a symbolic significance. The hierophantic nature of the altar's symbolism, with its hint of sacrificial rites, invokes a relationship to a higher power that remains unnamed throughout the *Fleurs du mal*. In addressing itself to this unknown God the poem expresses the desire for a surrender of self. But since the God addressed by the self remains hidden or unknown, what imparts significance to the altar's symbolism can only be the subjective relationship created by the act of prayer—a gesture of voluntary self-surrender. In suggesting such a relationship, Baudelaire implies only a need for it rather than any confirmed religious belief. Perhaps the mere sense of a relationship will suffice. As a source of emotional solace, the feeling of a divine presence within the self that apotheosizes consciousness through an aesthetic beatification of existence seems enough to justify the Baudelairean affirmation of faith.

Again the violin shudders like a heart one afflicts, but this time we are told it is "a tender heart, that hates the vast and black void." At the time of "Harmonie du soir," Flaubert's "Un Coeur simple" still lies in the future. Nevertheless, a common theme informs both pieces. The tenderness of a heart lies in its capacity to feel, to experience emotion from external impressions. With the loss of religious belief in the mid-nineteenth century, that capacity acquires immeasurably greater significance. For both Baudelaire and Flaubert, tenderness is what ensures the "humanness" of humanity. In "Harmonie du soir" the description of "un coeur tendre, qui hait le néant vaste et noir" becomes a defiant affirmation of the human capacity to feel in an inhuman universe lacking such consciousness.[9]

For Baudelaire the "néant" (nothingness, the void) represents the enemy of all human endeavor, an abyss that swallows up all attempts to construct or create. This "vast and black void" resembles night rather than twilight. But its existence on the other side of twilight shows that all creative activity (like reverie) takes place in a world bordering on silence and nothingness. Baudelaire retains invariably an awareness of the Pascalian void, of those "espaces infinis" that terrify and awe.[10] In his poem "Le Gouffre" he exclaims:

> En haut, en bas, partout, la profondeur, la grève,
> Le silence, l'espace affreux et captivant. . . .
>
> (*OC* 1:142)

> [Above, below, everywhere, depth, the strand,
> Silence, frightful and captivating space. . . .]

Elsewhere in the same poem he recognizes that "tout est abîme,— action, désir, rêve" (*OC* 1:142) [everything is an abyss—action, desire, dreams]. Of course the ultimate form of the "néant" is death. Perhaps that is why the poet has such a fear of sleep:

> J'ai peur du sommeil comme on a peur d'un grand trou,
> Tout plein de vague horreur, menant on ne sait où;
> Je ne vois qu'infini par toutes les fenêtres.
>
> (*OC* 1:143)

> [I am afraid of sleep as one is afraid of a deep hole,
> Full of vague horror, leading one knows not where;
> I see only the infinite at every window.]

As with Poe, windows signify for Baudelaire apertures of the soul. But the infinite he sees everywhere is no different from the "néant": if the sky appears through these windows, the sight is only one of a vast emptiness.

The equation of the shuddering violin with "a tender heart, that

hates the vast and black void" reveals a new aspect of the musical motif. Here it becomes clear that the violin's tortured sounds are not
merely a mechanical intensification of emotion but the expression of
a soul's agony. A new level of realism is thereby attained: the soul's
emotion is captured by means of sounds produced by an instrument,
but that instrument is in reality nothing other than the heart itself. Up
to now, we have taken the violin simply as an imaginative representation, its sounds a metaphor for emotion. These sounds depicted the
soul's feelings without actually pretending to express them. With the
additional qualification that the afflicted heart resembling a shuddering violin is specifically the tender heart that hates the vast and black
void, we recognize that the shuddering sounds we have heard are not
merely an embodiment of the new Romantic aesthetic but the soul's
own response to being acted upon by hostile forces. It is *the soul itself
that is being played upon by these forces*: the music they draw from it, an
expression of its fear of the void.

The ambiguity of the "one" who afflicts ("comme un coeur qu'on
afflige") now assumes a new and sinister meaning.[11] Its anonymity
guarantees protection, and if one equates the violin with the "coeur
tendre," one cannot but associate that "one" with the "néant" that
plays upon the heart. The impassivity of the "néant" seems curiously
at odds with what makes the violin shudder, but Baudelaire's point is
precisely that impassivity is merely an aggressive façade, a means by
which nothingness seeks to swallow up human tenderness within its
abyss. Like Flaubert, Baudelaire sees the "néant" as an active force,
one that corrodes the meanings residing in things. To affirm the heart
that suffers from these encroachments of the void represents his effort
to resist a nihilism the "néant" seeks to induce.

The repetition of "Le ciel est triste et beau comme un grand reposoir" *after* the shuddering violin's identification with the tender heart
completely alters the line's meaning. The sky now becomes an image
of impassive nature indifferent regarding human suffering. Elsewhere
in the *Fleurs du mal* Baudelaire describes this sky's more oppressive
aspect:

> Quand le ciel bas et lourd pèse comme un couvercle
> Sur l'esprit gémissant en proie aux longs ennuis,
> Et que de l'horizon embrassant tout le cercle
> Il nous verse un jour plus triste que les nuits
>
> (OC 1:74)
>
> [When the sky, low and heavy, weighs like a lid
> Upon the soul groaning as prey to long ennuis,

> And, embracing the whole circle of the horizon,
> It rains upon us a day sadder than nights.]

Passages elsewhere confirm that the "couvercle" Baudelaire speaks of here refers literally to a lid or pot-cover. The poem "Le Couvercle" exclaims

> Le Ciel! couvercle noir de la grande marmite
> Où bout l'imperceptible et vaste Humanité.
>
> (*OC* 1:141)

> [The Heavens! black lid of the great pot
> Where boils an imperceptible and vast Humanity.]

In this passage, the heavens' oppressive nature is even more apparent: a teeming humanity is kept from overflowing its prescribed limits by an immense lid or cover placed over the earth. If we equate the sky with the medium of human consciousness (as in "Le ciel est triste et beau"), depicting that sky as a lid necessarily implies its severe limits. In the "Spleen" poem Baudelaire describes the effect of this "lid": the sky is "low" and "heavy," it "weighs" upon the mind. Its effect is amplified by association with "longs ennuis." Even as it embraces the horizon's entire circle, the sky "rains upon us a day sadder than night." Its downward movement (like the falling of rain) portends its significance. The sadness of such a day ("plus triste que les nuits") amounts to dreariness. We see, in other words, only by a light that implies relinquishing any dreams of a better existence. The *falling* of day epitomizes our situation—one in which the beginning already carries the sense of an ending.

The infinite dreariness of the sky condemns the self to a life without meaning. But what if the very source of that life were to disappear? Baudelaire now contemplates this most terrifying of all possibilities: "The sun drowns itself [lit., "has drowned itself"] in its blood which congeals."[12] For Baudelaire the sun symbolizes the source of life. In "Le Soleil" he apostrophizes it as follows:

> Ce père nourricier, ennemi des chloroses,
> Éveille dans les champs les vers comme les roses;
> Il fait s'évaporer les soucis vers le ciel,
> Et remplit les cerveaux et les ruches de miel.
>
> (*OC* 1:83)

> [This foster-father, enemy of chloroses,
> Awakens the earthworms in the fields like roses;

> It makes the marigolds evaporate toward the sky,
> And fills brains and beehives with honey.]

The fact that the sun fills both "brains" and "beehives" with honey defines it as the source of all life, spiritual as well as material.[13] At the same time it also suggests the essential nature of life. In making the marigolds evaporate *toward* the sky, the sun seems to impart to the material or vegetal realm something like a spiritual impulse. But if even marigolds evaporate toward a sky which is also heaven (*le ciel*), they merely embody a virtually universal aspiration among all forms of life toward a higher state. We have seen earlier how in the nocturnal air of "Harmonie du soir" each flower "evaporates like a censer." From the standpoint supplied by "Le Soleil," we can now see this "evaporation" as expressive of spiritual aspiration. The association of evaporation with a censer endows the movement with a sacred quality. Given Baudelaire's opposition to pantheism, the sanctity adumbrated by the censer appears to apply not so much to the flowers themselves but rather to their movement of evaporation, or spiritual aspiration. Nevertheless even the flowers, "vibrating" upon their stems, had seemed endowed with a sensibility approaching that of the soul. In "Le Soleil," similarly, the "marigolds" (*soucis*) are also "cares" or "anxieties." In causing these "cares" or "anxieties" to "evaporate," the sun prepares minds for creative activity (i.e., the production of honey). Thus it "awakens" not only earthworms but also the "verses" (*vers*) produced by poets. In both "Le Soleil" and "Harmonie du soir," then, material and spiritual existence seem linked by a single impulse that informs both.

The source of this impulse, as we have seen, is the sun, the origin of all life. But the sun not only animates "brains and beehives"; it also imparts life to the emotions:

> C'est lui qui rajeunit les porteurs de béquilles
> Et les rend gais et doux comme des jeunes filles,
> Et commande aux moissons de croître et de mûrir
> Dans le coeur immortel qui toujours veut fleurir!

> (*OC* 1:83)

> [It is he who rejuvenates the bearers of crutches
> And makes them as gay and gentle as young girls,
> And commands the harvests to grow and ripen,
> In the immortal heart that wants always to flower!]

The desire of the "immortal heart" always to "flower" links "Le Soleil" even more closely to "Harmonie du soir." It now becomes apparent that the flowers which "evaporate" in the nocturnal air aptly symbolize the heart that seeks emotional fulfillment. According to "Le Soleil," however, such fulfillment can come only from the sun, which "commands the harvests to grow and ripen." Only the source of life, the life impulse itself, can impart to the emotions the primordial energy or joy (jouissance) that makes possible their coming to fulfillment. Like the sunlight that causes harvests to grow and ripen, then, the animation that the heart needs in order to flower presents itself not so much as mere emotion or mood, but rather as a more fundamental energy (the energy of life itself) that vitalizes all emotions. For the heart, this energy is that of the affections. In the nocturnal world of "Harmonie du soir," however, the affections are conspicuously absent. What the "tender heart" feels, rather, is the threatening presence of a "vast and black nothingness." It is this appalling prospect of a universe without affection, a universe without life, that causes the drowning of the self's own sun, its own affections, in emotional currents that congeal because they find no answering response. In this nocturnal world, a world without affections, the only hope for the self would seem to lie in those possibilities glimpsed at the end of another "nocturnal" poem, "Le Paysage," one that immediately precedes "Le Soleil":

> De tirer un soleil de mon coeur, et de faire
> De mes pensers brûlants une tiède atmosphère.
>
> (OC 1:82)
>
> [To draw a sun from my heart, and to make
> Out of my burning thoughts a warm atmosphere.]

But if the self is to be able to extract the sunlight of affection from its own heart, that light must ultimately come from another source. In "Le Paysage" Baudelaire suggests that this source is the imaginative faculty. It remains to be seen whether the imaginative faculty in "Harmonie du soir" possesses the means of realizing its possibilities.

Yet the sun's self-immersion manifests a conscious will. This manifestation of will *expresses* the self's own impulse. Like the violin that suffers in being played upon, the sun that drowns itself breaks through the façade of allegory. Its significance is not established without a figural violence: instead of merely signifying an emotion it becomes expressive of it. These violent disruptions of the allegorical surface of the poem reflect its specific aesthetic. Expressiveness lies precisely in being able to violate the norms of representation. In so doing, the imaginative faculty conveys the intensity of its *desire,* which is its ultimate objective. Viewed from this standpoint, the poem moves progressively toward a disruption of allegory or symbolism.[14] The opening quatrain begins with an image of the self's anxiety or hope: the flower vibrating upon its stem—the merest hint of instinctive life, nothing more. Clearly, the flower remains well within the limits of allegorical "representation." With the shuddering violin of the second quatrain, Baudelaire introduces explicit metaphorical association: the violin shudders "like a heart one afflicts." Only the expressive quality of the motif keeps it within the realm of music and representation. The third quatrain, however, disrupts representation with metaphorical violence: the shuddering violin is now equated specifically with a "tender heart, that hates the vast and black void." The violence within the text (the sadistic playing upon that tender heart by one who desires to torture it) corresponds to a violent rupture of representational limits. The self now appears *as itself* rather than through some form of representation. Having done so, it then intensifies the violence of the text: the image becomes a self-destructive force, the sun drowns itself in its blood as the final phase of this process. Its self-destructive act is a manifestation not only of will but of figural violence: through its immersion in its own blood, the metaphor of the sun literally obliterates itself as metaphor.

With the sun's disappearance the self too would seem to disappear, implying the end of the poem. But all along, at crucial moments, we have witnessed the repetition of an earlier line of the poem. What does it signify? In each instance, of course, the line acquires meaning from its new context, but the fact of the repetition must also be significant. In effect, it serves to characterize the poem as a musical sequence.

Now we recognize that each expression of emotion is both lyrical and—on account of its repetition—analogous to a musical theme. In his essay "Richard Wagner et *Tannhäuser* à Paris" Baudelaire observes of his experience in listening to Wagner's music that "des répétitions fréquentes des mêmes phrases mélodiques, dans des morceaux tirés du même opéra, impliquaient des intentions mystérieuses" (*OC* 2:786) [frequent repetitions of the same melodic phrases, in pieces drawn from the same opera, imply mysterious intentions]. Similarly, frequent repetitions of the same melodic phrases in "Harmonie du soir" might also imply a mysterious intention. With *Lohengrin,* as Baudelaire subsequently remarks in the same essay on Wagner, there is a rigorous correspondence between each character and the melody that "represents" or expresses it: "chaque personnage est, pour ainsi dire, blasonné par la mélodie qui représente son caractère moral et le rôle qu'il est appelé à jouer dans la fable" (*OC* 2:801) [each character is, so to speak, blazoned forth by the melody that represents its moral disposition and the role it is called upon to play in the fable]. Each melody, then, embodies a particular meaning or significance, iterated with each occurrence of that melody. In a similar fashion, each line of "Harmonie du soir" likewise suggests a particular symbolic meaning. This meaning, however, is also associated with a specific emotion. One might then conclude that each reiteration of the line involuntarily gives rise to that same emotion. But while such an effect does definitely occur, the repetition of a line also produces another result: a consciousness of the repetition itself, and hence of the line as part of a formal composition.

By this means, the poem evokes a consciousness of form. Because of the emotional associations of its symbolism, the consciousness of form in "Harmonie du soir" assumes a special quality. It consists of a sublimation of emotion to form. One might even go so far as to speak of what Charles Asselineau once called Baudelaire's "religion of form."[15] This "religion of form" implies a sacrifice of the emotion of a given moment to an awareness of the intrinsic form or pattern connecting this moment with others. Once aware of that pattern, it is no longer possible simply to feel the emotion of a particular moment. By reiterating the same lines, the poem precludes the possibility of experiencing pure emotion. Instead, the emotion associated with each symbolic image becomes, as the "experience" of a given moment, part of an implicit *sequence* of moments. But this sequence in turn suggests that the meaning of these moments lies in something other than the particular emotions to which they give rise. Hence the feeling of a "mysterious intention," corresponding to what Baudelaire himself had experienced in listening to Wagner. Thus the "harmony" of the poem results from a combination of the emotions associated with its various symbolic images in order to form a particular sequence. "Music" then appears in essence as a *sequence of emotions*. At this point the "intention" behind that sequence remains unclear. Nevertheless the presence of an intention seems manifest, from the particular pattern governing the repetition of images in the poem. But perhaps this sense of a definite intention (which nevertheless remains concealed) is precisely what the poem seeks to convey. It suggests a hidden "theme" permeating all the moments of an individual's existence, one that confers upon these a higher meaning. To be constantly in search of this meaning is the condition of the Baudelairean self.

The tender heart, hating the nihilism of the void, now turns to the past: "From the luminous past" it "collects every vestige." Its objective: to recover that past in all its implicit significance. Thus the image of a "luminous past" becomes symbolic of the preserving memory that retains what can be rescued of the extinguished sun. With particular emphasis, Baudelaire observes that the tender heart gathers *every* vestige of this past. Why such a total effort? Are we then to equate the "passé lumineux" with the entire past, or are there certain gaps, lapses of memory leaving significant lacunae?

We know how important a function memory plays in many of Baudelaire's poems.[16] Although evoked specifically only at the end of "Harmonie du soir," it figures throughout as an implied presence. The opening of the poem announces the arrival of those moments in which "each flower evaporates like a censer." For the speaker to describe such instances in the plural (*les temps*) suggests he knows them from previous experience, hence is able to recall them now through memory. But if his present experience of flowers "evaporating like a censer" is colored by memory, perhaps this might serve to explain why sounds and fragrances "revolve" (*tournent*) in the evening air: memory revolves them within itself, as if seeking through its manipulations to extract some hidden significance. The abrupt introduction of music ("valse mélancolique et langoureux vertige!") reflects an irruption of memory: the "valse mélancolique" shows how emotion suffuses the experience of these sounds and fragrances, originating from a memory of similar instances. This lyricism which is implicit in the reminiscences themselves "floats" the sounds and fragrances in a current of emotion. But that same current will also ultimately transform these impressions into elements of a work of art. By "floating" them it volatilizes them, lifting them out of the material realm and assimilating them into the creative medium of memory. Within that realm of memory, in turn, impressions become expressive, absorbing the emotion with which the mind invests them and subsequently emanating it like a luminous radiance.

At the same time, the "melancholy" quality of the waltz and the "languorous vertigo" hint specifically at a surfeit of reminiscences: precisely because the speaker remembers *too much,* his feeling is one of both oppressive or heavy melancholy (as if suffering under the burden of the past, which then induces languor) and vertigo, resulting from an inability to deal with the excess of memory. Consequently "the violin shudders like a heart one afflicts": because of the excess of reminiscence, emotion (the medium of memory) becomes painful. Its embodiment in an image, that of "the heart one afflicts," seems almost deliberately designed to produce a shock effect, as if by doing this the mind might somehow be able to break the spell induced by its own memories. Thus memory, when allowed to function without restraint, becomes inimical to the self. As we have seen earlier, the afflicted heart is actually the speaker's own. And, despite the fact that its suffering is being transformed into music and hence into something beautiful, there remains a danger of the self becoming lost in this process, of its inundation in an excess of emotion. The danger only intensifies with the announcement that "the sky is sad (*triste*) and beautiful like a grand altar," conveying the sense of a false serenity that belies the threatening possibility of a loss of self. As if trying to awaken to a realization of its imminent effacement, the mind reiterates the image of the heart: "A tender heart, that hates the vast and black void!" This reiteration of the heart image also opposes it explicitly to that which threatens its destruction. Finally, as we have seen, the poem projects the most terrifying of all possibilities—the sun (symbolic of life) drowning itself.

This ultimate image, of the sun drowning itself, appears to bring about something like a transformation of memory. When it resurfaces, collecting every vestige of "the luminous past," it no longer represents simply emotion. Despite its depiction as "a tender heart," it now performs a different function from that of merely imparting an emotional coloring to past moments. Whereas earlier the poem had implied an excess of reminiscences, what now confronts the "tender heart" is absence, nothingness, the void. Against such absence, memory (in the form of the "tender heart") seeks to collect every vestige of the "luminous past." But if the past has now become "luminous," its luminosity suggests that the emotion which earlier had formed an accompaniment to past experiences is now internalized within those experiences themselves. It is precisely this internalization of emotion within a memory that makes it luminous. But the internalized emotion of memory is not the same as the emotion we encountered earlier in "melancholy waltz and languorous vertigo." Whereas that earlier emotion had essentially expressed a transient mood, the present emotion possesses a different source. If the "tender heart" subsists within a universe of silence and nothingness, the only means by which it can recover the past is, in effect, to create it. This creation of the past through memory is what gives that past its radiance. In the act of creating (or recreating) its past, memory endows each recovered moment with the emotion that arises from its own creative consciousness. Through its ability to recover the past from the void of silence and nothingness, it affirms not only the significance of those moments composing its past but above all the creative capacity of memory itself. That capacity, in turn, suggests that memory need not be simply a means of preserving the past. Instead, through its ability to create a "luminous past,"

it clearly possesses the power to transform the speaker's earlier existence, making what had been merely life into something with the radiance of art.

The repetition at this point of "The sun drowns itself in its blood
which congeals" with an ellipsis appears to suggest an uncertain sequel. Its uncertainty arises in part, no doubt, from the fact that previously the sun's extinction had seemed to presage that of the self.
Earlier, faced with an indifferent universe, the self had looked to the
memory of past moments. Now, confronted with extinction, it turns
specifically to the last thing that remains to it: the remembrance of
affection. What now occurs instead represents a resurgence of the self:
"The memory of you in me gleams like a monstrance!" Like the "luminous past," this too gleams with an inner radiance. The suggestion
of spiritual transcendence that emerges here for the first time in the
poem has its origin, significantly, in our present existence rather than
in something beyond it.[17] The aura of the sacred (embodied in the
monstrance) surrounding reminiscence reflects its capacity to transform the self through the influence of affection. Instead of remaining
imprisoned within the solipsistic limits of its own consciousness, the
self now experiences awareness of an other: "The memory of you."

The fact that this marks the first explicit mention of an other in the
poem is doubtless revealing. Equally so perhaps is the mention of that
other only indirectly. "Ton souvenir": literally, "your remembrance"
(the remembrance of you), where the possessive fails even to signify
the other as such (i.e., as "you"), conceding the other's presence only
as a qualification of the remembrance. Nevertheless, the phrase "ton
souvenir" inescapably addresses the other: were the self not seeking to
invoke the other in some fashion, it would have been simpler and
more natural, obviously, to say "the remembrance of her" or "the remembrance of him." But the ambiguous position of the other in "Harmonie du soir," its indirect mention without being either addressed
or specified, defines precisely the special nature of the self's relationship to that other.

Throughout most of the poem, the other is conspicuously absent.
The violin that shudders "like a heart one afflicts" embodies an image
of the self as its own other: appearing initially merely as a poetic object, it becomes symbolic of some human sensibility by being likened
to "a heart one afflicts." But this human sensibility turns out to be
none other than that of the self—since the "melancholy waltz" of the
preceding stanza expresses the emotion of memory, its intensification
(through the shuddering violin) must also pertain to the same self that
experiences memory. Thus the violin becomes an image of the self,

but of the self seen as an other—which is to say, as an object that only turns out upon inference to be an embodiment of the self. The same applies to the sun that drowns itself in its own blood: another ostensibly external object, it too becomes an image of self upon inference by being associated in the third stanza with the shuddering violin and (more explicitly) "a tender heart." In the final stanza, the "death" of the sun (i.e., the self) becomes the necessary prelude to its resurgence in and through the memory of an other. If the sun represents only an image of the self as its own other, that image must then be "extinguished" (both literally and figuratively) in order for the self to resurface as a genuine other.

When the other finally appears in the last stanza of the poem, its appearance is inseparable from memory. But memory, as we have seen, is the image or embodiment of the self's emotion about its own past. In this sense, the other that figures in the final line of the poem is not a "real" other—it does not in any way resist the self, nor is it capable of thinking or feeling anything different from what the self experiences. Nevertheless it remains in one respect genuinely distinct from the self. Whereas the self embodies its emotion in one or another image (the violin, the sun), the emotion of the other remains identical with that other. As such it is not "expressed" anywhere in the poem. By being identified wholly with the other, then, it remains external to the self.

For the self to recover the other's emotion through memory thus becomes tantamount to a recovery of the other. But if in recovering the other's emotion the self in effect recovers that other, perhaps this can explain in part the ambiguity of the final line. "Ton souvenir en moi": it signifies, in one sense, "the remembrance of you in me," but in another sense "ton souvenir" might also mean "the remembrance that you possess," i.e., the remembrance preserved by the other—perhaps even the other's remembrance of the self. In this fashion, through memory, the self becomes one with the other. In so doing, however, it achieves nothing less than an imaginative *creation* of its own self through that other. If with the sun's drowning itself the self disappears, the gleam of the monstrance, by presenting the same light in another form, counts as its re-creation. Here the self, through what we might call a symbolic transference, appears once more, but in the form of an other. More precisely, its symbolic embodiment as light allows it to appear within the other. Yet the image of the monstrance, with the Eucharistic host at its center, depicts that other as enshrined within the self. But if the other is contained in this fashion within the self, that is only because its presence results from an act of the im-

aginative memory that brings it into existence. What the poem ultimately affirms, then, is the creative capacity of the imaginative faculty.
Insofar as the remembrance of the other is a creative act, however, it
becomes part of the larger act that is the creation of a "harmonie du
soir." In so doing, it embodies the assimilation of life into a work of
art.

2

"DE LA COULEUR"

On trouve dans la couleur l'harmonie, la mélodie et le contrepoint. . . .

La couleur est donc l'accord de deux tons. Le ton chaud et le ton froid, dans l'opposition desquels consiste toute la théorie, ne peuvent se définir d'une manière absolue: ils n'existent que relativement. (*OC* 2:423–24)

[One finds in color harmony, melody, and counterpoint. . . .

Color is thus the agreement of two tones. The warm tone and the cold tone, in the opposition of which consists all theory, cannot be defined in an absolute manner: they exist only relatively.]

In this fashion Baudelaire in his critique of the *Salon* of 1846 equates painting with music.[1] As a result color becomes primarily expressive.[2] We have already seen how music embodies the rhythm of passion: in "Harmonie du soir" the "shuddering" of a violin represents that of the heart one afflicts, while the "melancholy waltz" imparts a form to emotion. In such instances music appears essentially affective. A melody or theme creates a particular mood, conveying the allure of some indefinable longing. In so doing it conforms to a different ideal from that of a later era. Thus Pater finds music the supreme art because it achieves an identification of content and form. To Baudelaire, however, it evokes feelings of melancholy, longing, or passion that are ultimately independent of the actual music. Like all Romantic art, music aspires then to something beyond itself—a feeling that finally transcends all forms of expression.

For Baudelaire this feeling consists not of an apocalyptic consciousness of higher significance but rather of some ineffable emotion of the soul, a delicious languor or yearning for suprasensual bliss. By transposing an emotion into color, painting alters its nature.[3] In music, emotion offers pleasure precisely because of its transience—that evanescent quality of a mood which can be captured only in a particular melodic sequence (one that, because of its own fleeting aspect, inspires a nostalgia for the emotion's return). With painting the exact opposite occurs. Here the permanent presence of a color motif implies the possibility of perpetually retaining the emotion it suggests. Hence the necessity for some sort of dynamic equilibrium between different colors. The result of that equilibrium produces in turn an expressive harmony.

Color results from an "agreement" between two tones, each exercising a specific effect.[4] Thus color consists not of objective tints or hues but rather of certain subjective effects. "Warm" and "cold" tones exist only for the perceiving eye: to experience a color as either indicates its impression upon our aesthetic sensibility, or that faculty which associates a perception with various sensations of pleasure. To perceive a tone as warm suggests a certain intensity of emotion; a cold tone, on the other hand, greater subjective distance. But each of these, as Baudelaire observes, subsists only in relation to the other: without a cold tone the warm cannot be felt as such, and vice versa. Thus the whole concept of expressive intensity becomes relative. Without, say, a certain shade of dark green or blue, a lighter red (scarlet approximating vermilion) will not seem warm at all—will on the contrary appear simply faded. Here the intensity of a tint depends upon the mind's perception of it. Without the contrast of a surrounding dark green or blue (displaying not only darkness but an equally intense depth), the effect might easily be lost.

By noticing how necessary contrast is for any impression of intensity, Baudelaire might well observe the resemblance in terms of color between nature and art. That nature itself should consist of "aesthetic" effects—what is this if not justification for attempting to transform life into a work of art, a "composition" offering to the sensitive or observant eye an effect of harmony, of balance, of finer expressiveness? In his poem "Harmonie du soir" Baudelaire affirms the aesthetic nature of consciousness, its inherent tendency to arrange its impressions into a work of art. Earlier, in the *Salon de 1846,* he anticipates this view through his theory of color—specifically, the notion that *all* colors, including those we see in external nature, depend upon contrast and composition. Since the beauty of nature results from effects we have no part in creating, nature itself must be intrinsically "artistic." Yet if nature consists merely of various arrangements of color resulting in specific effects, it remains theoretically possible to exceed those effects by others.[5] A study of such effects and of the means of producing them would then amount to a comprehensive theory of color. For this reason Baudelaire can speak of "Le ton chaud et le ton froid, dans l'opposition desquels consiste toute la théorie."

But the relation of nature to art through the medium of a theory of color implies more than mere affinity between the external world and the artistic intelligence. To some extent, that would simply reaffirm the earlier Romantic concept of a correspondence between mind and nature, or—in its radically subjective form—the notion that the external world is a creation of the mind. Instead, by presenting the external world simply as an arrangement of colors, Baudelaire suggests the possibility of assimilating nature to art. Thus he observes that "Les affinités chimiques sont la raison pour laquelle la nature ne peut pas commettre de fautes dans l'arrangement de ces tons; car, pour elle, forme et couleur sont un" (*OC* 2:424). [The chemical affinities are the reason why nature cannot make mistakes in the arrangement of these tones; because, for nature, form and color are one.] But

> Le vrai coloriste ne peut pas en commettre non plus; et tout lui est permis parce qu'il connaît de naissance la gamme des tons, la force du ton, les résultats des mélanges, et toute la science du contrepoint, et qu'il peut ainsi faire une harmonie de vingt rouges différents. (*OC* 2:424)

> [The true colorist cannot make mistakes either; and everything is permitted him, because he knows from birth the gamut of tones, the force of a tone, the results of combinations, and all the science of counterpoint, and because he can thus create a harmony out of twenty different reds.]

To such an extent is this true that

> si un propriétaire anticoloriste s'avisait de repeindre sa campagne d'une manière absurde et dans un système de couleurs charivariques, le vernis épais et transparent de l'atmosphère et l'oeil savant de Véronèse redresseraient le tout et produiraient sur une toile un ensemble satisfaisant, conventionnel sans doute, mais logique. (*OC* 2:424)

> [If an anticoloristic proprietor were to take it into his head to repaint his countryside in an absurd manner and a charivaresque system of colors, the thick and transparent glaze of the atmosphere and the expert eye of Veronese would redress the whole and produce on the canvas a satisfying ensemble, conventional no doubt, but logical.]

Conventional in the sense of respecting the pictorial conventions for the depiction of skies and attempting to conform to these with the colors at its disposal; logical insofar as its arrangement results from a true knowledge of the harmonies between colors as well as of appropriate and expressive effects of composition.

Perhaps what is most significant about this passage is its suggestion that the "true colorist" might undertake to "repaint" nature itself. But why not, if nature consists merely of a certain arrangement of colors or tones? If one regards colors as analogous to notes in music, a variety of permutations becomes possible—all governed, of course, by a knowledge of the principles of color harmony, but availing themselves nevertheless of the freedom such principles permit. Which leads Baudelaire to the following inference: "Cela explique comment un coloriste peut être paradoxal dans sa manière d'exprimer la couleur, et comment l'étude de la nature conduit souvent à un résultat tout différent de la nature" (OC 2:424). [This explains how a colorist can be paradoxical in his manner of expressing color, and how the study of nature often leads to a result quite different from nature.] As long as the painter respects the principles of color harmony and composition, he is free to depart from nature's actual color schemes.

The "study of nature": for centuries, from Leonardo and Alberti down to the French realists, this had defined the program of European painting. In Leonardo, it amounts to something like a deification of nature, as evidenced by his notebooks. For Alberti and others, it leads to the science of perspective and similar disciplines. All, to be sure, had been aware of the necessity for departing from nature in order to achieve what we might call "l'effet de réel" (Roland Barthes). But nowhere before do we encounter anything quite like Baudelaire's intuition that nature itself might be regarded simply as an ensemble of aesthetic effects, capable of furnishing inspiration for yet more complex schemes of harmony and color. To some extent, the artistic consciousness had had to undergo the experience of Romanticism, with its subjective emphasis. But Baudelaire's intuition looks forward to something beyond even this: a vision, namely, of the external world and of life as contained within the sphere of our perceptions, and of the innate aesthetic tendency of all perception. We create the world by endowing it with splendid and vibrant life, in form, harmony, and color, and all the phenomena we perceive—the fragmentary yet vivid motifs of sound, light, and color—are but the elements that enter into the composition of our vision.

What separates Baudelaire from his predecessors is, above all, a sense of perception itself as a creation of the beautiful. The belief that perception amounts to nothing less than an arrangement of the impressions we receive—this legacy of Romanticism, which then leads to the Aesthetic idea of finding in that process, with its creative capacity, a

source of spiritual significance—such an idea has not yet led to the
flippancy that later permits a Wilde to claim nature did not know how
to create fogs in London until taught to do so by Impressionism. One
is still too close, with Baudelaire, to the original Impressionist insight—there is still, one might say, too deep an awareness of the pre-
carious and complex quality of perception to assimilate it so easily to
art. Thus, speaking of the effect of atmosphere on the relation between
a painter and his subject, Baudelaire observes:

> L'air joue un si grand rôle dans la théorie da la couleur, que, si
> un paysagiste peignait les feuilles des arbres telles qu'il les voit,
> il obtiendrait un ton faux; attendu qu'il y a un espace d'air bien
> moindre entre le spectateur et le tableau qu'entre le spectateur et
> la nature. (*OC* 2:425)

> [The air plays such a significant role in the theory of color that,
> if a landscapist were to paint the leaves of trees as he sees them,
> he would obtain a false tone—considering that there is a much
> lesser space of air between the spectator and the painting than
> between the spectator and nature.]

In other words, the distance between spectator and object must be
taken into account in both instances: if the painter depicts the color
of the leaves *as he perceives them,* he renders the color impression they
produce from a certain distance. But since the spectator of the painting
does not see the leaves from that same distance, this color impression
becomes "false" for him—it fails to reflect accurately the true color of
the leaves from his vantage point. The moral, according to Baudelaire:
"Les mensonges sont continuellement nécessaires, même pour arriver
au trompe-l'oeil" (*OC* 2:425). [Deceptions are continually necessary,
even to arrive at a trompe-l'oeil.]

With these remarks on the relation of art to nature, we arrive at the
essential principles of painting:

> L'harmonie est la base de la théorie de la couleur.
> La mélodie est l'unité dans la couleur, ou la couleur générale.
> La mélodie veut une conclusion; c'est un ensemble où tous
> les effets concourent à un effet général.
> Ainsi la mélodie laisse dans l'esprit un souvenir profond. (*OC*
> 2:425)

> [Harmony is the basis of the theory of color.
> Melody is unity in color, or the general color.

Melody wants a conclusion; it is an ensemble in which all the effects concur in a general effect.

Thus melody leaves in the soul a profound remembrance.]

In illustration of these principles one might perhaps consider the youthful Delacroix's celebrated entry for the *Salon* of 1822—*The Bark of Dante*.[6] It is difficult to define exactly the nature of color harmony: perhaps that is why Baudelaire merely offers some examples. Formally, it consists of the "agreement (*accord*) of two tones," one warm, the other cold. But the precise nature of their agreement remains difficult to specify, including as it does both opposition and concurrence. Baudelaire himself speaks of the "hand of a woman slightly ruddy, a little thin, and of a skin quite fine," in which one sees "a perfect harmony between the green of the large veins that furrow it [the hand] and the sanguinolent tones that mark the joints" (*OC* 2:423). This harmony of red and green, which recurs elsewhere in the *Salon de 1846,* plays a prominent role in the *Bark of Dante*.[7] It appears in the contrast between the Florentine's hood and his robe—the contrast of a flat red with a bright, almost metallic green tinted in various places with blue. There is something even mysterious in the harmony of these two colors: a red that, were it not for the presence of the green, would seem faded, and a green that without the red would seem even brighter, with a brilliant metallic sheen. But the effect of the robe's heavy folds actually intensifies the contrast with the poet's hood, which acquires an unearthly luminousness amid the dense mists of darkness shrouding the underworld. Even at its lightest, however, the green of Dante's robe remains incapable of achieving an effect of warmth comparable to that of the red—a result of what Baudelaire might call the respective "tonalities" of the different colors. In effect, the extreme contrast between the metallic brilliance of the green and the flatness of the red reaffirms Baudelaire's principle that the warmth or coldness of a color depends not so much upon its surface texture but upon its intrinsic chromatic quality.

With this we arrive at what defines for Baudelaire the very essence of harmony: the relationship between the different "tones" of various colors. Throughout *The Bark of Dante* one notices how colors are often juxtaposed for tonal contrast—as in the alternating sequence of warm and cold tints for the various naked bodies in the water, half of whom have a flesh tone mixed with orange, the other half with blue. Or there is the contrast between the cool green of Dante's robe and the warm reddish-brown of Virgil's. Even the atmosphere displays a similar tonal opposition, with the air of the burning city on Dante's right a warm amber while the halo above him shows a greenish-grayish tint. Such contrasts create the dynamic equilibrium necessary for pictorial expressiveness, which depends upon an impression of chromatic intensity.

For Baudelaire, however, harmony is but one of a painting's essential elements. The second, melody, consists of "unity in color, or the general color." Elsewhere in the *Salon de 1846* he writes that "La couleur est composée de masses colorées qui sont faites d'une infinité de tons, dont l'harmonie fait l'unité" (*OC* 2:455). [Color is composed of colored masses which consist of an infinity of tones, of which harmony makes the unity.] Thus the melody of a painting emerges out of its harmony: harmony creates unity in color, which is melody. By harmonizing various tones we arrive at the general color effect of a painting, what Baudelaire terms its "general color." This "general color" results from the chromatic impression produced by specific colors as an ensemble. Although the overall effect will be neither warm nor cold, the various colors will almost invariably share what one might call a fundamental qualitative resemblance. Thus both warm and cold tones can be characterized in terms of their relative "flatness" or "richness." "Flat" colors tend to form one kind of composition, "rich" ones another. A melody emerges from a painting as its color scheme takes on a specific significance. This occurs when it becomes expressive of a particular feeling. Just as a melody in music builds upon relationships between individual notes, so the melody of a color scheme begins with individual harmonies between various colors in order to create a composition conveying a particular emotion.

With *The Bark of Dante* we notice various harmonies that combine to form what Baudelaire would call its "melody." There is the harmony between two shades of red, that of Dante's hood and that of Virgil's robe, each juxtaposed against a contrasting green (in Virgil's case a dark laurel wreath about his head). A comparison is implicitly suggested between Dante's brighter red and the darker Virgilian hue, each finding its harmonic complement in a contrasting green. This comparison is then reinforced by the two poets' faces, Dante's somewhat tanned and Virgil's quite brown. Thus the colors of this central group of Dante and Virgil form a chromatic scale, culminating in the red of the Florentine's hood as its highest, most intense note. Set off against the cool green of the poet's robe on the one hand and the darker reddish-brown of Virgil's cloak on the other, this red of the hood becomes the one luminous spot around which everything else revolves, as if expressive of the stillness at the eye of the storm.

And in fact the suggestion of surrounding turbulence receives sig-

nificant emphasis from the movements of naked bodies in the water—
souls of the damned struggling to climb aboard the boat. From the
curved figure at the far left pulling itself up by clenching the stern
with its teeth to the one next to it who seems drawn by an irresistible
force in the opposite direction to the huddled figure attempting to
crawl into the vessel by bracing its right foot upon the abdomen of a
women who clutches at the bulwark with her arms in a backward
movement, the whole conveys a distinct impression of unbroken, violent swirling motion about a dramatic focal point.

We recall Baudelaire's assertion that "melody wants a conclusion"—
that it forms "an ensemble where all the effects concur in a general
effect." At what "conclusion," then, do the various complex harmonies
of *The Bark of Dante* finally arrive? We have seen how the swirling
movement of the painting revolves about a central spot, the luminous
red of Dante's hood. One might attribute to its radiance a kind of
spiritual significance: it suggests the mysterious aura that shone during
Troy's darkest night upon the head of Ascanius, symbolizing the promise
of a future Rome. Delacroix, well versed in classical sources, could not
fail to be familiar with this motif: by depicting Virgil as Dante's guide,
the painter emphasizes the Florentine's journey into the underworld
as a second quest comparable to that of Virgil's Aeneas for a new
spiritual homeland. Thus the radiance that shines upon Dante's head
here may be said to confer a similar significance. But whether or not
one accepts its literary associations, the expressive meaning of the color
scheme becomes manifest as an affirmation of a numinous radiance at
the center of the composition. Upon this motif all the numerous and
complex color harmonies converge. The central importance of a soli-
tary spot of color and its assertion of a spiritual aura—this, then, is
the "conclusion" or focal point of the color harmonies in *The Bark of
Dante*. Baudelaire had observed that melody "leaves within the soul a
profound remembrance (*souvenir*)." We recall how the same theme occurs at the end of his "Harmonie du soir": "Ton souvenir en moi luit
comme un ostensoir" [The memory of you in me gleams like a monstr-
ance]. And just as the memory of an other becomes endowed in that
poem with a religious significance, so here we might also be tempted
to read into Baudelaire's theory of color an affirmation of the sacred
quality of a work of art.

3

HISTORY AS A WORK OF ART

In his later years Jacob Burckhardt once recalled the impression made upon him by hearing Schelling lecture in Berlin. It had all seemed unintelligible—a mere display of abstract virtuosity. That these lectures should have struck him in this way is revealing. It indicates the gap separating Burckhardt's generation from its Romantic predecessors. We can imagine the moment: Friedrich Schelling, once in the vanguard of everything innovative in German idealism, when every subject he touched seemed to take on the luminous aura of his youthful brilliance, summoned now by a Prussian government after years of neglect to eradicate the Hegelianism that had supplanted him, speaking to an audience born under the shadow of the Congress of Vienna and disillusionment with the aftermath of 1830 and Louis-Philippe.

For Burckhardt, as for others, the Romantic concept that equates history with a progressive development of spirit had ceased to satisfy: but with this turning away from the discovery of self-consciousness as the ultimate aim of history what emerges is a new sense of the historical moment.[1] The disintegration of Romanticism's historical consciousness had in effect made it possible for Burckhardt, as for Ranke before him, to appreciate past epochs "aesthetically." Perhaps it was such aesthetic appreciation that had moved him to speak of the Renaissance, at the very beginning of his *Kultur der Renaissance in Italien*, as presenting a sort of image to the historical observer:

Die geistigen Umrisse einer Kulturepoche geben vielleicht für jedes Auge ein verschiedenes Bild, und wenn es sich vollends um eine Zivilisation handelt, welche als nächste Mutter der unsrigen noch jetzt fortwirkt, so muss sich das subjektive Urteilen und Empfinden jeden Augenblick beim Darsteller wie beim Leser einmischen. Auf dem weiten Meere, in welches wir uns hinauswagen, sind der möglichen Wege und Richtungen viele, und leicht könnten dieselben Studien, welche für diese Arbeit gemacht wur-

den, unter den Händen eines andern nicht nur eine ganz andere
Benützung und Behandlung erfahren, sondern auch zu wesent-
lich verschiedenen Schlüssen Anlass geben. . . . Einstweilen sind
wir zufrieden, wenn uns ein geduldiges Gehör gewährt und dieses
Buch als ein Ganzes aufgefasst wird. (*GW* 3:1)

[The spiritual outlines of a cultural epoch present perhaps to each
eye a different picture, and when it is a matter of treating comprehensively a civilization which as the nearest mother of our
own still works among us, so must the subjective judgments and
feelings intermingle at each instant both for the representer and
the reader. On the wide ocean upon which we venture, the possible ways and directions are many, and easily might the same
studies which were made for this work not only experience in
the hands of another a wholly different use and treatment but
also furnish occasion for essentially different conclusions. . . .
For the present, we are satisfied if a patient hearing be granted
us, and if this book be grasped as a whole.]

Significantly, Burckhardt even admits later that the categories into
which a great intellectual or spiritual continuum ("ein grosses geistiges
Kontinuum") must be broken up in order to make representation
(*Darstellung*) possible may seem quite arbitrary. His description of the
Renaissance as open to different interpretations reinforces his analogy
of a picture, which presents a different appearance when viewed from
different angles.[2] But perhaps most important is his insistence that his
work be grasped (*aufgefasst*) as a whole. Along with his admission of
possible arbitrariness in his categories, it suggests that the fidelity of
his—or any other—depiction of the Renaissance is not to be found
in its individual aspects but rather in their relation to each other—
which is to say, in their "composition."[3] But in fact Burckhardt does
not even claim objectivity for his composition as a whole. If the individual categories are necessarily subjective, their relations to each other
are equally so. By emphasizing the composition of his work as a whole,
Burckhardt seems to wish to avoid the whole problem of historical
objectivity altogether. As a result, a new kind of approach emerges,
one that seeks aesthetic rather than objective justification for its specific arrangement. In so doing, it attempts to emulate the formal coherence of a work of art.

The first section of Burckhardt's opus, "Der Staat als Kunstwerk"
("The State as a Work of Art"), represents Renaissance life as a whole,
since the State encompasses within itself all individual concerns.
Burckhardt describes the Renaissance State as "ein neues Lebendiges

in die Geschichte" [a new living thing in history], characterizing it as a "berechnete, bewusste Schöpfung, als Kunstwerk" [calculated, conscious creation, as a work of art]. In describing it as a "calculated, conscious creation," he describes the nature not only of all works of art but of his own historical treatment as well. The Renaissance State in *Die Kultur der Renaissance in Italien* possesses this special aspect, that it mirrors within itself the form of Burckhardt's own work. Like the Renaissance State, Burckhardt's essay is a "calculated, conscious creation." More than merely a naïve account of events or conditions, it manifests a consciousness of its own form as a work of art. This consciousness of form is reflected in the relation between various aspects of Burckhardt's work. But it was necessary first of all to introduce the aesthetic of form itself. Hence the portrait of the Renaissance State, which by disclosing the presence of form within the life of an epoch justifies form as the governing principle of Burckhardt's description. One might even ask whether a history that reproduces in its own form the form of its subject does not thereby lay claim to a higher objectivity than other historical analyses. Nowhere, however, do we find this claim made in *Die Kultur der Renaissance in Italien*. Perhaps the formal arrangement suffices in itself, as an embodiment of the work's aspiration toward an ideal of form.

The second section, "Entwicklung des Individuums" ("Development of the Individual"), exhibits both inward and outward aspects of the outlook of the Renaissance:

> Im Mittelalter lagen die beiden Seiten des Bewusstseins—nach der Welt hin und nach dem Innern des Menschen selbst—wie unter einem gemeinsamen Schleier träumend oder halbwach. Der Schleier war gewoben aus Glauben, Kindesbefangenheit und Wahn; durch ihn hindurchgesehen erschienen Welt und Geschichte wundersam gefärbt, der Mensch aber erkannte sich nur als Rasse, Volk, Partei, Korporation, Familie oder sonst in irgend einer Form des Allgemeinen. In Italien zuerst verweht dieser Schleier in die Lüfte; es erwacht eine *objektive* Betrachtung und Behandlung des Staates und der sämtlichen Dinge dieser Welt überhaupt; daneben aber erhebt sich mit voller Macht das *Subjektive*; der Mensch wird geistiges *Individuum* und erkennt sich als solches. (*GW* 3:89).

> [In the Middle Ages both sides of consciousness—that which was turned toward the world and that turned toward the inner realm of man himself —lay as if dreaming or half-awake beneath a common veil. The veil was woven of faith, childish prejudice,

and illusion; seen through it, the world and history appeared strangely colored, and man knew himself only as race, people, party, corporation, family, or any other form of the universal. In Italy this veil first blew away into the air; there awoke an *objective* consideration and treatment of the State and of all the things of this world in general; at the same time, however, the *subjective* asserted itself with fuller force; man became a spiritual *individual* and recognized himself as such.]

This outlook of the Renaissance determines the focus of Burckhardt's work, which concerns itself with objective as well as subjective aspects of Renaissance life, from the State as political structure to moral and religious beliefs of individuals, from pageants and festivals to the inherent social attitudes they exemplify. More specifically, this dual emphasis upon subjective and objective leads in the next section to "The Discovery of the World and of Man" ("Die Entdeckung der Welt und des Menschen"). The recognition of what defines an "objective consideration and treatment" first makes possible a discovery of the world. But it is also necessary to feel the subjective as subjective in order to recognize the distinctness of each individual. Unlike the Romantics, Burckhardt does not oppose subjective to objective and then seek in some fashion to reconcile their opposition. Instead subjective and objective become complementary aspects of consciousness, each necessary to the other. Their relation reflects that between the different aspects of Burckhardt's work, whose significance lies in its overall composition.

Both the discovery of the world and of man result in expansions of consciousness. Such is, similarly, the effect of "The Revival of Antiquity" ("Die Wiedererweckung des Altertums"), which might also be rendered "The Reawakening of Antiquity." Antiquity presents the possibility of a reawakening insofar as its essence consists not of a past epoch but rather of an earlier consciousness. Thus in speaking of the creation of an Italian culture Burckhardt can claim:

> allein wie das Bisherige so ist auch das Folgende doch von der Einwirkung der antiken Welt mannigfach gefärbt, und wo das Wesen der Dinge ohne dieselbe verständlich und vorhanden sein würde, da ist es doch die Äusserungsweise im Leben nur mit ihr und durch sie. (*GW* 3:116)

> [yet as is the preceding, so also is what follows variously colored by the influence of the ancient world, and where the essence of

things without this influence would still have been present and comprehensible, nevertheless the mode of expression in life occurs only with and through the classical influence.]

As style gives a form of expression to a theme, so classical antiquity offers the Renaissance a manner of expressing its new awareness of things. But a "mode of expression" (*Äusserungsweise*) is bound to affect the content it expresses. In so doing it also affects the Renaissance consciousness. In giving a particular form to the thoughts of that consciousness, it shapes the way in which the latter sees itself. Thus the Renaissance, in ushering in a new vision both of the external world and of the subjective self, sees itself through the image of classical antiquity, but in the process transforms antiquity into a reflection of itself.

The "discovery of the world and of man" are the results of the Renaissance's burgeoning awareness. If Burckhardt owes this formula ("la découverte du monde et la découverte de l'homme") to Michelet, his treatment of it differs nevertheless in a significant fashion.[4] For Burckhardt such discoveries are simply the outgrowth of a fundamentally altered perception of things. If classical antiquity affects the manner of expression (and hence the Renaissance's image of itself), the discovery of the world and of man represent the concrete embodiment of its empirical impulse. As such they make possible the Renaissance's expansion and development, by giving it specific forms. These forms offer the period new realms for exploration and become aspects of its self-expression. Just as classical antiquity had imparted to the Renaissance a mode of expression, of externalizing what is within itself, so the discovery of the world and of man are in some sense the *content* of that expression.

This externalizing of itself also defines the rationale of "Social Life and Festivals" ("Die Geselligkeit und die Feste"). What Burckhardt means by "Geselligkeit" are not simply the manifestations of social life but rather its underlying attitudes. These comprise the inner, subjective element of the social sphere. The festivals, conversely, make up its external, objective element. Thus the relation between these parallels that between the Renaissance consciousness and its embodiment in the discoveries of the world and of man. As these discoveries had endowed consciousness with external form, so in a similar fashion the festivals give visible expression to the social ideals of the Renaissance. Through their pageantry, however, festivals do more than simply express certain ideals. They also enhance and elevate them, by raising the relations embodied within them to a more formal level. As a result, the hier-

archical pattern they exhibit becomes a visible ideal for the social life
of the epoch.

The final section of the book, "Morals and Religion" ("Sitte und
Religion"), offers another, more subjective form of ideal. Earlier, in
depicting the reawakening of antiquity, Burckhardt had described how
the Renaissance sought in the classical world an embodiment of its
aspirations:

> sie bedurfte eines Führers, und als solchen bot sich das klassische
> Altertum dar mit seiner Fülle objektiver, evidenter Wahrheit in
> allen Gebieten des Geistes. . . . der zum Bewusstsein geweckte
> Geist aber war in Suchen nach einem neuen haltbaren Ideal be-
> griffen. . . . (*GW* 3:119)

> [it needed a guide, and as such classical antiquity offered itself,
> with its abundance of objective, evident truth in all realms of the
> spirit. . . . the spirit now awakened to consciousness, however,
> was in the process of searching for a new tangible ideal.]

Whereas classical antiquity might offer a "tangible ideal" for the
Renaissance, religion envisages something more elusive: a transformation of its inner consciousness. Because of its "abundance of objective, evident truth in all realms of the spirit," antiquity could indeed
present an external form in which consciousness might find an image
of itself. But insofar as the Renaissance seeks something other than
what it is in itself, antiquity could not satisfy it. In proposing an image
not of what it is but of what it could become, religion becomes for
the Renaissance a symbolic idea—one suggestive of a higher form of
existence. In implying the possibility of realizing that existence on earth,
Renaissance religion becomes expressive of the ideal of Aestheticism.

We have seen how the Renaissance State, as a "calculated, conscious
creation," represents a work of art. By subordinating all personal aspirations and desires to its own higher aims, the State sublimates individual consciousness to form. But this sublimation of consciousness
to a formal arrangement of life defines the meaning of all aspects of
existence. Thus the Renaissance State achieves the Aesthetic ideal—a
transformation of life into art. By its very formation, such a State suggests a plastic sense of the possibilities of human existence. From an
aesthetic standpoint, political alliances, war, administration, life at court,
all become part of a formal scheme in which the significance of each
aspect results from its relation to others. The whole, in turn, becomes
itself expressive of an idea: the permeation of life by "form." Thus life
itself, through its permeation by form, becomes the ultimate work of

art—the symbolic expression of a higher idea, that of the formative will's capacity to transform life into art.

If the creation of the Renaissance State assimilates life to form, the development of the individual implies, on the other hand, an intensified consciousness. We have seen how these two tendencies, the aestheticism of form and the aestheticism of consciousness, react unceasingly upon each other. Both are present in Burckhardt. A growing objective awareness arises from recognizing the beauty of the external world. Passionate curiosity about natural phenomena and a faithful reproduction of their varied appearances are symptoms of it. But whereas an increased objectivity might have been viewed as conflicting with the self's inner development, Burckhardt presents both as forms of a single impulse: the desire for a more intense experience of existence.

By becoming more responsive to external phenomena as well as to infinitely subtle shades of emotion, the Renaissance attempts to extract more from each passing moment. For no one is this need more urgent than for the tyrant or *condottiere,* but it applies to his dependents as well. Of such individuals Burckhardt remarks:

> Der Geist dieser Leute lernt notgedrungen alle seine innern Hilfsquellen kennen, die dauernden wie die des Augenblickes; auch ihr Lebensgenuss wird ein durch geistige Mittel erhöhter und konzentrierter, um einer vielleicht nur kurzen Zeit der Macht und des Einflusses einen grösstmöglichen Wert zu verleihen. (*GW* 3:90)

> [The mind of these people learned by necessity to know all its inner resources, the permanent as well as those of the moment; also, its pleasure in life was one enhanced and concentrated through intellectual means, in order to impart the greatest possible value to what might be only a brief time of power and influence.]

The discovery that mere sensual enjoyment quickly fades leads to an intellectualization of pleasure. The enhancement and concentration of pleasure through intellectual (*geistige*) means produces a refinement of sensations, one which also intensifies. Refinement implies an increase in both quantity and forms of sensation. These in effect multiply awareness, expanding the experience of each moment. But the expansion of a moment can only defer that moment's inevitable passing away. Through its quest for more intense forms of gratification, the Renaissance thus discovers the fundamental problem of pleasure: its inescapable transience. At the same time, it also realizes that by transmuting pleasure into thought, it preserves pleasure a little longer. But this intellectualization of pleasure also means translation of sensation into formal creation or art.

Even at its outset, then, the quest for pleasure encounters the implicit opposition between an aestheticism of consciousness and an aestheticism of form. Aestheticism of consciousness offers the voluptuousness of pure pleasure, all the forms of intellectual as well as material sensuousness, limitless intensity and depth of sensation. Only the finite capacity of the mind prevents it from experiencing more. Its essential problem, however, lies in its inability to feel the same stimulus repeatedly with equal intensity. Hence its recourse to intellectual pleasures, as a means of enhancing and concentrating its original experience. In adopting these, one raises a question: can any intellectualization of pleasure afford the same intensity as that of the original experience? And if not, does the mind's recourse to intellectual enjoyment and hence to an aestheticism of form necessarily preserve, in however diminished or altered a form, its original sensation? If not, does it represent anything more than another means of enhancing consciousness? What *Die Kultur der Renaissance in Italien* offers is not so much a resolution as an embodiment of this problem within the very form of the work. It thereby seeks to resolve this dilemma on the higher level comprised by such form—which is also simultaneously the "form" of the period it depicts.

The "reawakening of antiquity" manifests itself above all as an enhancement of Renaissance consciousness, a coloring that enables it to view the present in a new light. As such it presents a means of intensifying as well as aesthetically enriching its awareness. Of the individuals in the forefront of this endeavor Burckhardt observes:

> Die aktiven Träger derselben werden wichtige Personen, weil sie wissen, was die Alten gewusst haben, weil sie zu schreiben suchen, wie die Alten schreiben, weil sie zu denken und bald auch zu empfinden beginnen, wie die Alten dachten und empfanden. Die Tradition, der sie sich widmen, geht an tausend Stelle in die Reproduktion über. (*GW* 3:134–35)

> [Its active representatives became important persons, because they knew what the ancients had known, because they attempted to write as the ancients wrote, because they began to think and soon also to feel as the ancients thought and felt. The tradition to which they devoted themselves passed over at a thousand places into reproduction.]

But a revival of the antique consciousness is not the same thing as the original consciousness. For those individuals of the Renaissance who had assimilated the classical outlook, it was possible to feel it as something belonging to the past—a feeling not accessible to the ancients themselves, for whom this outlook represented all they knew. The feeling of antiquity that informs the Renaissance renewal of the classical consciousness imparts an added pleasure to its experience of the present moment, insofar as it can now feel its awareness of the present heightened by contrast with an earlier mode of feeling. At the same time, the presence of a modern sensibility makes possible the appreciation of those specific elements of a past outlook that give it its historical quality. The feeling of historicity that results becomes for the Renaissance something like an awareness of its own consciousness, to the extent that what it apprehends is not so much the actual past but rather its experience of that past. This "consciousness of consciousness" yields in turn a new pleasure by introducing one of the subtlest of all possible refinements, the sensation of our own experience of an impression.

The "discovery of the world and of man" offers the Renaissance new sources of impressions. The awakening of consciousness described in "The Development of the Individual" had made possible a new awareness of the beauty of external nature. Whereas previously that beauty, if perceived, had been either denied on account of monastic asceticism or assimilated to religious symbolism, it now becomes an object of pleasure in itself. Similarly, the beauty of the human face and figure and of various forms of social intercourse are now admitted as subjects of intrinsic interest. By reproducing the movement of daily life through literature it even becomes possible to enhance the delight received from minute observation. The same might also be said of the festivals, whose splendid pageants constitute yet another attempt to reproduce life in its various social relations. But the pageants, perhaps, even more so than literature or the other arts, exhibit a direct assimilation of life to form. What one sees in such pageants manifests above all a desire to give visible brilliance to those modes of social intercourse that define the life of an epoch. By means of these pageants, a State expresses ultimately the idea that the basic structure of its society represents a work of art.

In its various forms, Renaissance religion—in particular that of its most select spirits such as Lorenzo de' Medici and the Platonic Academy of Florence—endows Burckhardt's work with the culmination of its vision.[5] At the heart of this religion lies an apotheosis of the aesthetic consciousness, through an affirmation of the idea of a *Deus artifex,* God as maker, that raises the formative impulse to its highest

possible level. In the hymns of Lorenzo, "the highest result of that
school," is expressed a theism without reserve, one that proceeds "from
a perception which attempts to treat the world as one great moral and
physical cosmos" (*GW* 3:384). Against the pessimism of the Middle
Ages or the fatalism of the Renaissance it offers

> die Idee, dass die sichtbare Welt von Gott aus Liebe geschaffen,
> dass sie ein Abbild des in ihm praexistierenden Vorbildes sei,
> und dass er ihr dauernder Beweger und Fortschöpfer bleiben
> werde. Die Seele des einzelnen kann zunächst durch das Erken-
> nen Gottes *ihn* in ihre engen Schranken zusammenziehen, aber
> auch durch Liebe zu ihm *sich* ins Unendliche ausdehnen, und
> dies ist dann die Seligkeit auf Erden. (*GW* 3:384–85)

> [the idea that the visible world was created by God through love,
> that it is a copy of a pattern preexisting in him, and that he will
> remain its enduring mover and continuous creator. The soul of
> the individual can by perceiving God first draw *him* within its
> narrow limits, but it can also through love for him expand *itself*
> into the infinite, and this is then blessedness on earth.]

Such a soul will then see the formative impulse of aestheticism, its
desire to sublimate life to the form of a work of art, as but the reflection of a higher force, a plastic energy ceaselessly creating, ceaselessly conforming all things to its own divine scheme of perfect harmony. To feel a consciousness of that harmony by which the eternal
flux of life, its endless creative ferment, is brought to acquiesce in some
higher end is to realize that not even in life itself, the totality of all its
moments, can aestheticism find its highest fulfillment, but rather by
participating through consciousness in the creative activity of a divine
intelligence which it is the role of all earthly form finally to symbolize.

4

MUSIC AT TWILIGHT

In choice of subject, as in all besides, the *Concert* of the *Pitti* Palace is typical of everything that Giorgione, himself an admirable musician, touched with his influence. In sketch or finished picture, in various collections, we may follow it through many intricate variations—men fainting at music; music at the pool-side while people fish, or mingled with the sound of the pitcher in the well, or heard across running water, or among the flocks; the tuning of instruments; people with intent faces, as if listening, like those described by Plato in an ingenious passage of the Republic, to detect the smallest interval of musical sound, the smallest undulation in the air, or feeling for music in thought on a stringless instrument, ear and finger refining themselves infinitely, in the appetite for sweet sound; a momentary touch of an instrument in the twilight, as one passes through some unfamiliar room, in a chance company.

—Pater, *The Renaissance,* p. 119

It hardly matters that *The Concert* is now attributed to Titian rather than Giorgione. Pater himself had presented it only as an instance of the *Giorgionesque,* the characteristic expression of a style rather than of a specific painter.[1] What it offers is a glimpse of certain possibilities of imaginative apprehension—the sense of some hidden significance, like that of a musical theme, that runs like a leitmotiv through the whole of existence. This music heard amid the bustle of other, quite ordinary activities—fishing, for example, or tending a flock—also blends imperceptibly with the sound of running water or the delicate plash of a pitcher in a well. In all these instances it becomes part of our awareness of life, its rhythms and cadences.

Here music conveys something more than mere melody—as if those "people with intent faces" were listening for some hint of the meaning of their experiences: the "smallest undulation in the air," Pater tells us, yet that undulation might intimate a thought pregnant with recognitions. Thus the mind, "feeling for music in thought on a stringless instrument" as it moves among the confused array of its sensations and memories, searches for an idea to illuminate them. In the process we observe "ear and finger refining themselves infinitely, in the appetite for sweet sound," all our senses becoming more acute in the effort to grasp what lies behind external impressions. Hence the disclosure of previously unnoticed relations between various moments will have the semblance of "a momentary touch of an instrument in the twilight, as one passes through some unfamiliar room, in a chance company." We are always, one might say, dwelling in some indistinguishable twilight of consciousness, and our life consists symbolically of a passage through unfamiliar rooms inhabited by a chance company. These rooms that typify stages of our existence, the chance company composed of everyone we meet on our life's journey, including those dearest to us who yet remain distant through an unbridgeable subjective abyss—from all this, the momentary touch of fingers upon an instrument can liberate as if by a magical spell.[2]

In his novel *La Recherche de l'absolu,* Balzac had spoken of how at certain moments of intense emotion we become aware of an inner music in our lives. It is then that we feel time itself—perhaps this is, after all, the essence of music—as the emotions of those moments become detached from experience to assume a kind of independent existence. Through various scenes from Giorgione, similarly, a sense of music emerges like some mysterious allegory of life, so that fishing by the poolside or tending flocks or drawing water from a well become merely dreamlike rites of some inner drama. Thus the depiction of life becomes a tapestry, illustrating the passage of time and our experience of it. "In these then," as Pater observes, "the favorite incidents of Giorgione's school, music or the musical intervals in our existence, life itself is conceived as a sort of listening—listening to music, to the reading of Bandello's novels, to the sound of water, to time as it flies" (*The Renaissance,* p. 119).

There is, of course, a mute sensuousness when music blends with other sounds, especially that of running water, leading one to wonder about the deeper relation of these phenomena to each other: what meaning, for instance, are we to ascribe to the way music enters into scenes of ordinary life, its intervals of work and leisure, pleasure and reveries? Through all these runs a sense of the fleeting temporality of things: brief glimpses of beauty embodied in a gesture, a look, a smile, which yet are conscious of their own evanescence, the voiceless poetry of certain instants—"exquisite pauses in time," as Pater calls them, brimming with intense emotion, "in which, arrested thus, we seem to be spectators of all the fulness of existence and which are like some consummate extract or quintessence of life" (*The Renaissance,* p. 118).

Here, through a succession of such scenes, we become conscious of the passing of time. Simultaneously, however, music appeals to a higher sense. Like consciousness, it too concerns temporality, differing only in attempting to give form to our experience of time. In composing a specific theme, music creates a pattern that transcends the transitory nature of individual notes, altering the emphasis from specific moments to the sequence they form. With the apprehension of an intrinsic sequence, however, these moments become meaningful. From this standpoint, the presence of music in Giorgione's paintings attests to an implicit theme. Of such a theme we sometimes receive brief glimpses. Speaking of the protagonist of "The Child in the House," Pater observes:

> His way of conceiving religion came then to be in effect what it ever afterwards remained—a sacred history indeed, but still more a sacred ideal, a transcendent version or representation, under intenser and more expressive light and shade, of human life and its familiar or exceptional incidents, birth, death, marriage, youth, age, tears, joy, rest, sleep, waking—a mirror, towards which men might turn away their eyes from vanity and dullness, and see themselves therein as angels, with their daily meat and drink, even, become a kind of sacred transaction—a complementary strain or burden, applied to our every-day existence, whereby the stray snatches of music in it re-set themselves, and fall into the scheme of some higher and more consistent harmony. (*Miscellaneous Studies,* pp. 193–94)[3]

With "The Child in the House," the "complementary strain or burden" that enables brief intervals of audible music to "re-set themselves, and fall into the scheme of some higher and more consistent harmony" manifests a feeling of form—the intuition of disparate moments arranging themselves into something like a formal sequence. But this form is not imposed in any sense from without; like that of music, it seems to exist within our life itself. The *relation* of one moment to another—that is all we know of form, of the hidden arrangement that defines the sequence of our experiences. The sense of a relation between them conveys the feeling of special significance that we associate with harmony in music.

If music thus offers an apprehension of form through the experience of temporality, the same may be said, under different conditions, of painting.[4] Like music, painting assimilates subject matter to form. Nowhere does this occur more completely than with Giorgione. The combining of colors, like that of notes in music—a rich, sensuous dark red, for instance, with the mute splendor of amber or gold, or a shimmering green that blends with turquoise as part of a distant landscape—all this announces the special realm of Venetian painting, and of Giorgione in particular. To achieve a perfect concordance of colors within a painted scene, a symmetrical disposition of figures and objects modified by varying intensities of light—to idealize, in Pater's words, episodes of actual life "till they come to seem like glimpses of life from afar"—this is what is meant by subordinating substance to form. For Pater, however, what characterizes Giorgione above all is his capacity for selecting the ideal moment. By isolating the poetic element of a scene along with those conditions of light and shadow under which it occurs, painting expresses a higher harmony than any possible in actual life. Ideal moments can often involve an intense play of emotions. It is a measure of the supremacy of form in Giorgione's art that even emotion is sublimated to the requirements of composition, the luminousness of a look or gesture being combined with other motifs in a formal harmony of arrangement.

For Pater, the subordination of substance to form is not a result of the limitations of painting or any other art. Instead it exemplifies the indispensable condition of any higher expressiveness, any subtler or more complex vision. Here form comes to signify something more than merely an abstract program. For Pater what matters is rather the formal awareness that sees each object, each figure, each spot of color in relation to others. "Nothing," he asserts in *Plato and Platonism,* "nothing but the life-giving principle of cohesion is new; the new perspective, the resultant complexion, the expressiveness which familiar thoughts attain by novel juxtaposition. In other words, the *form* is new. But then, in the creation of philosophical literature, as in all other products of art, *form,* in the full signification of that word, is everything, and the mere matter is nothing" (*Plato and Platonism,* p. 8).

Hence the importance of form, and, consequently, of fusing form and substance in art:

> For while . . . it is possible to distinguish the matter from the form, and the understanding can always make this distinction, yet it is the constant effort of art to obliterate it. That the mere matter of a poem, for instance, its subject, namely, its given incidents or situation—that the mere matter of a picture, the actual circumstances of an event, the actual topography of a landscape—should be nothing without the form, the spirit, of the handling, that this form, this mode of handling, should become

an end in itself, should penetrate every part of the matter: this is what all art constantly strives after, and achieves in different degrees. (*The Renaissance,* p. 106).[5]

Thus all modes of pictorial treatment only emphasize the primacy of vision, the pure *seeing* of a subject by the artistic eye that disposes in accordance with its own formal requirements.[6] For Pater, ultimately, all form is nothing but this, the arrangement of things by a perceiving mind, and all art, finally, but a medium of the mind's vision:

Art, then, is thus always striving to be independent of the mere intelligence, to become a matter of pure perception, to get rid of its responsibilities to its subject or material; the ideal examples of poetry and painting being those in which the constituent elements of the composition are so welded together, that the material or subject no longer strikes the intellect only; nor the form, the eye or the ear only; but form and matter, in their union or identity, present one single effect to the "imaginative reason," that complex faculty for which every thought and feeling is twinborn with its sensible analogue or symbol. (*The Renaissance,* p. 109).

One art achieves this fusion of form and content more perfectly than all the rest:

It is the art of music which most completely realises this artistic ideal, this perfect identification of matter and form. In its consummate moments, the end is not distinct from the means, the form from the matter, the subject from the expression; they inhere in and completely saturate each other; and to it, therefore, to the condition of its perfect moments, all the arts may be supposed constantly to tend and aspire. In music, then, rather than in poetry, is to be found the true type or measure of perfected art. Therefore, although each art has its incommunicable element, its untranslatable order of impressions, its unique mode of reaching the "imaginative reason," yet the arts may be represented as continually struggling after the law or principle of music, to a condition which music alone completely realises; and one of the chief functions of aesthetic criticism, in dealing with the products of art, new or old, is to estimate the degree in which each of those products approaches, in this sense, to musical law. (*The Renaissance,* p. 109).

But if all the arts aspire to the condition of music, to a perfect fusion of form and substance, cannot the same be said of life? In life, however, we experience form only when our impressions come together in some arrangement expressive of a higher harmony or consistency. Thus the quest of life, like that of music, becomes one for form—a form encompassing life. For Pater, this "music" of life is one we find ourselves constantly striving to hear. Like some magical harmony that will reveal to us the meaning of all the disparate moments of our existence, it becomes audible only for the briefest intervals. Thus the posture of those figures in Giorgione whose faces, intent to detect "the smallest interval of musical sound," might aptly symbolize the human condition. But the music they are so intent on hearing represents something other than the harmony of emotions described by Baudelaire. In this respect, it is undoubtedly significant that the music Giorgione's players produce is a silent one—we hear nothing ourselves, we merely *see* them in the act of touching their instruments. But were it possible to hear it, such a harmony would impart a form to existence, endowing all our experiences with an awareness of their relation to each other. This harmony would in turn transform life into a work of art. But if life, under these conditions, becomes form, this is not to be understood in the sense in which, for Burckhardt, the Renaissance state assumes the structure of a work of art. That would be an instance of external form. But the form Pater imagines consists of a modification of perception rather than of external circumstances. Thus if the relation of different interludes is the result of an inner insight, the form we now speak of represents nothing more than a recognition of how life can assume the structure or arrangement of a composition—in other words, of music.

With Pater, the elements of a Giorgione exemplify such an arrangement. Here the expression of a look, a gesture, the gleam of armor, or the reflection of light in a pool of water become formal motifs: the spirit of their handling (to use Pater's term) is everything. Nevertheless, they do not enter into the music of the scene, that harmony which is always implied but never realized. Such harmony transcends that of the painting, existing only within the mind that views it. If we apply a similar principle to life, it becomes tantamount to saying that if we are to achieve an identification of form and matter, it can only be by apprehending the moments of our existence as we do those of a musical composition. What we then receive would be a sense of what Pater had termed the higher harmony or consistency of our existence.

To attain that harmony, it becomes necessary to separate ourselves from whatever there is of mere substance, i.e., emotion, in these moments. By their effect upon us, by the suffering or joy they cause us, they preclude the possibility of a purely aesthetic apprehension. This is not to imply that such an apprehension will be devoid of all relation to the human element of life. It suggests, rather, a different form of experience, in which the emotional coloring of our impressions becomes a part of aesthetic apprehension. Taken by themselves, our feelings ravage us, consuming our energies and our vital forces. Such, at least, had been the symbolic theme of Balzac's *La Peau de chagrin*. By disrupting the tranquillity of our inner life, these feelings render impossible any sense of what Pater defines as form. The intuition that all our disparate experiences might possess some deeper relationship to each other haunts us at various intervals of our lives. But "The world is too much with us"—as Wordsworth laments in one of his most famous sonnets. The same might be said, from an aesthetic standpoint, of our emotional life. We feel too deeply our engagement with others, we become too passionate in pursuit of our different objectives, to appreciate the beauty of those moments of intense consciousness that shed their radiance over our existence. The tremulous stillness of a look or a smile, as in certain scenes depicted by Giorgione; the mute passage of affection through a touch or a whisper, the record of "some brief and wholly concrete moment," into which, as Pater declares, "all the motives, all the interests and effects of a long history, have condensed themselves, and which seem to absorb past and future in an intense consciousness of the present"—all these fail to move us.

The beauty of such moments becomes apparent only when our vital engagement with them ceases—when we can withdraw to a more dispassionate distance to appreciate simply their aesthetic aspect. There is a poetry, of course, in the emotions we associate with past moments, but we become conscious of it only when they compose themselves into a larger sequence. A sense of composition, of each experience having a specific and appropriate place in some higher scheme, endows a given moment with a particular significance. This beauty of relation brings clarity into the chaos of our existence, producing its effect by an appeal to what our lives might be: an arrangement of disparate, disconnected impressions according to some finer consistency, some perception of intrinsic coherence, and a consciousness of form within the movement of time.

We are all familiar with the defense of "l'art pour l'art." That program had made possible a disengagement of interest from emotion and hence an appreciation of emotion in art simply for its intensity rather than for its specific associations. This could result in cultivation of the esoteric or remote, as in Flaubert's "Hérodias" or the "Légende de Saint Julien l'Hospitalier," as well as in the emotional aesthetic of "Un Coeur simple." But the proclamation of art for art's sake might also produce a yet higher appeal—of *life* for art's sake, which would mean not merely disengagement of form from social and moral interests but a subordination even of life itself to the canons of form.[7] To be sure, we do not find with Pater, as with Wilde, a concern with the external form of our existence. Pater's preoccupation is, rather, with the form of our perceptions. But, to the extent that this depends upon recognizing form in external phenomena, we must consider whether an arrangement of life into more formally pleasing modes might not yield a greater sense of harmony between different aspects of our existence. For Pater, the transformation of experience results above all from a transformation in perspective: to see our lives for their moments of beauty is, among other things, to see them as composing a formal sequence. Only with this sense of the moment as something dissociated from passion does it become possible to perceive its formal relation to other moments, other scenes. The appreciation of beauty, then, as a source of meaning in our experience of the moment awakens the mind to the possibilities in our life for form.

For Pater the desire for form in life, which proceeds from a sense of form in our external impressions, finds its highest expression in the period we call the Renaissance.[8] If life itself has always offered possibilities for form, only at specific moments does an awareness of these attain sufficient clarity to become expressive of an epoch. An epoch defines itself not by its external acts but by the manner in which it perceives them. Like the golden sheen or patina of a Venetian painting, such perception colors the whole life of its time, so that whatever one sees of that life inevitably appears through its medium. This medium in turn makes possible the aestheticism of the Renaissance, which is an aestheticism of perception. When it becomes concentrated enough to color significantly the various aspects of human existence, that vision also becomes conscious of itself. It then becomes expressive not only of what it sees but of its own medium. But the only form in which it can represent that medium is through a work of art. Thus the nature of Renaissance consciousness becomes for Pater that of a work of art.

In this respect, Pater's title for the first edition of his work may well be the most appropriate: *Studies in the History of the Renaissance.*[9] What it reveals is an attempt to define all of history in terms of works of art and the consciousness they manifest.[10] For Pater, each work embodies a particular sensibility—which is to say, a particular percep-

tion of life. But that perception, in turn, characterizes a specific historical moment, which is, after all, nothing but the experience of a
given moment through an individual subjective consciousness. Criticism, in its effort to recover that perception, ultimately identifies with
the artistic consciousness it seeks to represent, in order to reproduce
the work of art's plastic perception of the aesthetic possibilities of life.[11]
Where a painting or literary work sees Renaissance life in terms of its
capacity for aesthetic arrangement, historical interpretation will then
do the same. The result: a depiction of the history of the Renaissance
as a series of privileged moments of aesthetic perception. To think of
The Renaissance merely as *Studies in Art and Poetry* (Pater's later sub-
title) is therefore misleading. *Studies in the History of the Renaissance*
announces his larger ambition of transforming all of history into art.
But the transformation of history into art by the creation of a formal
sequence of privileged moments of consciousness ultimately suggests
a desire to transform life itself into a work of art.[12]

From this standpoint we might compare Pater's enterprise to that
of Jacob Burckhardt. But whereas Burckhardt had sought to impose
the form of a work of art upon the *life* of a historical epoch, what
Pater seeks is rather to define that epoch in terms of an aesthetic consciousness. Thus he begins by dissolving the historical moment into
subjective experience. By means of its experience, the artistic mind (which
represents for Pater the most sensitive medium of registration) unconsciously shapes what it sees so as to bring out the latent possibilities
of various phenomena, their susceptibility to arrangement in some more
expressive scheme. This perception already possesses the form of a work
of art; it does not need to impose form upon life. Thus while Burckhardt asserts the formal possibilities of life through their realization in
the Renaissance, what Pater presents is rather a sense of form within
the actual experience of Renaissance existence.[13] For him the "realization" of form achieves its highest expression not in life but in art.

Of course, the art Pater discusses in his *Renaissance* is itself a vision
of life, that is, of the life of its time. In this sense, it offers a perception
of the intrinsic possibilities for form in that existence, as well as a
formal consciousness of life. As a vision of life and its possibilities,
Renaissance art necessarily expresses an aesthetic ideal. That this ideal
should consist of a vision embodied within the period defines in turn
the unique form of Pater's work. Its particular source is the artistic
sense, which discloses (as in Giorgione) glimpses of a higher harmony
in human existence. Vision and form: we have felt their relation in
both Pater and his predecessors. What is significant here is how he
affirms that vision by situating it historically within the Renaissance.

Of course, Pater is not unaware of his work's interpretative aspect, the sense in which it elicits a vision from its sources. Nevertheless, that it should have been possible to ascribe a vision to the period at all pre-supposes the existence of those works of art from which it was for-mulated. By their very nature as art, these productions necessarily con-fer a consecration of form upon their subjects. Thus the *form* as well as vision of the aesthetic ideal lies within the Renaissance conscious-ness. Hence form, like vision, assumes a historical existence. Its exis-tence, in turn, lends the Renaissance its unique aspect by transforming history into a form-giving consciousness within the period itself.

It remains for us to consider the specific form of Pater's historical vision, the nature of its idealization of the Renaissance.[14] Such ideal-ization in effect internalizes the relation of life to art which forms the essence of aestheticism:

> The word *Renaissance,* indeed, is now generally used to denote not merely the revival of classical antiquity which took place in the fifteenth century, and to which the word was first supplied, but a whole complex movement, of which that revival of classical antiquity was but one element or symptom. For us the Renais-sance is the name of a many-sided but yet united movement, in which the love of the things of the intellect and the imagination for their own sake, the desire for a more liberal and comely way of conceiving life, make themselves felt, urging those who ex-perience this desire to search out first one and then another means of intellectual or imaginative enjoyment, and directing them not only to the discovery of old and forgotten sources of this enjoy-ment, but to the divination of fresh sources thereof—new ex-periences, new subjects of poetry, new forms of art. (*The Ren-aissance,* pp. 1–2)

"The love of the things of the intellect and the imagination for their own sake": like the pursuit of art for art's sake, this love signifies some-thing more than mere intellectualism.[15] We have seen how for Pater intellect and imagination become one in the mind of a sensitive ob-server of life. To love the things of the intellect, in the fashion of Abelard, is to feel a passionate desire for the highest forms of discrim-ination, where vision transcends the realm of visible objects to concern itself with those more abstract forms perceivable by the mind's eye alone. A feeling for the slightest shades of difference, a refinement of thought to the point where it becomes capable of registering the most complex impressions—this, then, is what a love of things of the in-tellect for their own sake implies. Such love finds itself inspired, above all, by a yearning for the beautiful. To believe that perception of the least tangible things is not an indifferent but rather the most passionate form of experience—to find in the subtlest discriminations a medium for the intenser consciousness—this would represent, perhaps, the most fascinating aestheticism of all, that of the intellect.

Here we might think of Pater's beautiful characterization of Abelard, who, dwelling in medieval Paris, "in such dreamy tranquillity, amid the bright and busy spectacle of the 'Island,' lived in a world of something like shadows; and that for one who knew so well how to assign its exact value to every abstract thought, those restraints which lie on the consciences of other men had been relaxed" (*The Renaissance,* pp. 3–4). The allure of a dreamlike awareness allowed to pass lightly over things—or to linger over moments that give it pleasure: such might be some of the attractions, for someone like Abelard, of the *vita contemplativa* as opposed to the *vita activa*. But if reverie moves within a realm of shadows, for the intellect there are additional pleasures—in particular, the fascination of concepts, those bright, iridescent objects whose apparition in the mind offers one of the highest forms of aesthetic stimulation. Pater would doubtless have been especially fond of the "intellectual sensuousness" (Henry Adams) of Renaissance neoplatonism, its peculiar fusion of the intellectual with the symbolic that endows the visible world with a higher significance and even ascribes to things of the mind the beauty of an epiphanic experience.

Clearly, then, a love of the things of the intellect includes rational thought as well as vision. Indeed, in its highest form, pursuit of intellectual truth becomes simply perception that embodies the highest discriminations—hence a life of intensified consciousness. But this definition merely reveals the intellect's role in any finer aestheticism, for which sensual pleasures fade by comparison with those we can never exhaust nor tire of. The notion that the Renaissance manifests a love of things of the intellect for their own sake thus places the whole of that epoch within an aesthetic perspective. Like the pursuit of art for art's sake, what lies at the basis of intellectual passion is, above all, a worship of form. Things of the intellect involve in essence an apprehension of form. To discern an inner coherence behind the chaos of external appearances is to perceive a higher harmony that unifies all the disparate moments of existence. If intellect, then, assumes the form of artistic vision, this is only to bring about, at some higher level, an assimilation of life to form. If intellectual things are among the most enduring, that is precisely because they display the highest degree of form. But the form they possess consists of an apprehension of relations between things. To discern these relations within our actual existence becomes then a means for the intellect to give form to life itself.

The desire for "a more liberal and comely way of conceiving life" is the desire, then, that life itself might be given over to form: born of a perception of life's higher harmony, it seeks to re-create that perception in terms of an ideal, as a vision of what our life ought to be. It need not affect that life externally, and it need not result in pursuit of a beauty of external forms: to experience the charm of a fleeting moment, a look, a gesture, the color of a sky or landscape might suffice, so long as it does not sacrifice the impression of that beauty to abstract imperatives. What this vision proposes, above all, is the mind's freedom to give form and color to its perceptions. All it asks for, its "liberality," so to speak, consists of this generosity, this freedom in treating its impressions. As with the arts (and the painting of Giorgione in particular) treatment rather than subject matter is everything. To be able to paint in the colors one chooses, to lend to the depiction of a given moment the effect of a certain atmosphere of light or shade— such is the freedom expression seeks, a freedom of composition.

The ideal of this freedom is what imparts to the idea of the Renaissance a glimpse of certain aesthetic possibilities. A more "comely" way of conceiving life—is this to suggest merely what pleases, or the appropriate and proper, or perhaps both? For pleasure now assumes a higher significance through its association with our experience of the beautiful. It is the beautiful, above all, which gives pleasure to our existence. Yet we know beauty can also be expressive of a deeper harmony. To propose a more comely way of conceiving life is then to advocate a different attitude toward pleasure, whereby the beauty of an experience becomes one's supreme objective. Whereas previously pleasure had been associated largely with sensual satisfactions, the significance in *The Renaissance* even of tendencies like those that express themselves in a "worship of the body" is to lead to a higher appreciation, whereby the experience of beauty becomes wholly one of mind. From this standpoint, pleasure consists above all of "intellectual or imaginative enjoyment," a delight in whatever gives most intensely the impression of harmony and form. For Pater the deep symbolic significance of form as we perceive it in works of art is undoubtedly its suggestion of a higher harmony in our existence. Instinctively, then, we feel ourselves drawn to whatever expresses that harmony, i.e., to plastic form, which allows the mind to shape its own impressions into something embodying form. This desire will also lead to a search for new sources of enjoyment, producing in turn new forms of consciousness. It all amounts to an effort to introduce beauty into our lives, but the highest form of the beautiful to result from this aspiration is perhaps that of the aesthetic ideal, i.e., an awareness of the possibilities of creating beauty within our existence. That this awareness should have belonged to the Renaissance defines for Pater its beauty as an epoch; in the recognition of that beauty lies the highest achievement of the historical consciousness.

5

ART AND LIFE

At the end of "The Critic as Artist," Gilbert notices that it is already dawn. He and Ernest have spent the night discussing the relation of criticism to art. Now it is time to draw back the curtains and open the windows for a breath of fresh air. "How cool the morning air is!" Gilbert exclaims. "Piccadilly lies at our feet like a long riband of silver. A faint purple mist hangs over the Park, and the shadows of the white houses are purple." It is too late for sleep: "Let us go down to Covent Garden and look at the roses. Come! I am tired of thought."

In this early morning stillness, as Oscar Wilde presents it, everything seems like a painting: the faint purple mist hovering over Hyde Park recalls the mists of Monet's depictions of the Seine near Giverny, while the purple shadows of houses bring to mind shadows of haystacks from the familiar scenes of southern France. After all, was it not Impressionism that had taught nature how to present herself? In Wilde's "Decay of Lying," Vivian declares: "That white quivering sunlight that one sees now in France, with its strange blotches of mauve, and its restless violet shadows, is [Art's] latest fancy, and, on the whole, Nature reproduces it quite admirably."

With art, perception becomes a pleasure. To see a landscape, a figure, an object under conditions that yield an aesthetic sensation leads to a heightened consciousness. In particular, intensified pleasure produces a sense of the beautiful. Many things can contribute to this: the charm of a fine wine (such as the Chambertin enjoyed by Gilbert and Ernest), the delicate harmony of a landscape, or the exhilaration of original thought. For Wilde, thought offers but one possible medium of pleasure—finer, of course, than others, because less ephemeral, but a medium of pleasure nevertheless, whether as the effect of a quickened awareness or as a delight in imaginative play weaving its gossamer veil of beautiful illusions.[1]

Regardless of their medium, the effect of such experiences is invariably one of pleasure. We might define it as resulting from a particular harmony in our sensations that enhances our receptive faculties, inducing a desire for more of the same sensation. In his *Paradis artificiels* Baudelaire had touched upon its essence: a certain delightful self-expansion, which assimilates the external world to the individual consciousness. But pleasure is, after all, only one means of intensifying consciousness. Its problem is that excessive stimulation can easily result in satiety and, finally, exhaustion. Hence the boredom or *ennui* described by Baudelaire and others as a peculiar affliction of modernity. It leads to a constant search for new forms of sensation. So Pater had claimed, but it remains for Wilde to attest through his own life to the truth of that claim. In *De Profundis* he recalls reading, during his first term at Oxford, Pater's *Renaissance*—"that book which has had such a strange influence over my life."[2] Do we not see its consequences borne out in his subsequent development? And if so, isn't this a testament to the strange, unique nature of that influence, even more perhaps than to the work itself? But the course of Wilde's life was to assume a shape far different from anything in Pater. In *De Profundis* Wilde declares:

> I treated Art as the supreme reality, and life as a mere mode of fiction: I awoke the imagination of my century so that it created myth and legend around me: I summed up all the systems in a phrase and all existence in an epigram. Along with these things, I had things that were different. I let myself be lured into long spells of senseless and sensual ease. I amused myself with being a *flâneur,* a dandy, a man of fashion. I surrounded myself with the smaller natures and the meaner minds. I became the spendthrift of my own genius, and to waste an eternal youth gave me a curious joy. Tired of being on the heights I deliberately went to the depths in the search for new sensations. What the paradox was to me in the sphere of thought, perversity became to me in the sphere of passion. Desire, at the end, was a malady, or a madness, or both. I grew careless of the lives of others. I took pleasure where it pleased me, and passed on. . . . I ceased to be Lord over myself. . . . I ended in horrible disgrace. (*Letters of Oscar Wilde,* p. 466)[3]

A desire no longer satisfied by its former sources must now seek gratification elsewhere, through some more esoteric means of fulfillment.[4] Thus one arrives at an aesthetic of bittersweet pleasures, of joys that mingle happiness with pain—in short, the aesthetic of des Esseintes in Huysmans's *À Rebours:*

Mais, en mettant même de côté les bienfaits de cet air fardé qui paraissait transfuser un nouveau sang sous les peaux défraîchies et usées par l'habitude des céruses et l'abus des nuits, il goûtait pour son propre compte, dans ce languissant milieu, des allégresses particulières, des plaisirs que rendaient extrêmes et qu'activaient, en quelque sorte, les souvenirs des maux passés, des ennuis défunts. (*OC* 7:16)

[But, even setting aside the benefits of this cosmetic air that appeared to transfuse new blood into a skin faded and worn out by the habit of ceruses and the abuse of nights, he tasted for himself, in this languorous milieu, particular joys, pleasures intensified and stirred up, in some sense, by memories of past evils, dead ennuis.][5]

In reviewing this novel, Barbey d'Aurevilly had been led to remark: "Après un tel livre, il ne reste plus à l'auteur qu'à choisir entre la bouche d'un pistolet ou les pieds de la croix" (from Huysmans's 1903 preface, *OC* 7:xxviii). [After such a book, it only remains for the author to choose between the muzzle of a pistol and the foot of the cross.]

Neither, however, was to be exactly the course adopted by Wilde: "I used to live entirely for pleasure. I shunned sorrow and suffering of every kind. I hated both. I resolved to ignore them as far as possible, to treat them, that is to say, as modes of imperfection. They were not part of my scheme of life. They had no place in my philosophy" (*Letters,* p. 472). And subsequently: "I don't regret for a single moment having lived for pleasure. I did it to the full, as one should do everything that one does to the full. There was no pleasure I did not experience. I threw the pearl of my soul into a cup of wine. I went down the primrose path to the sound of flutes. I lived on honeycomb." "But," he then observes, "to have continued the same life would have been wrong because it would have been limiting. I had to pass on. The other half of the garden had its secrets for me also" (ibid., p. 475).

With this we arrive at an important recognition: the pursuit of pleasure viewed as erroneous not on moral grounds but on the basis of an appeal to wider experience. To judge pleasure in moral terms is to see it merely from an external viewpoint. But that judgment is, in one sense, insufficient: it fails to question the validity of the moral standard from a hedonistic perspective. Even from the standpoint of pleasure, however, Wilde could adduce equally compelling reasons for pursuing a different course: "I remember when I was at Oxford saying to one of my friends—as we were strolling round Magdalen's narrow bird-haunted walks one morning in the June before I took my degree—

that I wanted to eat of the fruit of all the trees in the garden of the world, and that I was going out into the world with that passion in my soul. And so, indeed, I went out, and so I lived. My only mistake was that I confined myself so exclusively to the trees of what seemed to me the sun-gilt side of the garden, and shunned the other side for its shadow and its gloom" (*Letters*, p. 475).[6] In this fashion, an allegory of life is developed whereby eating from the tree of knowledge (i.e., of experience) becomes a positive act. The result: a revision of the very idea of moral values. Henceforth, something is "wrong" only insofar as it limits the possibilities of experience.[7]

With this concept a new ideal emerges. Whereas previously pleasure had seemed self-sufficient, Wilde now assimilates it to the higher aim of experience. In the process, the pursuit of pleasure is not so much rejected as transformed. We have seen how that quest, when carried to extremes, can lead to satiety and disgust. The feeling of pleasure invariably stimulates a desire for more pleasure. But that desire, if constantly indulged, becomes more demanding in its preferences. It is the very *nature* of desire that changes: from a longing for a particular object, it becomes less specific, less easily satisfiable. One might even say—in the case of a Don Giovanni, for instance—that it becomes more "abstract": less a desire for a specific individual than for some unattainable ideal. Hence the perpetual resurgence of appetite after each new "conquest." Under such circumstances, the original object no longer satisfies. On the contrary, it can even elicit a feeling of repulsion. What becomes manifest here is the *irrationality* of desire: after an initial stage, in which it represents simply a yearning for some specific object, desire begins to feed upon itself. Henceforth it can no longer be satisfied; it becomes in effect a desire *for desire*. As it seeks itself, its energy increases in attaining its object, thereby augmenting desire. The ostensible aim of its quest is now something abstract, impersonal—a fiction it proposes in order to attain its real objective: its own intensified emotion.

But, of course, desire cannot represent an ultimate end: by its very nature, it only heightens the original yearning. "Pleasure" now consists of a stimulus to desire, like a stimulus to the appetite. If one begins with the desire for a Chambertin, with repeated consumption this desire assumes a different nature. No longer a thirst for the Chambertin itself, it seeks the stimulus produced by the wine as an idea, the pleasure of a desire before its gratification. Perhaps one might even imagine a thirst for the pleasure of a Chambertin that dispenses with actually drinking it—such is the refinement at which desire arrives through a process of repeated gratification.

But intensified desire brings its own dilemma: what if that intensification should exhaust the capacity for desire itself? Thus the strain of unsatisfied desire—unsatisfied because unfulfillable by a specific object—leads to an irresolvable impasse, in which the self can neither relinquish its desire nor obtain satisfaction. The result: an aesthetic like that of Huysmans's *À Rebours,* in which the protagonist seeks pleasure from tendencies contrary to his normal desires.

But, as the outcome of Huysmans's novel makes clear, such conduct only leads to new complications. For the *décadent,* a certain pleasure arises from pursuing abnormal desires, even those that run directly counter to normal inclination. This pleasure derives from frustrating normal desire. The *décadent* seeks out an object of abnormal desire, provoking in the process resistance from normal desire. But that resistance only intensifies normal desire—which is precisely the sensation the *décadent* seeks to promote. Intensifying desire in this way, however, necessarily makes the experience of desire painful: brought on by unnatural inclinations, it produces an accumulated revulsion from the source of pain which, if it stimulates, also exhausts at the same time. Moreover, normal desire finds no satisfaction in the process— only a frustration that increases appetite. In attempting to promote abnormal desire, the *décadent* now forbids himself the simple pleasure of gratifying normal desires. The consequence can only be a *denaturalization* of desire itself, making its abnormal form the only one capable of gratification.

Should this occur, however, a problem arises. Whatever gratifies only by being opposed to normal desire (thus intensifying it) will necessarily stop doing so when that desire ceases to exist. With the disappearance of normal desire, all that remains is an artificial—because unnatural—desire, one without any emotional basis whatsoever. The illness of des Esseintes toward the end of *À Rebours* typifies the psychological and spiritual impasse he has reached as a result of his decadent fastidiousness. Unable at one point to digest any food at all, he submits to the prescriptions of a celebrated physician, who orders him to change his whole way of life. The change includes, among other things, renunciation of his aesthetic isolation at Fontenay for the turbulent life of Paris. In earlier days he had, to be sure, dwelt in the capital of luxury and fashion, but in a beautiful retreat far removed from the masses. Now his physician urges him to mingle with them, seeking out their pleasures and amusements. Driven by fear of a recurrence of his sickness, des Esseintes finally resolves to follow the physician's orders. Nevertheless, one cannot help finding this solution somewhat artificial (as does des Esseintes himself): given his earlier state of mind, there is no plausible road to the simple pleasures he is now told to seek out. Denaturalization of his desires has made this an impossibility. All that remain open to him are the possibilities suggested by Barbey d'Aurevilly.

From such a dilemma fate has, as it were, rescued Wilde. Perhaps nothing less than the catastrophic outcome of his suit against Lord Douglas would have sufficed to save him from the exhaustion that overtakes des Esseintes. Earlier Wilde had, as he tells us, sought out even the most depraved forms of pleasure: "Tired of being on the heights I deliberately went to the depths in the search for new sensations." How ironic, that Pater's high aspirations should come to this! Possibly, however, the object of Wilde's desires lies in his preceding admission: "I became the spendthrift of my own genius, and to waste an eternal youth gave me a curious joy." Similarly, in his *Twilight of the Idols,* Nietzsche remarks: "Das Genie—in Werk, in That—ist nothwendig ein Verschwender: *dass es sich ausgiebt,* ist seine Grösse . . ." (*Werke* 6:3:140). [The genius—in work, in deed—is necessarily a squanderer: *that he squanders himself* is his greatness.] Perhaps Wilde, after informing the New York customs officers that he had "nothing to declare but his genius," may have felt the right to lavish his wealth in this fashion. The "eternal youth" he professes to delight in wasting consists, in effect, of happiness. For happiness, there is neither yesterday nor tomorrow but only an eternal present. Elsewhere in *De Profundis* Wilde observes: "It was always springtime once in my heart. My temperament was akin to joy. I filled my life to the very brim with pleasure, as one might fill a cup to the very brim with wine" (*Letters,* p. 471).

To squander an eternal youth can give pleasure by making one more aware of one's wealth—hence, of one's happiness. And if feeling wealthy is, psychologically, tantamount to actually being so, why not squander? But Wilde had also harbored a desire "to eat of the fruit of all the trees in the garden of the world," a desire that assumes with him the proportions of a passion. In his mention of throwing "the pearl of his soul into a cup of wine," going "down the primrose path to the sound of flutes," lurks perhaps a subtle presentiment that the pursuit of pleasure must ultimately end by exhausting both mind and senses. In *The Brothers Karamazov* Ivan declares that he wishes to "drain the cup of life to the dregs until he is thirty and then dash it to the ground." Perhaps Wilde had felt animated by a similar impulse. A sense of fatality about one's existence can lead to a desire to exhaust all the sources of pleasure before catastrophe comes. Or it may even result in a secret wish for that catastrophe, as a means of ending things before desire has had time to pall.[8] In either case, the passion for pleasure can disregard all limits only if it tacitly relinquishes the possibility of prolonging pleasure indefinitely. "To have continued the same life would have been wrong because it would have been limiting," but it would also have been—as Wilde undoubtedly recognizes—impossible. One might even conjecture that his surrender to Lord Alfred Douglas's whims (which leads to Wilde's suing his companion's father) might have had its origin in this secret wish for a catastrophe—as a means of ending what would otherwise have exhausted itself. From such a standpoint, perhaps nothing can be worse than an incapacity for desire.

It seems only appropriate, then, that Wilde should seek to explore "the other half of the garden." No less appropriate, the fact that his doing so should have been "foreshadowed and prefigured in my art" (*Letters*, p. 475). Here, as elsewhere, art dictates to life. It anticipates the experience of a new sensation—the only one, perhaps, left to be experienced by the author, but also the most significant: "More than this, there is about Sorrow an intense, an extraordinary reality. . . . For the secret of life is suffering. It is what is hidden behind everything. When we begin to live, what is sweet is so sweet to us, and what is bitter so bitter, that we inevitably direct all our desires towards pleasures, and seek not merely for 'a month or twain to feed on honeycomb,' but for all our years to taste no other food, ignorant the while that we may be really starving the soul" (*Letters*, pp. 473–74). Earlier in the same work he had written:

> Suffering—curious as it may sound to you—is the means by which we exist, because it is the only means by which we become conscious of existing; and the remembrance of suffering in the past is necessary to us as the warrant, the evidence, of our continued identity. Between myself and the memory of joy lies a gulf no less deep than that between myself and joy in its actuality. Had our life together been as the world fancied it to be, one simply of pleasure, profligacy and laughter, I would not be able to recall a single passage in it. It is because it was full of moments and days tragic, bitter, sinister in their warnings, dull or dreadful in their monotonous scenes and unseemly violences, that I can see or hear each separate incident in its detail, can indeed see or hear little else. So much in this place do men live by pain that my friendship with you, in the way through which I am forced to remember it, appears to me always as a prelude consonant with those varying modes of anguish which each day I have to realise; nay more, to necessitate them even; as though my life,

whatever it had seemed to myself and to others, had all the while been a real Symphony of Sorrow, passing through its rhythmically-linked movements to its certain resolution, with that inevitableness that in Art characterises the treatment of every great theme. (*Letters,* pp. 435–36)

Suffering—or its emotional equivalent, sorrow—consists of feeling. Feeling alone, however, has no form. Only when we are able to associate it with particular scenes does it take on a more definite aspect. In this fashion, feeling assimilates itself to form—in other words: to art, which is, in essence, the form we give our emotions, thereby transmuting them from something passively suffered into an intellectual structure independent of ourselves.[9] For Wilde, form belongs to life rather than simply to our perception of it. As such it is external and expressive: it subsumes the various phases through which an individual passes in his or her development—experiences, acts, words heard or spoken, works conceived and created, moments of affection—in short, whatever has left some tangible trace upon the preserving memory. But the emphasis upon its external aspect cannot be mistaken: for Wilde the form of life lies in what can be perceived and felt by others as well as by the protagonist himself.

The externalization of form signifies, in effect, an externalization of self. By expressing itself through its life, the self becomes objective. But this objectivity is not merely expressive (as if one's inner nature could somehow remain unaltered). Instead, because various aspects of our life—our thoughts, emotions, and experiences—are part of us, in subsuming these within the form of a work of art, we redefine ourselves. To feel oneself fashioning one's experiences into a higher form, or elevating one's suffering to a level at which it assumes a hidden significance—for aestheticism all this becomes a fulfillment of its ideal, imparting a meaning to our existence that offers not only rare epiphanic moments but an unwavering sense of beauty that one might preserve always. "As though my life, whatever it had seemed to myself and to others, had all the while been a real Symphony of Sorrow, passing through its rhythmically-linked movements to its certain resolution, with that inevitableness that in Art characterises the treatment of every great theme." Here subjective impressions have ceased to matter, because life has taken on a form of its own. Whatever it had seemed to Wilde or others, it had been, all the while, shaping itself into a work of art.

With the notion of rhythmically linked movements, Wilde recalls the rhythms of passion that figure so prominently in Baudelaire's

"Harmonie du soir." The idea that passion can be defined by its rhythm, which becomes expressive like the rhythm of music, is hereby broadened to encompass an entire life whose variations of mood thus assume the form of an expressive sequence. As these move toward their final resolution, life achieves definitive objectivity, its ultimate form. Henceforth it becomes something independent of the self. The self suffers, but form acquires its own imperishable existence.

By perceiving life's formal possibilities, Wilde arrives at a recognition of his life in relation to art: "It [life] is, if I can fully attain to it, the ultimate realisation of the artistic life. For the artistic life is simple self-development" (*Letters,* p. 476). With this notion we arrive at a new sense of art. Whereas earlier the artistic life had been subordinated to the works it creates, Wilde now defines it as synonymous with its own creation: the supreme result of the artistic life *is* that life, seen as a process of "self-development." This development differs, however, from that of the Romantic self, which arrives at a higher consciousness embracing all the earlier stages of its existence in a moment of transcendent revelation. What distinguishes Wilde's notion of "self-development" above all is its sense of form. Like the "real Symphony of Sorrow" of which the various interludes of his life represent distinct movements, Wilde's identification of the artistic life with self-development implies a formal awareness of how different moments of an existence, like passages of a musical work, combine to establish a theme. Here the final result is a higher consciousness not so much of self as of composition—that is, of a work of art.

This insight into life's formal possibilities ultimately leads Wilde to differ from Pater. "In *Marius the Epicurean,*" Wilde observes, "Pater seeks to reconcile the artistic life with the life of religion in the deep, sweet and austere sense of the word. But Marius is little more than a spectator: an ideal spectator indeed, and one to whom it is given 'to contemplate the spectacle of life with appropriate emotions,' which Wordsworth defines as the poet's true aim: yet a spectator merely, and perhaps a little too much occupied with the comeliness of the vessels of the Sanctuary to notice that it is the Sanctuary of Sorrow that he is gazing at" (*Letters,* p. 476). For Wilde, life implies more than aesthetic impressions. Here his own experiences, of course, were bound to lead to a rejection of Pater.[10] Nevertheless, if we examine some of the assertions in *Intentions,* we see how closely they approximate Pater's. The whole idea of art as *subjective,* especially in movements like Impressionism (which *Intentions* espouses), ultimately results from equating the external world with our perception of it. For Pater, as we have seen, perception is simply the means by which we register our experiences. To treat it as mere "spectatorship" is to miss its deeper significance. Wilde's response to this aspect of Pater is revealing: it suggests the direction he himself was about to take. From the standpoint of *De Profundis,* the problem with Pater's assimilation of art to perception was its relegating too much to the subjective sphere. Art requires an external form. If life is to become one with art, it can do so only by attaining art's objectivity. What would perhaps have struck Wilde above all (as a result of his prison experiences) would be the necessity for transforming suffering into something like form. Suffering is passive. But in recalling and arranging our memories of it, we impart to these a form. In so doing, however, we give our experiences a different quality, so that they become expressive of a capacity to transform life into art. It is this transformation which, by affirming the higher principle of form, finally transcends the experience of suffering.

The relation of art to life can also raise the question of art's relation to religion. In *Marius the Epicurean,* Pater wonders whether religion might in fact represent the highest form of the aesthetic consciousness. To add pious awe to a sense of beauty—this might indeed yield the most rarified emotion, were it only possible to accede to those beliefs that impart to Christian worship the feeling of a genuine religious experience. For Wilde such faith is impossible. He admits: "Religion does not help me. The faith that others give to what is unseen, I give to what one can touch, and look at. . . . Only that is spiritual which makes its own form. If I may not find its secret within myself, I shall never find it. If I have not got it already, it will never come to me" (*Letters,* p. 468). The notion of the spiritual creating its own form inaugurates a new religion: the religion of life.[11] And the form of this religion can only be that of art. But if religion in the traditional sense cannot confer a higher form upon life, perhaps art can give form to religion. By this Wilde does not mean a mere "aestheticization" of religion, the appreciation of a cultus for the beauty of its ceremonies. What he seeks is, rather, a complete identification of art with religion through the medium of life.

If the objective of life is in some sense art (the achievement of form in our existence) one can likewise speak of religion (in effect, a way of life) as aspiring to form. The form religion seeks must be artistic, inasmuch as it attempts to bring into meaningful relation all our various experiences. Its aspiration, moreover, must be imaginative, involving a sympathetic identification with all modes of existence, all natures and passions. Perhaps one of the most remarkable developments in Wilde's entire *oeuvre* is his attempt to ascribe a supreme imaginative effort to the founder of the Christian religion, thus redefining radically not only Christianity but the very essense of religion: "Nor is it merely that we can discern in Christ that close union of personality with perfection which forms the real distinction between classical and romantic Art and makes Christ the true precursor of the romantic movement in life, but the very basis of his nature was the same as that of the nature of the artist, an intense and flamelike imagination. He realised in the entire sphere of human relations that imaginative sympathy which in the sphere of Art is the sole secret of creation" (*Letters,* p. 476).[12] "He understood," Wilde continues, "the leprosy of the leper, the darkness of the blind, the fierce misery of those who live for pleasure, the strange poverty of the rich." The form of this imaginative identification is sympathy, a sympathy involving compassion and love as well as mind.[13] For Wilde, love is one form of the artist's relation to the world. Through love the artistic intelligence identifies with different modes of human existence in order to bestow upon them a higher significance.[14] By means of "an intense and flamelike imagination" Christ is said to do the same. Here—as in so many other instances—we encounter once more an echo of Pater's *Renaissance.* In exhorting the imaginative nature to "burn with a hard, gem-like flame" (that much-ridiculed but little-understood phrase), Pater emphasizes intellectual clarity of perception. But the "flamelike imagination" Wilde ascribes to Christ signifies something much closer to the soft, lambent flame of love that appears so frequently in Dante's *Commedia.*

Perhaps the most daring of his imaginative acts, however, is that by which Christ takes upon himself the task of expiating all the sins of the world, an act of submission that figures in Christian doctrine as the Atonement: "There is still something to me almost incredible in the idea of a young Galilean peasant imagining that he could bear on his own shoulders the burden of the entire world: all that had been already done and suffered, and all that was yet to be done and suffered. . . . and not merely imagining this but actually achieving it, so that at the present moment all who come in contact with his personality . . . somehow find that the ugliness of their sin is taken away and the beauty of their sorrow revealed to them" (*Letters,* p. 477). This is, to be sure, not atonement in a mystical sense; it possesses nothing in common with the mysteries of the Church in orthodox belief. Wilde asserts that it is felt even by those who do not believe. It remains for him simply the profoundest imaginative act in the history of the world, the one moment of absolute sympathy that by its experience of others' pain deserves to count as a kind of benediction, thereby transforming pain's significance. "And the beauty of their sorrow [is] revealed to them": what before had been simply sorrow now becomes an occasion for compassion, of suffering freely accepted for another's sake. It represents the supreme imaginative act because it assimilates suffering, the most difficult of all aspects of life, to love, its highest virtue.

But the example of Christ possesses for Wilde another meaning as well. To have created out of his own life the highest work of art, highest because of its capacity to redeem not only his own suffering but, symbolically, that of others, by revealing its place in the "real Symphony of Sorrow" that is his life—in so doing the Galilean demonstrates the possibility of creating, even from what had seemed least justifiable in existence (i.e., suffering) a work of art that by its intrinsic relations redeems all of life with an infinite richness of meaning. Thus Wilde can say of him:

> But his entire life also is the most wonderful of poems. For "pity and terror" there is nothing in the entire cycle of Greek tragedy to touch it. The absolute purity of the protagonist raises the entire scheme to a height of romantic art from which the sufferings of "Thebes and Pelops' line" are by their very horror excluded. . . . Nor in Æschylus or Dante, those stern masters of tenderness, in Shakespeare, the most purely human of all the great artists, in the whole of Celtic myth and legend where the loveliness of the world is shown through a mist of tears, and the life of a man is no more than the life of a flower, is there anything that for sheer simplicity of pathos wedded and made one with sublimity of tragic effect can be said to equal or approach even the last act of Christ's Passion. The little supper with his companions, one of whom had already sold him for a price: the anguish in the quiet moonlit olive-garden: the false friend coming close to him so as to betray him with a kiss: the friend who still believed in him, and on whom as on a rock he had hoped to build a House of Refuge for Man denying him as the bird cried to the dawn: his own utter loneliness, his submission, his acceptance of everything: and along with it all such scenes as the high priest of Orthodoxy rending his raiment in wrath, and the Magistrate of Civil Justice calling for water in the vain hope of cleansing himself of that stain of innocent blood that makes him the scarlet figure of History: the coronation-ceremony of Sorrow, one of the most wonderful things in the whole of recorded time: the crucifixion of the Innocent One before the eyes of his mother and of the disciple whom he loved: the soldiers gambling and throwing dice for his clothes: the terrible death by which he gave

the world its most eternal symbol: and his final burial in the
tomb of the rich man, his body swathed in Egyptian linen with
costly spices and perfumes as though he had been a King's son—
when one contemplates all this from the point of view of Art
alone one cannot but be grateful that the supreme office of the
Church should be the playing of the tragedy without the shed-
ding of blood, the mystical presentation by means of dialogue
and costume and gesture even of the Passion of her Lord, and
it is always a source of pleasure and awe to me to remember that
the ultimate survival of the Greek Chorus, lost elsewhere to art,
is to be found in the servitor answering the priest at Mass. (*Letters*, pp. 477–78)[15]

We know from Gide's memoir that it was Wilde's habit to think in
stories.[16] And, in this light, perhaps we are justified in regarding the
rehearsal of Christ's Passion in *De Profundis* as Wilde's supreme story—
not only because it was to be his last (with the abandonment of his
plans for the plays *Pharoah* and *Ahab and Jezebel*), but because of the
particular resonance the Passion narrative comes to have for his own
life. As a result of his recent experiences, he could now approach such
a narrative with a new appreciation—one in which an unmediated
acceptance of that narrative's events becomes a means of accepting the
events of his own recent past. That acceptance leads in turn to an
imaginative re-creation of the narrative—in effect, the creation of a
new story. In the process, individual subjectivity (the memory of his
personal suffering) disappears. Not, however, in the sense of being
"forgotten"—on the contrary, it was necessary (as well as inescapable)
that it should be remembered as precisely as possible—but rather by
an imaginative identification with the protagonist of the Passion narrative through the memory of his own suffering, which enables him
(in a fashion not possible earlier) to experience pity for the Christ.
Through pity, the events of Christ's passion can assume for Wilde an
intense reality comparable to that of his own existence. But the effect
of this "realization" of Christ's life will not be (as one might expect)
merely catharsis. Instead, the sympathetic identification with Christ
makes possible an awareness of the profound and necessary relation
within the Innocent One's Passion of each event with every other.
Because of how Wilde relives these events, his awareness involves more
than mere intellectual apprehension. It becomes, rather, a felt experience of the meaning of each moment as part of a larger scheme. The
emotion of this experience is then assimilated into Wilde's own existence, transforming that existence into something like a work of art—

the perception of a significant relation that brings all the diverse moments of a life together.[17]

In his memoir Gide remarks that "the Gospel disturbed and trou-
bled the pagan Wilde. He could not forgive it its miracles" (*Oscar
Wilde*, pp. 32–33). Perhaps for this reason Wilde had found it easier
to accept the Passion narrative than any other part. Here the absence
of miracles, and indeed the wholly natural turn events take, as if compelled by an inner necessity, could produce a unique impression. For
Wilde, the Passion narrative calls for another kind of response from
those describing the miracles—not faith but simple acceptance. That
acceptance, however, will necessarily differ from what one accords Greek
tragedy. And here Wilde's admission to Gide seems significant: "I
thought, at first, that what would please me most would be Greek
literature, so I asked for Sophocles, but I could not get a relish for it"
(*Oscar Wilde*, p. 71). Ultimately, perhaps, the standpoint of Sopho-
clean tragedy remains external: if one is not asked to internalize the
events of a drama by identifying with the protagonist, the suffering of
the characters must also remain external to the spectator (hence the
possibility of catharsis). What was lacking in such an experience, for
Wilde, was "pity." "Have you ever learned how wonderful a thing pity
is? . . . I went into prison with a heart of stone, thinking only of my
own pleasure, but now my heart is utterly broken—pity has entered
into my heart. I have learned now that pity is the greatest and most
beautiful thing in the world" (*Oscar Wilde*, pp. 63–64). And subsequently: "You do not know how sweet that is, to feel that one is suffering for another."

Through pity the Other becomes more "real." And, as a result of
this intenser reality of the Other, experience itself becomes more real.
But that in turn is the "height of romantic art." For Wilde the "romantic" is always what is most real, what we experience with the most
intense consciousness. To experience the events of the Passion narrative through pity, then, is to experience them as life. In so doing,
Wilde can become aware of the relation of each event of the Passion
to others as belonging to the realm of the actual. At the same time,
there is a sense of the uniqueness of each event, its specific and necessary place within a larger scheme. This uniqueness of each event es-
tablishes the whole to which it belongs as a work of art. Thus Wilde
tells Gide that "one must never take up the same existence again. My
life is like a work of art. An artist never begins the same work twice,
or else it shows that he has not succeeded" (*Oscar Wilde*, p. 60).

The uniqueness of each event is an individual's life makes possible
that exact and necessary relation of the event to all others within the

same existence which defines a work of art. The sense of a specific
relation between different events of the Passion narrative thus becomes
the experience of a work of art which is, at the same time, life. And
that experience of exactitude is then carried over into Wilde's own life.
Consequently the precise recollection of each little detail in his relationship with Douglas possesses its own higher significance: on the
basis of such details the work of art that is his own life must be constructed. But when it is, he will have the feeling of fulfillment that
comes from experiencing the same necessary relation that connects the
events of the Passion to each other. It is this parallelism that he can
then go on to celebrate in the ceremony of the Mass, with the "participation" of the servitor who answers the priest and who, in so doing,
symbolizes for Wilde the participation of experiencing the Passion in
his own life, thereby elevating that life to the level of a work of art.
Consumatum est: the consummation of the Passion narrative then becomes the fulfillment of his own existence, transformed now into
something that transcends the past through the perduring significance
of form.

It remains for us to consider the form of *De Profundis*. Conceived
as a letter to Alfred Douglas, it begins by defining the personal relation
of author to recipient. But the address is only a prelude to describing
the author's past life with that recipient. The description opens by
attempting to explore the whole nature of their relationship, but it
progressively modulates into something quite different: the composition of a "real Symphony of Sorrow" in which the finale will come
"to its certain resolution, with that inevitableness that . . . characterises the treatment of every great theme." From a subjective relationship
between two individuals, the letter shifts to the external and objective.
It thus admits of no appeal from its recipient. Douglas's exclusion is
signalized, in a curious fashion, by Wilde's conclusion: "And the end
of it all is that I have got to forgive you." Such forgiveness, however,
results not so much from any feeling for Douglas but rather for Wilde
himself: "For my own sake I must forgive you." Forgiveness is then
both dismissal and appropriation. From now on, within the framework of Wilde's life, Douglas will figure merely as one of those forces
that, like characters in a drama, bring about its inevitable outcome.

In the letter's crucial middle section, Wilde turns to examine his
own self-development. Analyzing the inherent limits of a quest for
pleasure, he creates a rationale for the *peripeteia* of his life: the trial
leading to his imprisonment becomes his means of initiation into a
new and higher perspective, from which all moments of the past are
seen to have their appropriate significance as part of a supreme work

of art that is his life. But the recognition of their role belongs to *De Profundis:* within it, all past moments are finally collected and shaped into an artistic composition. Thus the work creates its own form by relating those moments to each other. For this, it was necessary for it to begin as a letter—in other words, as a document from life. Only then can it transform life into form. Nor is it any less appropriate for the work to end where it begins, with the relation of author to recipient. Now that relation too can be seen as part of a higher scheme, as part of the work of art that is the author's life.

6

A SENSE OF THE PAST

In his preface to *The Ambassadors* James described the incident that had furnished him with the germ for his novel. It had consisted of the words spoken to a friend of his by a "man of distinction, much his senior," in a charming garden in Paris on an afternoon in June: "Live all you can: it's a mistake not to. It doesn't so much matter what you do—but live. . . . I haven't done so—and now I'm too old. It's too late. . . . You have time. You are young. Live!"[1] The "man of distinction," as we know, was William Dean Howells, James's own friend who, late in life, had come over to Paris to see his son, a student at the Beaux Arts. Overwhelmed by all the possibilities of life revealed to him by his first real glimpse of Paris, Howells had been thus moved to express his realization to a friend. What had made the incident so richly suggestive to James however was not simply the fact of his friend Howells giving voice at such a time to such a realization, but the particular place in which he had felt compelled to do so: "What amplified the hint to more than the bulk of hints in general was the gift with it of the old Paris garden, for in that token were sealed up values infinitely precious" (1:vi–vii).

We know from the "Project of Novel" synopsis James sent to the Harpers in the autumn of 1900 that this garden was situated in the Faubourg St.-Germain ("a particularly old-fashioned and pleasantly quiet part of the town"). Of the garden itself James remarks: "The old houses of the Faubourg St.-Germain close round their gardens and shut them in, so that you don't see them from the street—only overlook them from all sorts of picturesque excrescences in the rear. I had a marked recollection of one of these wondrous concealed corners in especial, which was contiguous to the one mentioned by my friend: I used to know, many years ago, an ancient lady, long since dead, who lived in the house to which it belonged and whom, also on Sunday afternoons, I used to go to see" (*Complete Notebooks,* pp. 541–42). Thus this garden in which a friend (Jonathan Sturges) had encountered Howells could represent for James a tangible link with his own past, with the period of his literary apprenticeship decades earlier, when Paris had meant for him, among other things, the acquaintance of Flaubert, Turgenev, and Maupassant: the period, in other words, in which he had laid claim to the possibilities for life and art embodied in the European consciousness.

What James did not mention in his "Project of Novel" was the name of the mutual friend in whose garden Sturges had met Howells: James Abbott McNeill Whistler.[2] During his early years in London, James had first met Whistler, whose work he had reviewed anonymously (and not entirely favorably!) for the *Nation*. Whistler's Nocturnes and Arrangements had then seemed to him nothing more than "studio experiments," illustrating "the self-complacency of technicality." Now, years later, he could look back and survey the growth of a painter's reputation, its flowering into fame, and recognize that it had all been due to "the mere base maximum of cleverness," combined with an inexhaustible perseverance that could only come from a passion for art. Perhaps too there would have been for James a special poignancy in Whistler's being an American—one who, like himself, had had to confront the challenge of Europe and develop out of the encounter a unique, personal style. Now, as a result of his success, the painter had been able to obtain a house and garden in one of the oldest, most fashionable sections of Paris, one where every street seemed to speak of a historical consciousness consecrated by the passage of time. To think of Whistler as proprietor of a concrete embodiment of that consciousness could indeed assume a symbolic significance, suggestive of other, less tangible forms of appropriation—including the art of fiction.

But the symbolic suggestion contained in that appropriation would have to rest ultimately upon the significance of the garden. On one side of it, James recalled, was another, "visible from my old lady's windows, which was attached to a great convent of which I have forgotten the name, and which I think was one of the places of training for young missionary priests, whom we used to look down on as they strolled, always with a book in hand, in the straight alleys" (*Complete Notebooks,* p. 542). Here might be one of those direct, deep references of which Paris was invariably so full: a reference to the power of the Church, the role it had played in French life and in shaping a collective consciousness, a power based in the final analysis upon intellectual force (the book in hand) and upon a discipline that submitted figuratively as well as literally to walking in straight paths.

But the most moving note of the garden results from its association with the great dead: "It endeared to me, I recall, the house in question—the one where I used to call—that Madame Récamier had finally lived and died in an apartment of the *rez-de-chaussée*; that my ancient friend had known her and waited on her last days; and that the latter gave me a strange and touching image of her as she lay there dying, blind, and bereft of Chateaubriand, who was already dead" (*Complete Notebooks,* p. 542). Madame Récamier: one of the most brilliant women of the Empire, as celebrated for her charm as for her beauty, preserved for the memory of posterity through Chateaubriand's lifelong passion for her, she lives, like all the others of that time, in the radiance of Napoleonic legend. That James should have known someone who had known *her,* been with her, epitomizes what we might term tradition: the transmission from one generation to another of a knowledge consisting less of abstract principles than of an incomparable wealth of lived experience. And that this experience should have been of Madame Récamier not in the hour of her glory but in her lonely last days, stripped of all traces of the beauty that had made her so famous, facing the same inevitable end we all must face, gives to the remembrance a sense of something terribly real. Through that human sense of a lonely woman counting out her last days, the past may be said to live once more. And the process by which it comes to life, insofar as this depends on an imaginative apprehension of things, might be described as one of appreciation. That appreciation consists above all of vision. Thus James can conclude: "But I mention these slightly irrelevant things only to show that I *saw* the scene of my young friend's anecdote." To see is to appreciate, which means in turn: to discern the intimate inner life, consisting of all the remembered moments of passion that reside in things.

With this we arrive at the theme of *The Ambassadors*. In his preface to the novel, speaking of Lambert Strether's predicament, James observes: "he now at all events *sees*; so that the business of my tale and the march of my action, not to say the precious moral of everything, is just my demonstration of this process of vision" (1:vi). Here it seems revealing that the "demonstration of this process of vision" should count as "the precious moral of everything." In making such a claim, James in effect repudiates a moralistic standpoint. Even more, he affirms the moral significance of vision, which for him lies above all in "appreciation." "*The* false position," he remarks of Strether, "was obviously to have presented himself at the gate of that boundless menagerie primed with a moral scheme of the most approved pattern which was yet framed to break down on any approach to vivid facts; that is to any at all liberal appreciation of them" (1:xiii). "Appreciation" of this kind includes many things: a growing comprehension of the nature of Chad's relationship with Madame de Vionnet, a feeling for Madame de Vionnet herself, and, lastly, a glimpse of new possibilities of life as a result of the experience of Paris. It is a sense of these possibilities that James seeks to convey through Strether's vision. By making his novel nothing but the "demonstration" of its "process," James endows vision with thematic significance: to *see* is to appreciate, and to appreciate is to have attained the highest possible awareness.[3] It all amounts, then, to this: to experience things with the maximum intensity, to live for the higher awareness.

In his conclusion to *The Renaissance,* Pater had called for a life compressing "as many pulsations as possible into the given time." A life passionately lived ought to yield "this fruit of a quickened, multiplied consciousness." For James too a vision like Strether's leads to a similar result. At the same time, Jamesian aestheticism differs somewhat from Pater's in its definition of aesthetic experience. For Pater, as we have seen, all art aspires to the condition of music—i.e., to the purest embodiment of form. For James, on the other hand, nothing surpasses the drama of human suffering and emotion. At the end of *The Ambassadors* the devastating violence of Madame de Vionnet's passion for Chad becomes for Strether the most moving of all the impressions he will carry away with him. Obviously, an aestheticism that includes such experiences cannot be comprehended in terms of purely formal criteria. Nevertheless even the experience of suffering can become beautiful, if by beauty we mean simply whatever yields the most intense impressions. This standpoint permits James to return to the moral sphere, after initially appearing to reject it. The high point of Jamesian aestheticism now becomes one of moral appreciation precisely because it endows a moment with the greatest possible awareness. Thus aestheticism, which begins as *l'art pour l'art,* becomes for James an affirmation of the moral sense, a feeling for the human significance of our relations to each other, which his predecessors had sought in some fashion to deny. Yet the Jamesian standpoint is not, in itself, moral. Instead, it seeks to embrace the moral sphere within an aestheticism for which the moral sense exemplifies only the highest possible form of awareness.

In Book Fifth of *The Ambassadors,* Lambert Strether, having met the celebrated sculptor Gloriani at a garden party at Gloriani's house (where he also sees Madame de Vionnet for the first time) allows his impressions to overflow in the famous exhortation to little Bilham.[4] In yielding, as James puts it in the preface, to "the charming admonition of that crisis," Strether feels the immense effect of everything he has heard and seen since his arrival in Paris. Now, finding himself in Gloriani's beautiful garden in the heart of the Faubourg Saint-Germain, quiet, rare, and wonderful, its tall trees alive with twittering birds and, all around, the high walls that make for privacy amid distinguished edifices of another age, Strether can only feel more acutely than ever a consciousness that makes his present impressions of Paris a renewal of the past, with all its particular significance:

> All the same don't forget that you're young—blessedly young; be glad of it on the contrary and live up to it. Live all you can; it's a mistake not to. It does n't so much matter what you do in particular so long as you have your life. If you have n't had that what *have* you had? This place and these impressions—mild as you may find them to wind a man up so; all my impressions of Chad and of people I've seen at *his* place—well, have had their abundant message for me, have just dropped *that* into my mind. I see it now. I have n't done so enough before—and now I'm old; too old at any rate for what I see. Oh I *do* see, at least; and more than you'd believe or I can express. . . . What one loses one loses; make no mistake about that. The affair—I mean the affair of life—could n't no doubt, have been different for me. . . . Still, one has the illusion of freedom; therefore don't be, like me, without the memory of that illusion. I was either, at the right time, too stupid or too intelligent to have it; I don't quite know which. Of course at present I'm a case of reaction against the mistake; and the voice of reaction should, no doubt, always be taken with an allowance. But that does n't affect the point that the right time is now yours. . . . Do what you like so long as you don't make *my* mistake. For it was a mistake. Live! (1:217–18)

For Strether, speaking now to little Bilham, to be young is less a matter of years than of one's openness to life. At various moments in the sequel, he will wonder if he himself isn't too old for what he sees, for the possibilities of life represented by Paris. The color, the immediacy of its impressions—all this, he feels, might well be lost on one unable to respond to them as they deserve. The substance of his exhortation to little Bilham, then, is not to fail of that full measure of response—to live up to the challenge implied in one's experiences. For Strether, little Bilham is young not just in years but primarily because he possesses the intenser consciousness. To live with that consciousness, to breathe constantly a rarefied air in which impressions assume a brighter, more vivid form—this, for Strether, is what it means to be blessedly young. To possess such perception strikes him as a gift—with all the sense of sacred obligation it confers.

In his conclusion to *The Renaissance* Pater had spoken of what it meant to live aesthetically. Addressing little Bilham, Strether too has in mind the need for compressing as much as possible into the briefest interval. But he stresses also the necessity for awareness: "It does n't so much matter what you do in particular so long as you have your life." Here experience is distinguished from action. That too can yield its own intensities of emotion. Not less passionate, in a different fashion, is the feeling of having a richer relation to one's existence through an intenser consciousness.[5] To be aware of the nature of our experiences yields us the richest treasures of the moment, the fruit of experience. It all comes back, as James might say, to appreciation: to feel pleasure through appreciation of what a moment has to offer, and, in so doing, to discern—for however brief a span—the presence of beauty in our existence.

We begin and end with consciousness. All that we possess comes to us through its medium. To lack consciousness is thus to forego all the rest. "If you have n't had that what *have* you had?" Not to "have" one's life signifies, then, a failure of appreciation, a lack of awareness of our own vision. Simply to recognize how consciousness makes possible a fuller experience of our whole existence—that would be, in itself, the measure of a finer perception.

Among Strether's deepest impressions is that of his meeting with Gloriani. A sculptor whose features exhibit a "medal-like Italian face" (suggestive of a Pisanello), he evokes an aura of the Italian Renaissance, in which (as Pater might say) life assumes something of the comeliness of art. But the Italian Renaissance can also signify, as we have seen, an age in which all of life is lived more passionately. Here the relation between the Renaissance and aestheticism lies not simply in the idea of life assuming the form of a work of art (Burckhardt) but also in the intensity with which a period experiences each individual moment. Specifically it had seemed to Strether that "the deep human expertness in Gloriani's charming smile—oh the terrible life behind it!—was flashed upon him as a test of his stuff." Such "deep human expertness" can only come from an acute awareness whose allure beckons to Strether from the impression of his encounter with the artist.

But he will also have been drawn almost equally to Chad—happy, fortunate Chad, whose own life manifests, even more than Gloriani's, the advantages of discrimination. For what Chad's existence amounts to, more than anything else, is appreciation—of Paris itself and of the human "values" represented by the varied circle of his acquaintances. And why, for that matter, should Strether's tribute not include little Bilham—to whom Strether so handsomely alludes in his reference to the "people he's seen at Chad's place?" More than anyone else Strether knows, little Bilham embodies the virtue of appreciation carried to its furthest extreme, where it approaches artistic vision. A dilettante in painting, he appreciates the process by which art creates an image of the beautiful without, however, surrendering himself to it. If in one sense Chad bridges the worlds of Gloriani and Strether, the same might be said of little Bilham. Hence Strether's impression of him as "blessed," which is also the reason why he, as well as Chad's other acquaintances, can press for Strether the spring of the realization he now seeks to impart.

To Strether, it all forms part of a larger recognition of certain possibilities awakened by seeing Paris. From the early moments when he strolls through the Tuileries or sits on a penny chair in the Luxembourg Gardens watching little women in white caps and playful girls "compose" a picture to the more recent period of his deeper initiation, climaxed by his visit to Gloriani's house in the Faubourg Saint-Germain, with its distinguished appearance and the even more brilliant human "note" of Gloriani's asssembled acquaintances, Strether must take into account an accumulating quantity of impressions. They lead in turn to a deepening sense of a way of life for which perception comes to represent the medium of an intenser awareness—one that forms, in fact, the essence of aestheticism. For this reason too it seems important to him to tell little Bilham that he now, at all events, *sees*— "and more than you'd believe or I can express." What he sees is, above all, the importance of seeing, the belatedness of which only intensifies perception.

To "see" is, in itself, a sufficient response to the challenge posed by his recent experiences. To see is to appreciate, and to appreciate is to allow the beauty of his vision to sink into himself, to loom expressively with its own "precious moral," which is, quite simply, that vision is not a means but an end when it achieves a transformation of consciousness. To this end, each individual impression contributes (as James would say) its special note, its special intensity, whether of form, color, or passion. The demonstration of this process which forms the central concern of *The Ambassadors* is precisely the record of Strether's assimilation of his impressions, the process by which they acquire, for him, their special relevance. It consists then not only of his impressions but

Eugène Atget, *Luxembourg* (1923–26).

of the resonances they awaken in him. In brooding over these, the mind attains brief intensities of recognition that amount to an experience of the beautiful.

Such is the result of Strether's first visit to Madame de Vionnet— a sense of the beautiful in which the brush of human feelings counts for the most poignant note.[6] It marks a new phase of his initiation into Paris and into what he has now become accustomed to thinking of as a life of the intenser awareness. From the moment he finds himself in Madame de Vionnet's drawing room, this awareness will operate in him to especially vivid effect. He has had, we learn, access to her apartment in the rue de Bellechasse through an old clean court: "The court was large and open, full of revelations, for our friend, of the habit of privacy, the peace of intervals, the dignity of distances and approaches" (1:243). With this feeling of space in the midst of a crowded metropolis comes, first of all, a sense of freedom as well as serenity. Whoever has walked along the narrow streets of Paris will undoubtedly have noticed large courtyards into which the high entrance doors facing a street sometimes open. Vistas of peace are thus disclosed, affording welcome relief from a crowding that had already begun to develop in the early nineteenth century as a result of the daily movements of huge urban masses. In contrast to such crowding, the privacy Strether encounters here can easily have for him an air of high distinction. The habit of privacy, moreover, marks a transmission of inherited values, of feelings and manners now become instinctive. In the "peace of intervals" and the "dignity of distances and approaches," he perceives the preserving of inner spaces as well, spaces of contemplation and reverie that now mean so much to his own existence.

To place an interval between entrance gate and house, or between edifice and edifice—what is this but to allow time for the forming of impressions, for assimilating the architectural effect of a building, its harmony and possibly grandeur? An adequate presentation only affirms the intrinsic dignity of an edifice and its owners. The house itself, in "the high, homely style of an elder day, and the ancient Paris that [Strether] was always looking for," embodies moreover earlier values. James's consistent refusal, throughout *The Ambassadors,* to associate modernity with Madame de Vionnet deserves notice. One might speculate as to what it implies—above all, perhaps, a sense of how accumulated associations can yield, with the passage of time, a richer, more complex awareness. The finer vision—how much this depends, for James, upon the assimilation of impressions! It involves discrimination (in the preface to *The Ambassadors* he describes Strether's development as "a drama of discrimination") but also memory, through which impressions achieve a cumulative effect. What results is a feeling for the meaning of a person or place based upon the sum of its various associations.

In Madame de Vionnet's apartment, then, Strether encounters the Paris of another age, in the "immemorial polish of the wide waxed staircase and in the fine *boiseries,* the medallions, mouldings, mirrors, great clear spaces, of the greyish-white salon into which he had been shown." Here the "boiseries" or paneling possess for the reader of James a personal note. We know from Edith Wharton's *A Backward Glance* of James's fondness for the Georgian paneling of his own Lamb House at Rye and of his modest pride in exhibiting it to visitors.[7] With its other ornaments, however, its "medallions" and "mouldings," Madame de Vionnet's apartment manifests not merely the charm of another era but an air of high dignity, of the classic in taste and style. The mirrors and the "great clear spaces" of the salon are its tribute to lucidity of consciousness. And, in fact, the impression of lucidity is one that will remain with Strether through all his subsequent encounters with Madame de Vionnet. To fail of that lucidity would be nothing less, for her, than a failure of dignity.

But the "great clear spaces" also exemplify an economy of taste in which no ornament must appear superfluous, no object of decor excessive. One has only to recall the burdensome overdecoration of fin-de-siècle houses (severely criticized in Edith Wharton's *The Decoration of Houses*) to realize the appeal of the classic austerity James invokes here. It remains the keynote, for Strether, of any form of the finer appreciation. In the grayish-white color of Madame de Vionnet's salon, he discovers the ideal medium for such appreciation. Its cool, restrained effect, the conspicuous absence of any emotional emphasis from some warmer tone sets off by contrast the human presence of its occupant—a perfect setting for a "drama of discrimination."

As he glances about Madame de Vionnet's apartment, Strether finds himself making out, "as a background of its occupant," "some glory, some prosperity of the First Empire, some Napoleonic glamour, some dim lustre of the great legend; elements clinging still to all the consular chairs and mythological brasses and sphinxes' heads and faded surfaces of satin striped with alternate silk" (1:244). To the end of the nineteenth century, the "glory" of the First Empire could indeed shine by comparison with the debacle of Napoleon III. The Romantic grandeur of its aspirations, remote now after decades of subsequent vicissitudes, sheds its radiance over a period when all things had seemed possible. Emerging out of the ferment of the French Revolution, whose turbulent energies it assimilated, the Empire had dedicated itself to the accomplishment of tasks a later age might regard as visionary but whose heroic dimensions it could not deny. From the fin-de-siècle standpoint of Strether and James, the "glory" sought by the First Consul and his contemporaries becomes a defining characteristic of the whole Romantic epoch.[8] As the memory of its specific political struggles fades, what remains of Napoleonic France almost a century later is an object of nostalgia for its passionate ardor, the high sense of drama in which it lives and moves. Surveying all the "consular chairs and mythological brasses and sphinxes' heads and faded surfaces of satin," Strether will recall many things—the strange classicism of the period (a legacy from the republicanism of the early days of the French Revolution) and its taste for the antique, intensified by Napoleon's Egyptian expedition.

But, beyond its oddities of taste or fancy, what remain for Strether are the emotions of an earlier epoch. That is the precious human "note" in such relics: the tangible, cherishable fragrance of passions that once animated the life of another time. To appreciate these relics is to feel what James (speaking of old English country houses) had described as "accumulations of expression," the historical associations that convey a meaning to the sensitive observer (*Complete Notebooks*, p. 224).[9] For Strether, these associations become a part of his impression of Madame de Vionnet. They reflect about her "some dim lustre of the great legend," making him see in her similar "accumulations of expression." They enable him to find in her the special note of value missed even by Chad—that of inherited forms of sensibility. Every richness, every enhancement of emotion that results from accumulated recognitions becomes a source of that "beauty of sentiment" (*The Golden Bowl*) of which Madame de Vionnet offers a brilliant example.

While in her salon Strether recognizes that the apartment itself dates from an earlier time, before the Revolution. "But the post-revolutionary period, the world he vaguely thought of as the world of Chateaubriand, of Madame de Staël, even of the young Lamartine, had left its stamp of harps and urns and torches, a stamp impressed on sundry small objects, ornaments, and relics" (1:244). Once more we encounter the Empire note, albeit in a slightly different fashion. For what these figures evoke above all is Romantic passion. Here one has only to think of Chateaubriand's René, with his incestuous love for a sister who enters a convent to avoid confessing to similar feelings for him (a motif James had employed earlier in *The American*). Perhaps an even more prominent presence might be that of Madame de Staël's Corinne, with the devastating effects of her love for Lord Nelvil. We know James himself could savor fully the intensity of these Romantic passions—the loves, for instance, of George Sand, for whom he had made the pilgrimage to Nohant. For Strether, the memory of such passions is what lives in Madame de Vionnet's apartment, as an air of association indescribably precious: "all the life of the past," as James says elsewhere, now becoming expressive of the beauty of a sentiment.

Through its various relics—"little old miniatures, medallions, pictures, books; books in leather bindings, pinkish and greenish, with gilt garlands on the back, ranged, together with other promiscuous properties, under the glass of brass-mounted cabinets"—the world of Romantic sensibility still breathes in the atmosphere of Madame de Vionnet's apartment. As relics of sacred emotion Strether takes them "all tenderly into account." To be sure, they are not terribly attractive, with their somewhat garish colors and odd decorative fancies. James is also no doubt aware of the somewhat jarring impression they make in a room whose cool gray-white spaces reflect the measure of its own austere classicism. But the beauty of *The Ambassadors* is of another sort: what appreciation seeks is not so much surface appearances (though these too can count for something) but rather the life of feeling that still emanates from historic objects. As relics they serve to crystallize another consciousness. Because aestheticism consists of an appreciation of life, at times artistic beauty in the narrower sense will cease to matter, becoming absorbed in a larger relation to experience. At that moment the various "promiscuous properties" no longer signify in themselves: now their effect is only one of association, of the remembrances they awaken of the sacred past.

That past is what Strether sees above all in Madame de Vionnet, in her relation to her possessions and what they represent. "Hereditary, cherished, charming": so Strether characterizes them to himself, distinguishing simultaneously the nature of her tenure of them. In thus taking them into account he makes out for himself the difference between her apartment and Maria Gostrey's "little museum of bargains" or even "Chad's lovely home": "he recognised it as founded much more on old accumulations that had possibly from time to time shrunken than on any contemporary method of acquisition or form of curiosity" (1:245). "Accumulations": we have encountered this term before, in James's description of the great English country houses. In its present context, it embraces more than just material accumulation. For Strether, possession of these relics symbolically expresses something much greater—a sensibility which they reflect. Whereas Chad and Maria Gostrey had "rummaged and purchased and picked up and exchanged, sifting, selecting, comparing," Madame de Vionnet had, by contrast, been "beautifully passive under the spell of transmission." This "spell" implies a process by which certain attitudes are transmitted along with

their material counterparts. For Strether, the process indeed amounts
to a spell, with the mind not fully conscious of the means by which
it comes to think and feel in certain ways. The beauty of Madame de
Vionnet's passivity consists simply of what Strether earlier termed "the
common unattainable art of taking things as they came" (1:83). An
acceptance that implies having only "received, accepted, and been
quiet"—but in that acceptance there is also, involuntarily, affirmation
of what one accepts.

For Strether, such affirmation is what distinguishes Madame de
Vionnet from his compatriots Chad and Maria Gostrey: to "sift, select,
compare"—what is this, after all, but to refuse to submit to *any* spell
of transmission, to insist on one's right to choose one's impressions?
But then one loses something: the feeling that informs what one receives when the inheritance itself typifies a particular mode of life, the
fruit of various "accumulations of expression." Of course, neither Chad
nor Maria Gostrey nor, for that matter, Strether himself, can simply
receive: for them, pursuit of the beautiful necessarily implies (in Pater's
phrase) "for ever curiously testing new opinions and courting new
impressions." The objective of their quest is the beauty of a moment,
its immediate sensuous appeal. What Madame de Vionnet offers Strether,
however, is "something for which he had no name on the spot quite
ready, but something he would have come nearest to naming in speaking of it as the air of supreme respectability, the consciousness, small,
still, reserved, but none the less distinct and diffused, of private honour" (1:245–46). What Strether thus so quaintly figures to himself
under the rubric of "supreme respectability" is precisely the result of
age-old "accumulations." Embodied in the relics around him, it revives
a past consciousness: "He would have answered for it at the end of a
quarter of an hour that some of the glass cases contained swords and
epaulettes of ancient colonels and generals; medals and orders once
pinned over hearts that had long since ceased to beat; snuff-boxes be-
stowed on ministers and envoys; copies of works presented, with in-
scriptions, by authors now classic."

Yet even with his impressions of all these things, what remains with
Strether most is a sense of Madame de Vionnet herself:

> She was seated, near the fire, on a small stuffed and fringed chair,
> one of the few modern articles in the room; and she leaned back
> in it with her hands clasped in her lap and no movement, in all
> her person, but the fine prompt play of her deep young face.
> The fire, under the low white marble, undraped and academic,
> had burnt down to the silver ashes of light wood; one of the

> windows, at a distance, stood open to the mildness and stillness, out of which, in the short pauses, came the faint sound, pleasant and homely, almost rustic, of a plash and a clatter of *sabots* from some coach-house on the other side of the court. (1:247)

The suggestion of comfort here speaks significantly about Madame de Vionnet's relation to her past. The absence of any movement but "the fine prompt play" of her face displays the concentrated attentiveness Strether will learn to recognize as her distinctive feature. All her acute feeling for nuances of tone, all her fine sense for discriminations of meaning, all the unfailing alertness by which she will always seem to him never less than completely *there*—these will affect him with a quite special meaning: the refusal to allow a sense of the past to overcome one's sense of the present.

A special beauty manifests itself as the note of her "deep young face": deep because of all her accumulations of expression, young because she can still give herself to what she feels with the passionate intensity of youth. We recall how Strether had described little Bilham as "blessedly young" in his openness to experience; the same might also be said of Madame de Vionnet. But in her case the contrast between her youth and the accumulations surrounding her make it especially significant. Strether will later think of her, under the pressure of certain moments, as "old"—less responsive, in other words, because of what she has suffered. Nevertheless, her willingness to suffer yet more on behalf of the person she loves attests finally to her being still young.

It remains for Strether to register one final perception of Madame de Vionnet. His appreciation of her possessions now becomes part of his relation to her, and in particular to everything that seems to him most vulnerable—and hence most human—in her:

> She was the poor lady for Strether now because clearly she had some trouble, and her appeal to him could only mean that her trouble was deep. He could n't help it; it was n't his fault; he had done nothing; but by a turn of the hand she had somehow made their encounter a relation. And the relation profited by a mass of things that were not strictly in it or of it; by the very air in which they sat, by the high cold delicate room, by the world outside and the little plash in the court, by the First Empire and the relics in the stiff cabinets, by matters as far off as those and by others as near as the unbroken clasp of her hands in her lap and the look her expression had of being most natural when her eyes were most fixed. (1:249)

This relation of Strether's to Madame de Vionnet amounts to nothing more than the acknowledgment of a relation. But, by that acknowledgment, Strether recognizes the human reality of their situation, and of hers with Chad—a recognition that implies the breakdown of "a moral scheme of the most approved pattern" on "any approach to vivid facts"; which is to say: "to any at all liberal appreciation of them." But what is this appreciation if not a perception of what Madame de Vionnet has done for Chad, by way of refinement, of developing his sensibility? What Strether sees as a result of visiting her is what he has been seeing ever since his arrival in Paris: how experiences like the simple observance of sunlight as it passes through a grove of trees, the feel of a sea breeze and the appearance of sails on foam-flecked waves, or the grandeur of a cathedral at sunset, can impart a meaning to particular moments of our lives. This meaning, in turn, replaces the "moral scheme of the most approved pattern" with which he was sent over. To accept the experience of beauty, however, as a sufficient source of meaning for our existence—what is this but to affirm the Aesthetic belief? Throughout his visit with Madame de Vionnet, Strether has felt how his sense of a relation to her "profited by a mass of things that were not strictly in it or of it." To appreciate them is to affirm, tacitly, what Strether has been expected to deny. His conclusion seems inescapable: how deny what one cannot help appreciating if one has any sensibility at all? And what, in fact, has the whole "process of Strether's vision" been, if not a deepening appreciation of the significance of various impressions—in short, of everything Paris offers the sensitive observer?

If the process of vision amounts to a process of appreciation, the result must be a specific recognition: to witness the beauty of a sunset on the Seine or a morning on the Île de la Cité is to know all we can know of the meaning of our existence. That meaning can only come from the intensity with which various impressions affect us. In his preface to *The Ambassadors* James affirms a similar principle with regard to fiction. In restricting his novel to Strether's perspective, he finds that "a full observance of the rich rigour I speak of would give me more of the effect I should be most 'after' than all other possible observances together." This effect is "the grace of intensity"—"the grace to which the enlightened story-teller will at any time, for his interest, sacrifice if need be all other graces whatever" (1:xv). And, later in the same preface: "Since, however, all art is *expression*, and is thereby vividness, one was to find the door open here to any amount of delightful dissimulation" (1:xxi). Vividness of expression produces an effect corresponding to the impressions we feel in our actual existence. The immediacy of *The Ambassadors* results from an attempt to re-create the effect of similar impressions upon Strether.

Here James's standpoint differs substantially from his earlier pronouncements in "The Art of Fiction." The earlier essay had emphasized art's capacity for representation.[10] To expand representational limits, to enable art to encompass more of life, had seemed a sufficient aim. If art differs fundamentally from life, representation becomes imaginative as well as suggestive. For the later James, however, art no longer differs so much from life. Permeating both is a subjective consciousness for which things become meaningful by the intensity of their impression. But that intensity requires art to become expressive so as to create a similar effect. What art offers, then, is the intensity of our moments of highest awareness. For Strether, at least, such intensities are simply those of his impressions. His appreciation of them mirrors the larger process of appreciation that is the theme of *The Ambassadors*.

This small struggle sprang not a little, in its way, from the same impulse that had now carried him across to Notre Dame; the impulse to let things be, to give them time to justify themselves or at least to pass. He was aware of having no errand in such a place but the desire not to be, for the hour, in certain other places; a sense of safety, of simplification, which each time he yielded to it he amused himself by thinking of as a private concession to cowardice. The great church had no altar for his worship, no direct voice for his soul; but it was none the less soothing even to sanctity; for he could feel while there what he could n't elsewhere, that he was a plain tired man taking the holiday he had earned. He was tired, but he was n't plain—that was the pity and the trouble of it; he was able, however, to drop his problem at the door very much as if it had been the copper piece that he deposited, on the threshold, in the receptacle of the inveterate blind beggar. He trod the long dim nave, sat in the splendid choir, paused before the clustered chapels of the east end, and the mighty monument laid upon him its spell. He might have been a student under the charm of a museum—which was exactly what, in a foreign town, in the afternoon of life, he would have liked to be free to be. This form of sacrifice did at any rate for the occasion as well as another; it made him quite sufficiently understand how, within the precinct, for the real refugee, the things of the world could fall into abeyance. That was the cowardice, probably—to dodge them, to beg the question, not to

Eugène Atget, *Notre-Dame* (March 1922).

deal with it in the hard outer light; but his own oblivions were too brief, too vain, to hurt any one but himself, and he had a vague and fanciful kindness for certain persons whom he met, figures of mystery and anxiety, and whom, with observation for his pastime, he ranked as those who were fleeing from justice. Justice was outside, in the hard light, and injustice too; but one was as absent as the other from the air of the long aisles and the brightness of the many altars. (2:4–5)

The impulse that carries Strether across the river to Notre Dame corresponds to the one that, at the end of *The Golden Bowl*, floats Maggie's vision across the drawing-room at Portland Place to where her father stands silently looking at the painting he had given her for her marriage, the "early Florentine sacred subject." By an involuntary movement expressive of the heart's deepest desire, what Strether now feels is a need, a longing, for refuge. The "impulse to let things be, to give them time to justify themselves or at least to pass" has operated within him before, albeit to a different purpose. Then it allowed him to absorb the full splendor of the scene before him; now he knows no desire but to escape from the pressure of those intensities of impression he has recently had only too much of. "World-weariness," Pater might have called it: for Strether it results from an excessive brilliance of phenomena, a surfeit of emotion. Under such circumstances, the mind longs for the peculiar sweetness of seclusion, the pleasure of a "sense of safety, of simplification" obtainable from an hour in Notre Dame.

It is precisely this mood of longing that allows religious associations to make their most poignant appeal.[11] The charm of the cloister, of a sheltered existence, invariably exercises a seductive effect upon whoever seeks relief from worldly complexities. This charm is not simply one of solitude but also of reflection or reverie. In his *Apologia Pro Vita Sua*, Cardinal Newman had attested to the cloister's allure. What religious worship offers is the pleasure of immersing oneself in a collective consciousness, the accumulated emotion of countless generations. All those "accumulations of expression" that Strether notices in Madame de Vionnet's apartment have never been more manifest than here, in the great cathedral.[12] The sheer awareness of presences that continue to make themselves felt in spite of any passage of time, filling the very atmosphere with their aura, suffices to impart a kind of sacredness to this place that Strether cannot help but acknowledge. "The great church had no altar for his worship, no direct voice for his soul; but it was none the less soothing even to sanctity. . . ."

If it is impossible to share the beliefs embodied in this edifice, if one is not sufficiently engaged to either affirm or deny them, it remains possible nevertheless to sense in the church a human presence and all that it implies.[13] From its beginnings, Aestheticism had been preoccupied with the question of sanctity. After early affirmations of the sacredness of life (e.g., Rossetti's *House of Life*), it shifts to an emphasis upon liturgy and ritual (*Marius the Epicurean*), concerning itself less with a ceremony's intrinsic meaning than with the aesthetic impression it produces. Attempting to depict the "world-weariness" of the Roman mind in the early Christian centuries as well as its anxious search for new beliefs to replace a waning tradition, Pater had sought to capture the experience of discovering Christianity. What had interested him above all was its sense of renewal, of awakening to a new existence, the immersion in a strange new world of ceremonies and practices, where events become endowed with a different kind of meaning—that of the sublime mystery of transubstantiation, for instance, and other, equally paradoxical mysteries of faith. For the sensitive Roman observer, such ceremonies could yield a sensuous *frisson* through initiation into a hitherto-unsuspected realm of beauty and symbolism.

But the complex relation of that Roman world to the end of the nineteenth century, with its similar world-weariness, its comparable loss of religious belief, and its anguished search for new sources of meaning, does not permit of any easy identification. Missing from the fin-de-siècle is a new religion that could rejuvenate its outlook. As a result, it must approach existing forms of belief from a different standpoint. For Pater (as for many others) this was to be the road leading ultimately to Rome. The aesthetic possibilities offered by Roman Catholicism through its symbolic rites exercise an attraction against which Protestantism had nothing comparable to offer. The attraction includes the pleasure of contemplating centuries of religious art but also something less tangible, yet equally significant: a consciousness of tradition.

For Pater, as for other aesthetes, tradition assumes a human form. To know that the liturgy one employs has been preserved unaltered for more than a thousand years—the thought of countless others with all their hopes and aspirations celebrating the same sacrament with similar emotions, the consciousness of a silent communion uniting one to all those for whom this ceremony expressed their deepest, most cherished beliefs—such a consciousness can indeed induce a feeling of the sacredness of that ceremony and of the faith it symbolizes. For Cardinal Newman, a similar recognition had prompted his return to the creed of Rome. That the belief of the majority should constitute, in some ineffable sense, the will of the living Church had been the decisive factor leading to his conversion. If it seems difficult historically to recover certain aspects of Newman's viewpoint, it remains possible to comprehend what a lay convert or even a dispassionate observer (such as Strether) might feel.

Previously, Christian symbolism had conferred a consecration upon ceremonial rites through belief in a literal presence of the divine within the human sphere. With the progressive loss of belief, what remains is simply the rite itself and its material appurtenances. Through their association with Christian observances, however, these remain endowed with an aura of sanctity even for the casual observer. Their associations thus become a religious equivalent to the accumulations of expression James had ascribed to certain English houses. This impression of sanctity that remains when its original source has disappeared locates the feeling of sacredness within religious emotion, its nature of pious awe. If Strether cannot share the original faith, he can experience something of what Hawthorne had felt in St. Peter's in Rome—a yearning for relief from the burden of individual conscience and a wish to merge oneself with the vast collective consciousness of humanity. The relief Strether now feels comes, then, from assimilating his individual mood to the hallowed space of the vast cathedral.

"He trod the long dim nave, sat in the splendid choir, paused before the clustered chapels of the east end, and the mighty monument laid upon him its spell." We recall how Madame de Vionnet had remained "beautifully passive" under the "spell of transmission" that had brought her her Empire relics and surrounded her with something of the glory of the Napoleonic era. In a similar fashion, Strether too can now remain beautifully passive: what is imparted to him, however, is not the Empire's dim lustre but a sense of humanity itself, the feelings and aspirations of those who have worshipped in the great cathedral. Here the dimness of the nave might afford a refuge to one eager to lose himself amid the shadows. But the "splendid choir" and the "clustered chapels of the east end" can also inspire another kind of emotion. Amid the brilliant spectacle of architectural harmony, the radiant light of stained glass windows, and the gleaming gold of the altars it becomes easy to surrender oneself to a feeling of aesthetic grandeur. That grandeur, however, encompasses the beauty not only of the monument itself but of what it evokes as well.

With the splendor of the choir, a fusion of visible and invisible becomes manifest. For those dwelling like Strether in the twilight of a declining faith, symbolism possesses a special allure: with the loss of belief, it becomes possible to appreciate in a different fashion the *beauty* of that belief. If to feel intrinsically a hierarchical relation between the mind and God is impossible, by means of a harmony in architectural gradations of nave and choir one can yet obtain a sense of it. At the same time, the nature of this apprehension is necessarily aesthetic, its form wholly defined by that of a vault or nave. Thus what had been experienced before as "life" now becomes an appreciation of spiritual conditions in terms of form. In his magisterial *History,* Henry Adams had spoken of Jefferson's concern with the form of his writings—"a sure sign," Adams remarks, "of intellectual sensuousness" (*History* 1:100). Here one might ascribe a similar inclination to Aestheticism. This concern with the form of expression reflects an aesthetic pleasure in intellectual structure. It implies an appreciation of how form affects thought, an apprehension of beauty in discursive arrangement that allows one idea to illuminate another, the impression of composition produced by a whole, a sense of architecture, of ideal harmony. Perhaps Strether's vision of the great cathedral amounts to no more than this—a feeling for how architecture might give form to the religious aspiration for unity that Henry Adams was to describe almost simultaneously in his *Mont Saint Michel and Chartres*.

We are told that the atmosphere of the church had proved "soothing even to sanctity" for Strether, and in his final impression this note predominates: "Justice was outside, in the hard light, and injustice too; but one was as absent as the other from the air of the long aisles and the brightness of the many altars." An awareness of those human questions concerning Chad, Madame de Vionnet, and himself remains with Strether even here. At the same time, if only dimly, he receives a glimpse of what will become the dominant theme of *The Golden Bowl*: the possibility of assimilating life into form and the redeeming significance of that form. What the "air of the long aisles" offers is a sense of order— the perception of all things having their appropriate place in some higher scheme of beauty and harmony. But James's principal concern in *The Ambassadors* remains with what we might call the phenomenology of "the affair of life"—an analysis of the process of vision by which external impressions are transmuted into recognitions of beauty and significance. We have seen how *The Ambassadors* lends itself to a theory of impressionism that traces our experience of the beautiful to the effect of our impressions. In so doing, it makes a plea for appreciation of the beautiful in life, of everything embodied in the immediacy of our impressions. That appreciation will take account of not only the beauty of impressions but also their significance—which means their relation to the consciousness that perceives them.

It seems both touching and ironic that Strether's one excursion into the countryside mentioned by the narrative should have been in pursuit of a vision formed many years earlier from a small landscape by Lambinet, seen in a Boston gallery. Here one cannot help recalling Wilde's remark in *Intentions* about nature's ability to imitate art and the appearance of fogs in London after Whistler and others had painted them. The idea that art gives us a fresh perception of nature can lead to higher aspirations: a desire, for instance, to assimilate nature to art, to create from external impressions a composition conforming to the painter's eye—this, then, is what prompts Strether to his little excursion into the *banlieues* of Paris.

We have seen how the process of Strether's vision defines the central theme of *The Ambassadors*. Nowhere does this become more apparent then in the shock with which he registers what he sees on the little stream that winds past the pavilion from which he surveys its course. The vision that presents itself to him at that moment demonstrates decisively the impossibility of assimilating life to art—that the composition Strether attempts to create for himself out of a summer's day in the French countryside cannot suffice to encompass all of life. But if James himself is not yet prepared to sublimate life to form (as he will do in *The Golden Bowl*), what remains conspicuous in Strether's attempt is that even this—the discovery he makes—belongs to his process of vision. Its shock, and the deepening awareness which comes as that shock recedes, can only enrich his sense of the human drama he now witnesses. What his vision amounts to, as much as anything else, is an increased appreciation of the complexity of Chad's relation to Madame de Vionnet. If it ruptures even with violence his interpretation of what he has seen, it also makes for greater fullness of vision and an intensified awareness.

But if Strether's awareness governs the aestheticism of *The Ambassadors*, the effect upon him of what he sees on the stream is not in fact a denial of the relation of art to life but rather its highest realization. Thus while his attempt to assimilate the landscape before him to a Lambinet fails to take into account all the richness and complexity of the actual scene, a deeper recognition springs from what he sees and how it transforms his idea of Chad's relationship with Madame de Vionnet. In one respect, of course, Strether feels himself "sold"—he who had asserted the "virtuous" character of their attachment. But the knowledge he attains initiates him into the nature of human passion—its strange mixture of desire and tenderness, opportunism with affection. That knowledge, in turn, forms the culmination of a process of vision that began with his arrival in Paris.

Equated with vision, art becomes identified with the possibility of a virtually limitless depth of impression, what Edith Wharton would call in *The Age of Innocence* the "long echoes of beauty" that art awakens (*Novels*, p. 1299). For *The Ambassadors,* at least, this is what aestheticism consists of: an appreciation of impressions in all their depth and fullness. But if art is equated with vision rather than with form, the distinction between art and the aesthetic of experience also ceases. Even more than before, art now becomes merely our finest medium of awareness, a means of registering our most varied impressions.[14]

If art has nothing more to offer than what is implied in the process of vision, its responsibility then is simply to affirm that vision. By basing *The Ambassadors* upon the process of Strether's vision, James in effect abjures the possibility of an inner architectonics, presenting instead a continuous intensification of awareness. Moreover, if the form of the novel is solely that of Strether's vision, its theme is the nature of art. As a phenomenology of vision, the narration of Strether's experiences is also an analysis of the mind's apprehension of external phenomena: hence consciousness, so to speak, becomes one with art. In describing Strether's experiences, James equates art with the formation of an impression. Art becomes then the *form* of our relation to life, i.e., to our impressions. The process by which vision elicits from these impressions an experience of the beautiful is art.

We have seen how Strether's attempt to assimilate the French countryside to his remembrance of a Lambinet implies a loss of various complexities of the scene. His attempt, nevertheless, is both instructive and revealing. What it demonstrates is the aesthetic nature of vision itself, its intrinsic tendency to compose in pictorial terms: "The oblong gilt frame disposed its enclosing lines; the poplars and willows, the reeds and river—a river of which he did n't know, and did n't want to know, the name—fell into a composition, full of felicity, within them; the sky was silver and turquoise and varnish; the village on the left was white and the church on the right was grey; it was all there, in short—it was what he wanted: it was Tremont Street, it was France, it was Lambinet" (2:247).

The "oblong gilt frame" indicates the limits of pictorial vision. Within its compass it embraces abundant suggestions of nature—poplars, willows, reeds, and a river. Their colors are carefully complemented by others: "silver and turquoise and varnish." Nowhere do we find a simple blue, which might disrupt the harmony by introducing a strong primary color. Instead, turquoise represents the blue one naturally looks for from the sky on such a clear and sunny day. At the same time, touches of silver impart a precious effect, one quite appropriate to the painterly quality of the vision. The "varnish" only adds emphasis—an allusion, to be sure, to the actual canvas, but also possibly to the sky's glazed aspect, which reflects its silver light.

"Full of felicity," in any case, Strether's vision is said to be, in a manner that does not distinguish between his emotion and the scene's own harmonious composition. This failure to distinguish highlights an affinity between consciousness and artistic vision. The whiteness of the village on the left and the gray of the church on the right recall similar juxtapositions from various Impressionist works, especially in winter pictures contrasting the whiteness of snow with gray walls and slate-colored roofs of houses. Neoclassical painting had sought to obtain an equilibrium by disposing its masses in an appropriate fashion; the Impressionist discovery that color in itself suffices to create such an equilibrium marks a new stage in the development of pictorial technique. The rightness of this equilibrium for Strether is implied in his conclusion: "it was Tremont Street, it was France, it was Lambinet." The vision of a remembered past (Tremont Street) is thus superimposed, like a palimpsest, upon the present (France), which in turn is assimilated to a pictorial image of that present (Lambinet). The superimposition reveals the capacity of Strether's vision to accumulate impressions that mutually enrich each other.

Thus Strether's remembered past—an impression of refreshing coolness offered by a painted landscape on a hot, dusty Boston day—materializes now in the summer air of the French countryside. Conversely, how could the present not be suffused by the past, its gleam of remembered vision that imparts a greater brightness to all his present impressions? Without doubt, the feeling that permeates his encounter with this landscape results from the "taste of idleness" that comes with the Pococks' departure as well as from the holiday atmosphere that had informed his seeing of the Lambinet many years earlier. Then there is the Lambinet itself, which transforms consciousness into a work of the painter's eye. Such a transformation necessarily yields a heightened pleasure, by allowing one to experience the process by which one's aesthetic impressions are formed: "He really continued in the picture—that being for himself his situation—all the rest of this rambling day; so that the charm was still, was indeed more than ever upon him when, toward six o'clock, he found himself amicably engaged with a stout white-capped deep-voiced woman at the door of the *auberge* of the biggest village, a village that affected him as a thing of whiteness, blueness and crookedness, set in coppery green, and that had the river flowing behind or before it—one could n't say which; at the bottom, in particular, of the inn-garden" (2:251–52).

This episode and others that remind him of Maupassant all contribute to his "jour à la campagne," with its summer atmosphere, conversations with country people, and aimless but enjoyable peregrina-
tions. The rendering of his circumstances by pictorial means need not
be literal: what remains expressive is its evocation of large leisure, the
luxury of simply observing. In addition, the anecdotal quality so well
captured in various Impressionist works—a glimpse of interrupted activity or a brief, relaxing interlude—presents itself as a subject for
composition. For Strether, the village in which he finds himself at the
end of his day's rambles "affected him as a thing of whiteness, blueness
and crookedness, set in coppery green." Here color is not distinguished from form: both are simply impressionistic effects. The delight
the eye experiences in whiteness or blueness, the surface of a wall or
door or window shutter, is enhanced by the angular perspective of a
road or roof. Above all, there is the pleasure of reproducing concrete
edifices through motifs of color that yield a sensuous pleasure not to
be found in the actual appearances.

Here color consists of rendering an *impression*: to the extent that
what we see in a picture is not an object but our impression of it,
what painting makes possible is a heightened consciousness of that
impression and hence of the process of vision by which we create for
ourselves an apprehension of the beautiful. To see this apprehension
emerge from a chaos of form, light, and color is the profound and
moving experience of all pictorial art. Strether's own vision, to be
sure, is mild enough, as he himself readily recognizes: an interpretation
of the scene before him through the eyes of a minor nineteenth-century landscape painter. But if so, it only represents more clearly the
essential miracle of painting, its transformation of external appearances
into an experience of the beautiful. The means by which form and
color suffuse a landscape with emotion, this imperceptible art of creating an atmosphere out of a natural scene, epitomizes the pictorial
process.

But there remains for Strether a further depth of awareness, one
that permeates even pictorial appreciation with a sense of the moment's capacity for drama: "For this had been all day at bottom the
spell of the picture—that it was essentially more than anything else a
scene and a stage, that the very air of the play was in the rustle of the
willows and the tone of the sky. The play and the characters had, without his knowing it till now, peopled all his space for him, and it seemed
somehow quite happy that they should offer themselves, in the conditions so supplied, with a kind of inevitability" (2:253).

These elements that Strether sees become stage properties as a result of his sense of other, unrepresented human agencies. Perhaps this is the essence of drama: an awareness of the relation between the scene we see and things not present which give that scene its particular meaning. Thus Strether is aware of how the elements of his vision become part of a larger account. And we are told, quite surprisingly, that together they constitute *the thing* even more than Madame de Vionnet's great salon, where "the ghost of the Empire walked." This capacity to create an aura of suggestion by what it implies represents art's highest resource. As Strether sits at the pavilion by the water's edge and gazes across the stream, he receives a glimpse of artistic possibilities: "The valley on the further side was all copper-green level and glazed pearly sky, a sky hatched across with screens of trimmed trees, which looked flat like espaliers; and though the rest of the village straggled away in the near quarter the view had an emptiness that made one of the boats suggestive. Such a river set one afloat almost before one could take up the oars—the idle play of which would be moreover the aid to the full impression" (2:255).

Like the turquoise and silver, the "copper-green level" suggests something artificial and precious, as does the "glazed pearly sky." Other pictorial motifs abound: the cross-hatching of the sky by "screens" of trimmed trees which "looked flat, like espaliers," evoking the style of a fine-point drawing; or the emptiness of the foreground, which makes one of the boats "suggestive." The recognition that "such a river set one afloat almost before one could take up the oars" hints at a pleasure-seeking impulse within vision itself. The motive for movement, however, could only originate in the mind that perceives this scene, while the disposition of that scene, with its flagrant appeal to a desire for luxurious idleness and the charm of aimless divagations (like the motions of reverie) results from an aspiration for what Baudelaire had described as "luxe, calme, et volupté." The vision is explicitly self-conscious: the "idle play" of the oars, we are told, would be "the aid to the full impression." Thus the maximum possible intensity of impression, which James had called the highest grace of art, emerges as an accompaniment to the present vision. In the spectator's quest for intensity, the idle play of the oars forms an expressive note. The appreciation of similar effects defines this vision as "aesthetic."

But one feels also the presence of something else besides what Strether had earlier termed the "art of taking things as they come." Implied is a feeling for the arrangement of our impressions, what we might call "composition." This sense of form signifies, then, the ultimate result of the aesthetic consciousness. Within the thematic economy of *The Ambassadors,* as we have seen, it figures as something less than the

whole of art's relation to life. For there remains something deeper—
the drama of human relationships that informs the spectacle Strether
is now called upon to witness, which is both ironic and, at the same
time, the highest possible "subject" for appreciation:

> What he saw was exactly the right thing—a boat advancing round
> the bend and containing a man who held the paddles and a lady,
> at the stern, with a pink parasol. It was suddenly as if these fig-
> ures, or something like them, had been wanted in the picture,
> had been wanted more or less all day, and had now drifted into
> sight, with the slow current, on purpose to fill up the measure.
> They came slowly, floating down, evidently directed to the land-
> ing-place near their spectator and presenting themselves to him
> not less clearly as the two persons for whom his hostess was al-
> ready preparing a meal. For two very happy persons he found
> himself straightway taking them—a young man in shirt-sleeves,
> a young woman easy and fair, who had pulled pleasantly up from
> some other place and, being acquainted with the neighbour-
> hood, had known what this particular retreat could offer them.
> The air quite thickened, at their approach, with further intima-
> tions; the intimation that they were expert, familiar, frequent—
> that this would n't at all events be the first time. They knew how
> to do it, he vaguely felt—and it made them but the more idyllic,
> though at the very moment of the impression, as happened, their
> boat seemed to have begun to drift wide, the oarsman letting it
> go. It had by this time none the less come much nearer—near
> enough for Strether to dream the lady in the stern had for some
> reason taken account of his being there to watch them. She had
> remarked on it sharply, yet her companion had n't turned round;
> it was in fact almost as if our friend had felt her bid him keep
> still. She had taken in something as a result of which their course
> had wavered, and it continued to waver while they just stood
> off. This little effect was sudden and rapid, so rapid that Streth-
> er's sense of it was separate only for an instant from a sharp start
> of his own. He too had within the minute taken in something,
> taken in that he knew the lady whose parasol, shifting as if to
> hide her face, made so fine a pink point in the shining scene. It
> was too prodigious, a chance in a million, but, if he knew the
> lady, the gentleman, who still presented his back and kept off,
> the gentleman, the coatless hero of the idyll, who had responded
> to her start, was, to match the marvel, none other than Chad.
> (2:256–57)

The luminous pink point of the parasol becomes a kind of center, a focal point, about which the whole shimmering scene revolves. It exercises a special effect upon Strether, the one bright touch of color within his field of vision, vibrant not only because of its beauty but because it awakens at the same time other, more human recognitions: the recognition, in particular, of Madame de Vionnet as the parasol's owner, and with this, a sense of arrested movement—as if the flow of thought typified by the winding current of the stream now comes abruptly to a standstill. Vision concentrates intensely upon the "pink point" of the parasol because it crystallizes the mind's impressions of both beauty and pain. The beauty of color, of whatever vivifies perception, imparting pleasure to its vision of the external world, infuses the scene with its special brightness, making one aware once more that if forms express the thought of perception, color expresses its emotion and its joy. Pain, on the other hand, comes from acknowledging the relation between what is now perceived and other, far different scenes.

There neither is nor can be any pain in the shining apparition of the actual scene. All sense of pain comes rather from those intimations that inform the scene. The air "quite thickens" with them, creating a sense of drama where what had existed previously had been only a visual tableau. Yet that tableau by itself cannot suffice: "these figures, or something like them, had been wanted in the picture, had been wanted more or less all day," and they now appear "on purpose to fill up the measure." By an involuntary movement of desire, the mind seeks to discover some human interest in these figures, developing its own suppositions or conjectures: that they are acquainted with this neighborhood, that they are even "expert, familiar, frequent"; finally that "this would n't at all events be the first time."

But with its human interest and its increasing intimations of relation, even of knowledge, there comes, suddenly, a shock of recognition. From the instant it occurs, thought can no longer sustain its movement: the boat begins to drift, falling away from its course; a moment of awkwardness ensues. The composition to which these figures in the boat were to have added the consummate touch is abruptly rent, with a violence that leaves the luminous pink spot as its sole expressive motif. Within itself, however, that pink spot absorbs all the consciousness, the entire impression of the scene, its experience both of beauty and of pain, allowing them to interfuse and in the process to enrich each other. In so doing, the "fine pink point" of the "shining scene" intensifies emotion beyond anything imaginable from a purely pictorial standpoint. But how could any purely pictorial impression offer anything comparable? The consciousness now embodied within the luminous pink spot of Madame de Vionnet's parasol contains not only the fullest appreciation of color or light but also that deeper sense which comes only with moral awareness, a feeling for the sacredness of trust and affection, for the awful realities of betrayal and suffering. His pursuit of a life of intenser consciousness will have led Strether to this—the paradoxical realization that our moral impressions afford the highest, because most intense, medium of experience. Nothing else—neither sensual pleasures nor the more refined and complex ones of art—can claim a similar permanence. And, for complexity, what possibly to compare with the infinite multiplicity of intimations, insights, awarenesses, and realizations issuing from the discovery of a single moment's recognition whose circumstances remain in the mind forever?

From the standpoint afforded by this moment, it becomes possible to look forward to Strether's subsequent meeting in Paris with Madame de Vionnet, when he will find her looking haggard and old, and witness her devastation at the prospect of Chad's departure. What Strether then sees he realizes he will carry with him always: the memory of passion, violent, uncontrollable, yet human in its awareness, its capacity to feel. Perhaps nothing in the novel quite exceeds the tenderness of those moments of his final visit with Madame de Vionnet, a tenderness all the more eloquent because unexpressed, confronting the reality of Chad's loss of attachment, when Strether finds himself compelled to make a final appeal on behalf not of beauty, interest, or appreciation but of moral responsibility. If that appeal is perhaps doomed to failure, something else survives: the remembrance, consecrated like some sacred trust, of human suffering and the life of the emotions, upon which it touches. Because nothing, ultimately, elicits a greater intensity of response than the expression of human emotion: but with this realization comes a recognition of moral awareness as the highest, most intense consciousness of all.

7

THE TRIUMPH OF FORM

We have seen how *The Ambassadors* looms with the presence of a city expressive of all the aesthetic possibilities of life: Paris. In its own more somber fashion, *The Golden Bowl* also reflects the sense of a particular place: London. But the London of *The Golden Bowl* is a London of the mind, its position as commercial capital of the nineteenth century transmuted into a suggestion of other, less tangible forms of influence. What it suggests to the Prince in particular at the beginning of the novel is Rome: "The Prince had always liked his London, when it had come to him; he was one of the Modern Romans who find by the Thames a more convincing image of the truth of the ancient state than any they have left by the Tiber" (1:3). Like the "ancient state," the modern capital manifests an aura of *Imperium*, of power based upon the capacity for conquest.[1] What the Roman legions had accomplished for the Eternal City, the British metropolis now achieves by other means. Thus, "brought up on the legend of the City to which the world paid tribute," the Prince "recognised in the present London much more than in contemporary Rome the real dimensions of such a case."

In either instance, the idea of empire implies aggression, the transgression of natural limits to appropriate what belongs to another. Thus conquest leads to possession, and possession, in turn, to enjoyment: "If it was a question of an *Imperium*, he said to himself, and if one wished, as a Roman, to recover a little the sense of that, the place to do so was on London Bridge, or even, on a fine afternoon in May, at Hyde Park Corner." From London Bridge one might view the spectacle of the Thames, with its busy commercial traffic, signifying the prosperity of the empire. Hyde Park Corner presents a somewhat different appearance: the sight of ladies and gentlemen of the upper classes, on foot or in carriages, enjoying the air of a fine May afternoon affords a suggestion of a material splendor consisting of both wealth and leisure. In a sense these are the rewards of empire, elements whose en-

Alvin Langdon Coburn, *London Bridge,* 1905.

joyment is the objective of conquest. Together they enhance, more than anything else, the sense of possession which is the requisite of particular forms of pleasure.

But it is not at either of these places that we find the Prince as the novel opens. Instead the "grounds of his predilection" have guided him elsewhere: "he had strayed simply enough into Bond Street, where his imagination, working at comparatively short range, caused him now and then to stop before a window in which objects massive and lump-ish, in silver and gold, in the forms to which precious stones contrib-ute, or in leather, steel, brass, applied to a hundred uses and abuses, were as tumbled together as if, in the insolence of the Empire, they had been the loot of far-off victories." We are told that the "grounds of his predilection" were "after all sufficiently vague"; combined with his "straying" into Bond Street, they hint at an involuntary movement, the manifestation of an unconscious desire. That desire would be for wealth, for the pleasure of possession. And, indeed, the "objects" at which the Prince gazes, concrete attestations of wealth, are reduced to their most elemental aspect, the material of which they consist: silver, gold, precious stones, leather, steel, brass. To reduce them in this fash-ion to their material essence emphasizes the abstract idea of wealth. These objects have no value in themselves; their only value accrues from the desire to possess them. "Tumbled together," they adumbrate an excess which is the hallmark of wealth.

At the same time they are compared to "the loot of far-off victo-ries," representing the spoils of violent conquest. Conquest of whom, though, or of what? It is a sign of the "insolence of the Empire" that it does not concern itself with such questions. This indifference to the fate of others is precisely the standpoint that makes possible the cre-ation of empire. But the spoils of conquest, however enjoyable in themselves, are merely a symbol of something else: the fact of pos-session—not only of these objects, of course, but in effect of the peo-ple to whom they once belonged, who now have lost their capacity to possess, who have themselves become nothing more than a pos-session. The desire to possess others is then perhaps the ultimate ob-jective of empire. In possessing them one possesses all they have and all they are capable of producing—the very source of their wealth.

Yet it is not any of these forms of wealth that finally attracts the Prince: "The young man's movements, however, betrayed no consis-tency of attention—not even, for that matter, when one of his arrests had proceeded from possibilities in faces shaded, as they passed him on the pavement, by huge beribboned hats, or more delicately tinted still under the tense silk of parasols held at perverse angles in waiting victorias" (1:3–4). The failure to maintain consistent attention can often indicate a surfeit of desire. Nevertheless, the Prince's eye continues to experience "arrests"—as if the impulse for conquest, now become instinctive, persists in pursuing even after desire has been satiated. What he pursues are "possibilities," in faces shaded by huge feminine hats or concealed by parasols in waiting carriages. The specific sense of "possibilities" remains unspecified, but the fact that what gives the Prince pause are not the faces but their "possibilities" is suggestive. In light of the theme of Imperium, the word appears to imply possibilities for possession. One feels the irritation of a desire frustrated in its efforts to see these faces, to determine whether they are beautiful and whether it is worth pursuing them. From that standpoint, the hats and parasols can only be obstructions to a voyeuristic eye seeking to consume its objects simply by seeing them. In the waving and bobbing of "huge beribboned hats" the eye tends to get lost, while the "perverse angles" of parasols seem deliberately set on frustrating desire. That desire sees, moreover, objects rather than beings— "faces" rather than personalities, without the mention of even a look or smile. It is capable of appreciating subtle nuances of appearance (the delicate tinting of a face by the reflection of color from a parasol). But the fundamental nature of this desire precludes its sensing any emotion in its objects. To do so would be to acknowledge their existence as something more than objects: as others capable of experiencing feeling (even desire) like the self, and hence no longer capable of being possessed as objects.

What the self seeks from its objects, however, is not a response but simply the pleasure of possessing them. This pleasure consists of the sensations these objects excite. The sight of a beautiful face can yield a certain pleasure to the eye. But desire (as in the Prince's case) also seeks all the other sensual pleasures that face can give. In addition to a greater variety of pleasures, possession suggests the possibility of having them whenever one wants. Unlike Strether's fleeting impressions of the beautiful in *The Ambassadors,* the pleasures that result from possession offer a prospect of constant gratification. In attempting to possess them the Prince seeks to attain the permanence that had eluded Strether. The prospect of constant gratification offers something like a transcendence of time, were it possible always to receive the same sensation from a particular object. But, even without this prospect, there remains the pleasure of having in one's grasp not only a desired sensation but the source of that sensation as well. To possess the source of a pleasure, however, is to possess the possibility of endlessly renewing it. And indeed the thought of renewing one's pleasures offers, perhaps, the subtlest pleasure of all.

In his quest the Prince is by no means alone. What his excursion into Bond Street reveals, among other things, is an entire world animated by a similar desire: "And the Prince's undirected thought was not a little symptomatic, since, though the turn of the season had come and the flush of the streets begun to fade, the possibilities of faces, on the August afternoon, were still one of the notes of the scene." Though the "season" has begun to wane, desire persists in pursuing its object, animated by an involuntary instinct. The "flush" of the streets suggests a heightening both of color and, by implication, of passion. If these have begun to fade, the "possibilities" of faces nevertheless remain. That such possibilities should not be ascribed solely to the Prince's individual eye but objectively asserted is undoubtedly significant. It implies a kind of collective voyeurism, in which each individual consciousness regards all others as prospects for possession. These possibilities remain, we are told, one of the "notes" of the scene: in this fashion the aesthetic pleasure of an expressive motif (a "note") is assimilated to a quest for possession. Whereas in *The Ambassadors* an expressive note or impression becomes a subject of appreciation, the present world seeks simply to subsume it. Thus possibilities cease to remain such when the desire for them disappears.

That is precisely what now happens with the Prince: "He was too restless—that was the fact—for any concentration, and the last idea that would just now have occurred to him in any connexion was the idea of pursuit" (1:4). But if the idea of pursuit does not explicitly occur here, we have seen how desire nevertheless follows an instinctive movement. The subconscious movement of desire, even when not (ostensibly) pursuing an object, attests to its constant presence. For the Prince it remains always a need to be satisfied—hence his identification with the Imperium and its ambition for conquest. What the Imperium signifies, above all, is the prospect of conquest, of constant appropriation rather than simply of possession. Thus the pleasure of possession need not depend upon attaining a specific object; it results instead from the act of conquest, by which the self seeks to possess the ultimate object—another self.

But in the first half of the novel the Prince is not the only one who attempts to possess. Possession assumes different forms, and if the economy of his desire allows only for certain forms, it leaves various possibilities open to others—most of all to Charlotte, whose long voyage to London from America is made solely to have him to herself for an hour, before his marriage. "I don't want to pretend, and I can't

pretend a moment longer," she tells him as they enter the park together. "You may think of me what you will, but I don't care. I knew
I should n't and I find now how little. I came back for this. Not really
for anything else. For this." Behind her candor there is, finally, indifference—indifference to what he should think of her. What matters
to her most (the only thing that really matters to her) is simply having
him, compelling him to listen to her speak of her relation to him and
of her feeling for him. Compared to such possession, to "having" him
in this sense, what he thinks of her cannot matter: it is, after all, only
his emotion, which in no way affects the fact of possession. By simply
acquiescing in her proposal of an hour alone together, he allows her
to "have" him, acknowledging with that acquiescence her precedence
over any such emotions. To be indifferent to those emotions, then, is
not necessarily to lack feeling; it attests rather to her possession of him,
since only on account of that possession can she ignore what he might
feel. And, at this particular moment, it is important both that she not
care what he feels (the sign of her possession) and that she should
state this fact, and in so doing clinch her possession:

> I don't care what you make of it, and I don't ask anything what-
> ever of you—anything but this. I want to have said it—that's
> all; I want not to have failed to say it. To see you once and be
> with you, to be as we are now and as we used to be, for one
> small hour. . . . I mean, of course, to get it *before*—before what
> you're going to do. . . . If I could n't have come now I prob-
> ably should n't have come at all—perhaps even ever. . . . *Af-
> ter*—oh I did n't want that! . . . This is different. This is what
> I wanted. This is what I've got. This is what I shall always
> have. . . . I did n't want simply to get my time with you, but
> I wanted you to know. . . . I wanted you to understand. I wanted
> you, that is, to hear. I don't care, I think, whether you under-
> stand or not. If I ask nothing of you I don't—I may n't—ask
> even so much as that. What you may think of me—that does n't
> in the least matter. What I want is that it shall always be with
> you—so that you'll never be able quite to get rid of it—that I
> *did*. I won't say that *you* did—you may make as little of that as
> you like. But that I was here with you where we are and *as* we
> are—I just saying this. Giving myself, in other words, away—
> and perfectly willing to do it for nothing. That's all. (1:97–98)

"To see you once and be with you, to be as we are now and as we
used to be": for the Prince to accept her being with him is tantamount,
then, to accepting her possession of him, precisely because in being

with him she needn't say anything—anything, that is, except that she had wanted to have an hour with him "as we are now and as we used to be." To say just that is to leave him with nothing besides the reality of her emotion, her desire, her feeling for him. For him to accept these, in turn, as she presents them, without demur, without qualification, is to accept them as she sees them—as the sign of her possession of him. To be "as we are now" means being "as we used to be." And if, on the eve of his marriage, with his commitment to another already fully resolved upon, it is still possible for him to be with Charlotte "as we used to be," this can only signify that in a sense they will always be in this way with each other. As long as they can still be "as we used to be," nothing has changed. And if so, then the past is not the past but rather a perpetual condition for both of them.

Thus Charlotte can demonstrate for him the steps of her desire's fulfillment: "This is what I wanted. This is what I've got. This is what I shall always have." If the Prince does nothing to impede the movement from desire to its fulfillment, his refusal to act becomes, for her, a tacit acquiescence in her possession of him. If for her to desire something from him is equivalent to obtaining it, that equivalence exists because she possesses him. It implies that his feelings cannot count in the passage from the inception of a desire to its fulfillment. And if not, their failure to do so testifies to his being for her an object she owns.

But there remains for Charlotte even in her possession of the Prince a sense of solemn commitment: the sense that, for her, "having" him is everything, and that without this there can be nothing at all. If she could not see him "as we used to be," she would not have seen him at all—"perhaps even ever." But that would mean, for her, giving up what matters most, the one person whom her "having" counts as everything. In this sense, then, "having" him cannot be distinguished from loving him. In pledging herself to "one hour alone" with him, she renews her pledge, the committing of her very self to him. To surrender herself to the possibility, the hope, of having one hour alone with him is to let him know that for her nothing else matters. And the act of letting him know this becomes more significant than anything: "I wanted you to understand. I wanted you, that is, to hear." In the end, whether he understands does not matter. What matters is simply that he should know that, in coming to see him as she has, she surrenders her self to him. "Giving myself, in other words, away—and perfectly willing to do it for nothing." In giving herself away, in his presence and with his tacit consent, she confirms her possession of him: she compels him to acknowledge what she is now doing, an ac-

knowledgment that can only be based on a sense of their prior relationship. She asks for nothing from him—to do so would be to con-
tradict her affirmation of possession, making her dependent on his
response. Instead, by simply giving herself away, she forces him to
accept her act and thus to confirm that she still possesses him, that
she still lives in his affections. That this knowledge "shall always be
with you" then becomes both a legacy of and testament to her possession.

At the moment she "gives herself away," Charlotte cannot, of course,
know the circumstances that will later make possible a renewal of her
relationship with the Prince. Those circumstances, in turn, depend upon
a gesture of private honor: after receiving Adam Verver's marriage
proposal, she cables to the Prince, and on receiving his response offers
to show it to her suitor. His refusal to see this response and innumerable other events and conditions result in Charlotte's marriage to
him and hence in a relationship between the two couples that sees
father and daughter spending much time with each other. Near the
end of volume 1, Charlotte unexpectedly arrives by herself one rainy
afternoon at Portland Place. In her ensuing talk with the Prince she
traces the various causes of their present situation. The closeness of
father and daughter, Charlotte's failure to have a child with Adam,
bring about imperceptibly an exclusion from her husband, whose closest, most intimate attachment remains to Maggie. But surely Charlotte, "as a decent harmless wife," or "the best stepmother that really
ever was," or simply as a *maîtresse de maison,* deserves better. Here
something of her hurt, a genuine sense of wrong and bitterness, becomes apparent. Yet, if father and daughter are "extraordinarily happy,"
then "what else can we [Charlotte and the Prince] do, what in all the
world else," other than spend time with each other? To do so is to
"protect" father and daughter, to preserve *their* intimacy. Thus Charlotte and the Prince justify their own intimacy with each other: "And
so for a minute they stood together as strongly held and as closely
confronted as any hour of their easier past even had seen them" (1:312).

What holds them is the perfect "rightness" of their being together,
of their being with each other under the circumstances. This rightness
amounts almost to a moral imperative: to lapse at all from that duty
would be to fail father and daughter. With such "rightness," however,
they find themselves "as closely confronted" as in the past: the situation compels them not only into their specific places but to a forced
intimacy with each other, not through any desire of their own but
simply by the pressure of circumstances. But their being so "strongly
held" and "closely confronted" inevitably suggests a physical intimacy,

reinforced by the clasp of their hands. Behind the rightness of their situation, they themselves now hold and confront each other: "They were silent at first, only facing and faced, only grasping and grasped, only meeting and met."

What before had only a suggested physical quality now becomes explicit: their situation cannot face them in this way, nor grasp them. It is they who face each other, grasp each other. Their silence bespeaks their passion: facing each other, holding each other, they cannot put their emotion into words. It is embodied wholly in their physical awareness of each other. In silence finally they are "meeting and met." At this point feeling concurs with feeling, desire with desire. With such concurrence, they cease to be separate from each other: one no longer knows who is facing and who faced, who meeting and who met. Each of them is both, and that is the measure of their union with each other.

"It's sacred," he tells her, and she breathes the same back to him. This sacredness of their union results from the intensity of their passion. To feel something so intensely that the effect will be like a sudden arrest of time; to achieve a fullness of consummation that transcends the moment and our quest to save what must inevitably disappear; to feel oneself elevated to a point where desire can have nothing more to ask for—this is to sense the presence of something sacred in an emotion. If the nature of our existence is to search constantly for new impressions, whatever achieves a transformation of consciousness so that we experience a moment in a different fashion from all others can impart a feeling of the sacred to our lives. This feeling Charlotte and the Prince now share. As a result, they can lose their sense of self, of consciousness which is the embodiment of our unsatisfied quest for a single, supreme moment:

> They vowed it, gave it out and took it in, drawn, by their intensity, more closely together. Then of a sudden, through this tightened circle, as at the issue of a narrow strait into the sea beyond, everything broke up, broke down, gave way, melted and mingled. Their lips sought their lips, their pressure their response and their response their pressure; with a violence that had sighed itself the next moment to the longest and deepest of stillnesses they passionately sealed their pledge. (1:312)

Their intensity draws them "more closely together," each seeking to possess the other fully. Yet the "tightened circle" and "narrow strait" might figure not simply as intensified awareness of each other but also as the tortuous reasoning by which they have sought to justify their

passion. Once beyond the "narrow strait," passion dissolves everything. Whereas earlier the description of "grasping and grasped" had
suggested their physical closeness, even that closeness now disappears
in a complete communion that becomes liquescent: passing into the
"sea" beyond, everything "broke up, broke down, gave way, melted
and mingled." Within a "sea" of passion, all solid orientations cease
to exist—to break up or to break down are one and the same. What
"gives way" is the self's last resistance to possession by another. And
with the breakdown of that resistance each self then ceases to exist
as something separate from the other. All that remains now is their
passion.

Whereas earlier Charlotte had told the Prince she wanted nothing
from him, each now seeks a response from the other. That response
consists of the other's passion. At moments of this intensity, one can
no longer feel one's own desire: only the sensation of another's desire
for oneself can now satisfy. But if that desire is itself an emptiness
seeking fulfillment, the effect as each attempts to find satisfaction becomes a sort of violence. The silence that follows represents appease-
ment, consummation, fulfillment. It embodies the communion these
two now have with each other, a communion of feeling. Neither at
this point seeks to know the other's thoughts: what is between them
is the reality of their passion, contained and expressed in the "longest
and deepest of stillnesses." In sealing their "pledge" they affirm that
passion as the medium henceforth of their relation to each other. This
pledge becomes in turn the "consecration" of their communion: through
it they announce their commitment to each other. As something based
on passion, however, such a commitment necessarily depends upon a
continuance of that passion. Thus a decline in passion, by altering conditions, suffices to abolish the commitment.

Passion demands possession. Among various moments of passion
in the first half of the novel, perhaps none represents a more consummate fulfillment than that which the Prince and Charlotte achieve at
Matcham. As he waits for her on the terrace of the country house,
gazing at the ancient towers of Gloucester in the distance (a "brave
darker wash of far-away watercolour," as James so beautifully puts it),
he recognizes "why he had from the first of his marriage tried with
such patience for such conformity." "It had all been," he tells himself,
"just in order that his—well, what on earth should he call it but his
freedom?—should at present be as perfect and rounded and lustrous
as some huge precious pearl. He had n't struggled nor snatched; he
was taking but what had been given him; the pearl dropped itself, with
its exquisite quality and rarity, straight into his hand. Here precisely

it was, incarnate; its size and its value grew as Mrs. Verver appeared, afar off, in one of the smaller doorways. She came toward him in silence while he moved to meet her; the great scale of this particular front, at Matcham, multiplied thus, in the golden morning, the stages of their meeting and the successions of their consciousness" (1:358).

His freedom appears as an object ("some huge precious pearl") because he feels it as something he now possesses. This freedom can indeed be palpably weighed, felt, and handled. Its essence is one of possibility awaiting fulfillment; merely to contemplate it gives pleasure. Perhaps the utmost refinement of that pleasure is its being one of anticipation. In anticipation enjoyment progressively increases. Thus we are told that the "size and value" of the pearl symbolizing the Prince's freedom "grew as Mrs. Verver appeared, afar off, in one of the smaller doorways." She comes toward him moreover in silence, recalling that "longest and deepest of stillnesses" with which they sealed their pledge at Portland Place.

But it is the "great scale" of the front at Matcham, above all, that amplifies the Prince's enjoyment; it "multiplied thus, in the golden morning, the stages of their meeting and the successions of their consciousness." Reflecting his image and Charlotte's, the numerous windows of the façade "multiply" the stages of their meeting. But this multiplication is only a visible image of the "successions of their consciousness." Such "successions," by isolating and arresting each fractional instant that brings them closer to each other, expand the moment of pleasure. Thus the scene fulfills the injunction of Pater's *Renaissance*, in "expanding that interval, in getting as many pulsations as possible into the given time." And passion, as Pater had said, could yield precisely "this fruit of a quickened, multiplied consciousness."[2]

If a desire for possession characterizes both the Prince and Charlotte, one might wonder about the form it assumes in Adam Verver, i.e., in the mind of a "collector."[3] To collect is of course to possess, but unlike the possession of passion, collecting neither exhausts nor consumes. If the Prince and Charlotte hope to obtain from each other a certain quantity of intense sensations, the function of the collector is simply to appreciate. We have seen in *The Ambassadors* how "appreciation" signifies respect for the integrity of an object: in Madame de Vionnet's salon, Strether takes her properties "all tenderly into account." But if appreciation originally inspires an impulse to collect, the collector's vision must consist of something more. In the mind of a great collector like Adam Verver, it signifies a feeling not only for each object but also for its possible combination with others. What results is an arrangement suggestive of some higher harmony, a consistency of taste affirmed through the perfect rightness of its judgments. In its quest for order, symmetry, and composition, that arrangement ultimately becomes an expression of form. Thus it implies that the impulse to possess in a collector of the highest type is at bottom a desire for form. In seeking this, the collector attempts to discover some principle of coherence to which one might subordinate all individual objects. The discovery of that principle marks the perception of form.

At the same time James himself notes the seeming strangeness of the collector's passion. Pushed to its logical extreme, it encompasses a desire to collect human beings as well as objects. Speaking of Adam Verver, he observes: "Nothing perhaps might affect us as queerer, had we time to look into it, than this application of the same measure of value to such different pieces of property as old Persian carpets, say, and new human acquisitions . . ." (1:196). It would be all too easy to fall into the temptation of describing such an impulse as immoral. But the absence of any accusation in the passage itself (which exhibits even a touch of humor in noticing how Adam Verver is, as a "taster of life," "economically constructed") warns against it. Application of the same "measure of value" to Persian carpets and "human acquisitions" need not imply a disregard for the humanness of individuals. It all depends upon what "measure of value" one employs. And, considering that any such measure results from a desire to appreciate rather than to possess, it remains quite possible to discover in individuals and in Persian carpets some similar principle of fineness or excellence.

Perception of that fineness rests, of course, with the collector. For this reason, nothing can be more necessary than a corresponding fineness in perception—which Adam Verver exemplifies: "He put into his one little glass everything he raised to his lips, and it was as if he had always carried in his pocket, like a tool of his trade, this receptacle, a little glass cut with a fineness of which the art had long since been lost, and kept in an old morocco case stamped in uneffaceable gilt with the arms of a deposed dynasty" (1:196). Here the fin-de-siècle equation of knowledge with sensations (as in Henry Adams's lessons of color and taste) can lend to Adam Verver's tasting a deeper significance. Everything he experiences becomes a subject of "appreciation," and the measure of his capacity for appreciation becomes a measure of his capacity for experience. For him there can be no experience that does not involve taste: the intellectual quality or sensuous appeal of an object is inherent in the very process by which we perceive it. To refine sensibility to the point at which it becomes responsive to the slightest degree of beauty in an object thus becomes the requirement of all higher appreciation.

The metaphoric "little glass" Adam Verver is said to carry with him, "cut with a fineness of which the art had long since been lost," exemplifies the height of his refinement. In describing this instrument, James might have been speaking of his own art. We are told that the little glass is "kept in an old morocco case stamped in uneffaceable gilt with the arms of a deposed dynasty." The "uneffaceable gilt" attests to an enduring quality in the art that has traced those letters, and, by implication, to that of all great art.[4] The "arms of a deposed dynasty" point to the moral of that art: dynasties pass away, but "a thing of beauty is a joy forever." Here art is nothing other than the perceiving medium which makes possible all appreciation. But the perceiving medium within *The Golden Bowl* is in some sense the work's own vision. What the Jamesian perspective attempts to offer, then, is the highest possible appreciation of its subject, which consists of the characters and scenes it presents. From this standpoint, the collector's passion in Adam Verver assumes a special value as an expression of the same art that informs the novel. It is all a matter of "appreciation," and in this sense both "old Persian carpets" and "new human acquisitions" can exercise a particular appeal: "As it had served him to satisfy himself, so to speak, both about Amerigo and about the Bernardino Luini he had happened to come to knowledge of at the time he was consenting to the announcement of his daughter's betrothal, so it served him at present to satisfy himself about Charlotte Stant and an extraordinary set of oriental tiles of which he had lately got wind . . ." (1:197). This is not to say that in each instance he equates the one with the other, the "human acquisition" with the material object. It only implies that the same fine glass, the same medium of perception, measures both. As an object of value, in human terms, one of the highest for Adam Verver and his daughter is the Prince, whose lineage endows him with the richest associations. "Appreciation" of such associations can itself be an art: Walter Berry once remarked of Edith Wharton that she saw in a count or duke not only the individual himself but his entire ancestral history.

Of the nature of this faculty of appreciation the narrative goes on to assert: "It was all at bottom in him, the aesthetic principle, planted where it could burn with a cold still flame; where it fed almost wholly on the material directly involved, on the idea (followed by appropriation) of plastic beauty, of the thing visibly perfect in its kind. . . ." In his "Conclusion" to *The Renaissance* Pater had declared, "To burn

always with this hard, gem-like flame, to maintain this ecstasy, is success in life." For James, like Pater, the appreciative "flame" implies an
absence of emotion in the Romantic sense.[5] Its "cold still" aspect signifies the ability to regard objects without the distorting coloration
emotion imposes, a capacity for pristine apprehension that preserves
the beauty of these objects in themselves. But it is the "idea" of an
object, above all, that appreciation seeks, the "idea of beauty" that is
the concept of "the thing visibly perfect in its kind." Here what matters is not so much the sensations an object excites but the idea the
mind discerns within it. As a result, unlike other forms of possession,
appreciation does not consume its object in a quest for the sensations
that object can give. Instead it attempts to achieve simply the perfect
apprehension of its object, within the clearest, most refined medium
possible.

What most attracts appreciation is the "plastic" quality of the object.
This plastic quality engages the mind's formative impulse, inviting it
to place that object within some expressive scheme. "Appropriation"
however leaves the object intact, trying only to situate it in its proper
light, and in so doing to create a formal arrangement in which that
object finds its splendor enhanced by association with others and by
the larger design of which it forms a part. From this standpoint, the
specific significance of Adam Verver's "new human acquisitions," the
individuals with whom he and his daughter have now allied their lives,
lies in an attempt to give form to life. If "plastic beauty" counts as the
highest value of life, its finest expression must be that which gives
form to life in the largest sense: a shaping of the most intimate relations between one human being and another.

Adam Verver's marriage thus represents the culmination of his am-
bitions as a collector—as appropriator and composer of the beautiful.
If behind any act of appropriation there exists for the collector an idea
of the object's fitness within some larger scheme, the idea behind his
marriage embodies the very highest possibilities:

> The sharp point to which all his light converged was that the
> whole call of his future to him as a father would be in his so
> managing that Maggie would less and less appear to herself to
> have forsaken him. And it not only would n't be decently hu-
> mane, decently possible, not to make this relief easy to her—the
> idea shone upon him, more than that, as exciting, inspiring,
> uplifting. It fell in so beautifully with what might be otherwise
> possible; it stood there absolutely confronted with the material
> way in which it might be met. The way in which it might be

met was by his putting his child at peace, and the way to put
her at peace was to provide for his future—that is for hers—by
marriage, by a marriage as good, speaking proportionately, as
hers had been. . . . It was n't only moreover that the word,
with a click, so fitted the riddle, but that the riddle, in such perfection, fitted the word. He might have been equally in want
and yet not have had his remedy. Oh if Charlotte did n't accept
him the remedy of course would fail; but, as everything had fallen
together, it was at least there to be tried. And success would be
great—that was his last throb—if the measure of relief effected
for Maggie should at all prove to have been given by his own
actual sense of felicity. (1:207–8)

The ultimate arrangements in life are those that affect its form. In
creating the conditions of our existence, they shape our very consciousness. Consequently they provoke the deepest moral questions,
questions concerning the nature of our relationships with others: in
seeking to arrange these, we touch upon what is most sacred in our
lives. Attempting to manage things so that Maggie "would less and
less appear to herself to have forsaken him," Adam Verver conceives
of a scheme that offers more than the "decently humane," the "decently
possible." It appears even "exciting, inspiring, uplifting" because "it
fell in so beautifully . . . with the material way in which it might be
met." The "falling in" of need with fulfillment gives his solution its
inspiring quality. By speaking of it as "uplifting," James even imparts
to it a moral resonance: it reveals how form (here the form of marriage) creates meaning by transforming our relation to others and hence
our consciousness of those others. If Maggie's relation to her father
after her marriage lacks form through the difference between her married and his unmarried state, his marriage with Charlotte restores the
balance.

But if marriage presents a means of resolving the problem of father
and daughter, it remains to be seen what it does for Charlotte. From
Adam Verver's standpoint, "it was n't only moreover that the word,
with a click, so fitted the riddle, but that the riddle, in such perfection,
fitted the word." Earlier we are told that "he had seen that Charlotte
could contribute—what he had n't seen was what she could contribute
to." If "the riddle, in such perfection, fitted the word," this implies
that marriage gives Charlotte the purpose she has been in need of.
One can question, of course, the accuracy of Adam Verver's assessment
of her situation. But the fact remains that she, in full view of all the
complications involved, accepts his proposal. Her doing so suggests

(and nothing she subsequently says really invalidates this) that she herself had sincerely believed in the possibility of her own happiness. To be sure, Adam Verver is then in large measure ignorant of the complications. Nevertheless they do not in themselves nullify the meaning marriage gives to his life and Charlotte's, as well as to Maggie's and the Prince's. They simply present some of the obstacles to be overcome in a process by which both Adam and Maggie grow increasingly aware of marriage's moral exigencies.

In *A Backward Glance* Edith Wharton recalls reading the celebrated night scene from *The Portrait of a Lady* in which Isabel Archer stares at the fading embers of a fire, brooding over the failure of her marriage with Osmond. Wharton then goes on to compare it to what she terms James's far greater "night-piece" in *The Golden Bowl*—the bridge party at Fawns.[6] If *The Golden Bowl* is about relationships that define the form of our existence, the bridge game played by four of the novel's principal personae assumes a symbolic significance. With Adam Verver, the Prince, Charlotte, and Fanny Assingham engaged in the game while Maggie surveys their play, James embodies in a highly visible form the deeper relationships of his novel.

It is only appropriate that the four should be depicted playing a game: in a larger sense this is exactly what they do in the second half of the novel. Equally appropriate is Maggie's being somewhat apart from the rest, as the medium through which we observe what happens. Nor is it less fitting that Adam Verver should be described as "a high adept, one of the greatest," while the Prince "excelled easily, as he understood and practised every art that could beguile large leisure." In the more serious game of life, Adam Verver's mastery becomes quietly evident: later Maggie will witness how he appears to have Charlotte on a silken halter that, regardless of how much "play" it affords, never allows her to escape his control (2:287). He ranks as "a high adept, one of the greatest" because of his ability to mask the motives behind his acts. To the end, even Maggie can wonder whether he knows of the Prince's infidelity with Charlotte. The Prince, on the other hand, though he "excelled easily," is less committed to the game: he can sacrifice Charlotte when necessary, though he tells himself earlier that his freedom to be with her is precisely the reason for conforming so scrupulously through all the years of his marriage. Yet he is as willing to play Maggie's game in the second half of the novel as to play Charlotte's in the first. All he needs, as Maggie observes, is to understand what he is supposed to do, the role he is to assume. Charlotte and Fanny Assingham, by comparison, are "as 'good' as members

Alvin Langdon Coburn, *Portland Place, London,* 1906.

of a sex incapable of the nobler consistency could be" (is the conde-
scension Adam Verver's or James's?). Condescending or not, the judgment is nevertheless appropriate here. Both Charlotte and Fanny have
sought to play the larger game with only limited facility compared to
that of Adam Verver or the Prince. Thus Charlotte in the second half
of the novel fails to grasp why her relations with the Prince have changed,
while Fanny seems unable to foresee the consequences of her policy
with either Maggie or the Prince.

In a similar fashion, Maggie's being outside the game must also be
judged significant. On a deeper level, of course, she is as much in it
as anyone. But her isolation from the visible, external game points to
how the others are themselves the elements of *her* game. Her role,
then, is to play *with* them, setting them off against each other or using
the resources of each to act upon another. As she tells Fanny: "And
that's how I make them do what I like!" (2:115). In the novel's second
half, she acts upon others but is herself hardly acted upon at all.[7] A
distance separates her from them: "Silent and discreet she bent a vague
mild face upon them as if to signify that little as she followed their
doings she wished them well." In the game they now play, their relations to each other are crucial. For Maggie, however, what matters
is her relation to their game and the attempt that, figuratively speaking, she makes to direct it. As disposer of their destinies, she assumes
the role of *Deus artifex*, of God as maker, or, on another plane, that
of "author":

> They might have been—really charming as they showed in the
> beautiful room, and Charlotte certainly, as always, magnificently
> handsome and supremely distinguished—they might have been
> figures rehearsing some play of which she herself was the author;
> they might even, for the happy appearance they continued to
> present, have been such figures as would by the strong note of
> character in each fill any author with the certitude of success,
> especially of their own histrionic. They might in short have rep-
> resented any mystery they would; the point being predominantly
> that the key to the mystery, the key that could wind and unwind
> it without a snap of the spring, was there in her pocket—or
> rather, no doubt, clasped at this crisis in her hand and pressed,
> as she walked back and forth, to her breast. She walked to the
> end and far out of the light; she returned and saw the others
> still where she had left them; she passed round the house and
> looked into the drawing-room, lighted also, but empty now, and
> seeming to speak the more in its own voice of all the possibilities

she controlled. Spacious and splendid, like a stage again awaiting a drama, it was a scene she might people, by the press of her spring, either with serenities and dignities and decencies, or with terrors and shames and ruins, things as ugly as those formless fragments of her golden bowl she was trying so hard to pick up. (2:236).

We have encountered earlier in Adam Verver the collector's appreciation of the high value of his "new human acquisitions." Here Maggie too shares in that appreciation: removed from the game, she can take in the players' magnificent appearances. Yet to her their value is something other than that of human acquisitions, however precious. For her they represent dramatic resources, "such figures as would by the strong note of character in each fill any author with the certitude of success." By their "strong note of character," they reveal their capacity for action. To Maggie, who seeks to move them to act in a particular fashion, this gives a "certitude of success." Removed from the scene of their activity, she can justly estimate their resourcefulness. The reality of their emotions, their density and complexity, have a quality that strikes her, the spectator of their human drama, as plastic in the highest sense. Like the "cold still flame" of Adam Verver's appreciation, Maggie's vision now sees them without passion. For her, it is only natural that they should possess dramatic reality. They might have been "figures rehearsing some play"—rehearsing rather than performing, since in rehearsal the plastic sense is most palpable, the feeling of arranging appearances and actions.

With the decade of his efforts at conquest of the London stage now behind him, James could recall the whole theatrical experience as comparable to what he had called in *The Ambassadors* "the affair of life."[8] On account of the special nature of its medium (live actors, the actuality of a stage), drama offers the possibility of creating something that approximates life. The resultant sense of power, of being able to shape the actual substance of human existence could impart to an author a fresh awareness of life's plastic possibilities, its capacity for aesthetic form.[9] Just as Adam Verver's finely cut glass had symbolized the medium of this novel, so Maggie as "author" might now represent James himself. But if we are to identify Maggie with James the author, her sense of "histrionic" possibilities must then be not dissimilar from his own.

And in fact the subsequent development of the work bears this out: the form of the second half is essentially dramatic, defined by a sequence of major scenes that move inexorably toward their conclusion.

If it is the essence of drama to suggest the importance of what is absent to the visible scene, the essence of dramatic action might be defined as that which creates a feeling of inevitability, of the relentless progression toward a climax or resolution. And in large part this is the atmosphere that pervades the second half of *The Golden Bowl*. If Maggie's sense of her life thus corresponds to the work's authorial consciousness, her sense of capacity to arrange the histrionic circumstances of her drama becomes expressive of James's own sense of art's capacity to give form to life. And just as her concern is with the most intimate personal relationships, so in these above all do we find embodied the essence of form.[10]

The "formless fragments of her golden bowl" that "she was trying so hard to pick up" symbolize Maggie's broken relationship with her husband. The fragments are "ugly" precisely because they are formless. Of course, they are not formless in the literal sense. What the narrative means is that they do not contribute toward a recognizable aesthetic form. Their ugliness signifies the mind's inability to give them a form corresponding to that of the relationships that make our existence meaningful. But if the "formless fragments" are at bottom no different from the "terrors and shames and ruins" of drama, their substance must be histrionic—which means: capable of shaping, of being changed. And indeed, as Maggie realizes, she herself has the power to people her scene "either with serenities and dignities and decencies, or with terrors and shames and ruins." These "ruins" have characterized the first half of the novel, with its progressive descent into chaos that culminates in a complete negation of form (marriage) by the events at Matcham. From that point on, Maggie's quest throughout the second half to restore her marriage represents an attempt to attain the "serenities and dignities and decencies" of form.

Through her "authorial" relation with others, Maggie's attitude toward them will necessarily differ from that of simple appreciation. If the nature of drama results in sympathy, Maggie's relation to others is also sympathetic—not, however, from pity or compassion (though she can feel both for Charlotte), but rather from vicarious experience of another's situation. Thus Maggie can fully appreciate Charlotte, "magnificently handsome and supremely distinguished." That appreciation includes awareness of Charlotte's suffering, her torment in not knowing why the Prince has begun to turn away from her. But the dramatic consciousness that now fills Maggie looks beyond that suffering, seeing in it finally only a condition of our existence, capable, like the conditions of drama, of being transformed so as to give that existence a different aspect.

This "plastic" consciousness of how conditions may be shaped allows Maggie to dissimulate to Charlotte in the immediate sequel to the bridge party that takes place "under the old lustres of Venice" in the drawing room at Fawns. "I've been wanting," Charlotte begins, "to put a question to you for which no opportunity has seemed to me yet quite so good as this." But even as she hears these "few straight words" of Charlotte's, Maggie is already feeling the "scene of life" of which they form a part. Earlier she had seen the same drawing room as "spacious and splendid, like a stage again awaiting a drama." What occurs now will not alter that sense. We have seen how drama involves the feeling of an inevitable movement toward a conclusion. If Maggie has already seen the drawing room as a stage awaiting its drama, the present moment only fulfills her anticipation. And nothing "was now absent from her consciousness of the part she was called on to play in it" (2:246–47).

When Charlotte then asks, "Have you any ground of complaint of me? Is there any wrong you consider I've done you?" Maggie can only think of how to avoid answering her. But Charlotte is not to be put off: "I've seen, week after week, that *you* seemed to be thinking—of something that perplexed or worried you. Is it anything for which I'm in any degree responsible?" At this point we are told Maggie "summoned all her powers." Like a great actress, she must give exactly the right emphasis to her response: "What in the world *should* it be?" Here Maggie does not actually lie to Charlotte. Instead she allows Charlotte to answer her question herself: "Ah that's not for me to imagine, and I should be very sorry to have to try to say! I'm aware of no point whatever at which I may have failed you. . . . If I've been guilty of some fault I've committed it all unconsciously, and am only anxious to hear from you honestly about it." In allowing Charlotte to respond for her, Maggie assumes the role of dramatic artificer who simply elicits from a persona its "strong note of character." She sees Charlotte has already decided on which course to pursue, and this in turn helps Maggie to help *her*. As she does so, Maggie can think to herself: "she had kept in tune with the right, and something certainly, something that might resemble a rare flower snatched from an impossible ledge, would, and possibly soon, come of it for her. The right, the right— yes, it took this extraordinary form of humbugging, as she had called it, to the end. It was only a question of not by a hair's breadth deflecting into the truth" (2:250–51).

Thus Maggie appears distinctly conscious of the moral problem in dissimulating to Charlotte. To think of what she has done as keeping "in tune with the right" suggests that her very idea of "the right" has now been transformed. No longer can one equate it simply with "the good," with what is moral in a traditional sense. Instead the "rightness" Maggie now seeks is something like the "rightness" of art, in which all the elements of a work concur. This "rightness" is then the sense of form that brings all the events of a drama into agreement with each other. In pursuing such "rightness," however, her objective is not simply form but something else: the "rare flower snatched from an impossible ledge." This "rare flower" signifies the sense of meaning that form will give her existence. By seeking to restore her marriage with the Prince (and her father's with Charlotte as well), Maggie attempts to recover a form shattered earlier into the "formless fragments of her golden bowl." In recovering that form she will attain a sense of rightness which comes from being able to endow one's deepest relationships with a permanence based on something higher than feeling: the commitment to a symbolic structure (marriage) transcending all our individual desires.

We have seen how Maggie's attempt to "keep in tune with the right" causes her to deviate from a traditional moral standpoint. But if she does not give Charlotte the benefit of the "straight view," neither does she allow it to herself: "She might fairly, as she watched them, have missed it as a lost thing; have yearned for it, for the straight vindictive view, the rights of resentment, the rages of jealousy, the protests of passion, as for something she had been cheated of not least: a range of feelings which for many women would have meant so much, but which for *her* husband's wife, for her father's daughter, figured nothing nearer to experience than a wild eastern caravan, looming into view with crude colours in the sun, fierce pipes in the air, high spears against the sky, all a thrill, a natural joy to mingle with, but turning off short before it reached her and plunging into other defiles" (2:236–37). In surveying the bridge players absorbed in their game she realizes that "to feel about them in any of the immediate, inevitable, assuaging ways, the ways usually open to innocence outraged and generosity betrayed, would have been to give them up, and that giving them up was, marvelously, not to be thought of" (2:237). To "give them up" is inconceivable because it implies relinquishing any attempt at imparting form to her existence.[11] Without form, her existence becomes meaningless. Thus Maggie, in spite of everything she suffers in the process, must seek to recover that form by restoring her marriage—not for the Prince, not even for herself, but for the sake of a form through which her life can become meaningful. For Maggie, then, it is really no longer a question of right and wrong, of justice and injustice, but rather of meaning as opposed to its absence. In not "giving up" her people, she is like an author who refuses to give up on his or her characters. But in order not to "give them up," Maggie must find an appropriate form in which all of them (including herself) achieve their rightful place.

James once remarked that for him the most beautiful words in English were "summer afternoon." In this light it seems only appropriate that the image conjured up by these words should set the scene for one of the most moving episodes of *The Golden Bowl*. In "the golden air that toward six o'clock of a July afternoon hung about the massed Kentish woods," Adam Verver and his daughter set off for a stroll to confront their recent past and the question of their future. Here the "golden air" of late afternoon might almost appear as an objective counterpart to the emotional aura of the scene. In contrast to the great "night-piece" before it, this splendid episode will carry throughout a sense of luminous assurance diametrically opposite to the dramatic atmosphere surrounding the bridge party and its sequel. If its intensity matches its predecessor's, it remains of a different kind. What it presents is a drama of sacrifice, a surrender of the deepest affections James believes human nature to be capable of. That surrender, in turn, represents in some measure the cost of a quest for form.

It is quite fitting that the present summer afternoon revives the memory of an earlier autumn afternoon when Maggie and her father surveyed what then seemed their crisis. By recalling certain aspects of their situation then, Maggie attempts to introduce the topic she wishes to discuss now. In this scene one becomes conscious of the need for an indirect approach, necessary on account of the intimacy between father and daughter. Because of it, Maggie must begin by speaking about what they once lacked without realizing it—what Fanny Assingham had called a "position." By means of this discussion she anticipates the topic she wishes to bring up: her "selfishness." The similarity between these two conditions lies in their both embodying a lack one is unaware of. By reminding her father of their previous deficiency (which he had been unable to see at the time), she hopes to persuade him of their present one (or, if he won't have this, of *her* present one). Her means of persuasion are, obviously, psychological rather than rational: their earlier blindness need not necessarily imply their blindness now. What she hopes to awaken in her father, however, is a sense of his blindness as something he has ceased to be aware of. This loss of awareness of one's own blindness will then become proof of his present blindness, the "omission" covering a lapse that has been lost sight of.

Thematically too the first deficiency resembles the second. Maggie begins by telling her father how he has always had a position, one that, moreover, has always been the same. She then goes on to notice how she had lost hers by marriage, appending the curious remark that "that one—I know how I saw it—would never come back. I had done something *to* it—I did n't quite know what; given it away somehow and yet not as then appeared really got my return" (2:260). This "position" is nothing less than her independence, her ability to define her relation to others. What she surrenders to the Prince is the power to determine that relation: as a result of her marriage she comes to exist only for him. In surrendering this power, however, she fails to acquire a reciprocal one over him—he remains free to form whatever relation he chooses with Charlotte. In describing her attempts to regain her position she speaks in terms of "waking up." Since her position is not external but psychological, to maintain it requires an effort of will. Her struggle to recover it is like that of someone trying to wake up who must contend against the desire to go on sleeping, of remaining in the voluptuous state of dream consciousness. Nevertheless, she *can* recover her position, just as (so she wishes to imply) they can fill their present deficiency by a similar effort of will. In both instances the implied theme is the necessity of recovering independence: hers vis-à-vis the Prince, and now that of the two couples (Maggie and the Prince, her father and Charlotte) vis-à-vis each other.

Significantly, as Adam Verver remembers, the struggle to recover her "position" is the only thing about which Maggie has ever made anything of a difficulty. Ironically, what made it difficult was precisely her "happiness." Maggie now intensifies this irony further by claiming it is just her "happiness" that has made them "selfish." Carefully, she attempts to establish a basis for her claim by situating it in the past: already, at *that* time, the question of their "selfishness" had come up between them. What she means by "selfishness" is not a failure to give or do for others but rather a refusal to go outside themselves, to be for others what they are for each other. Even their marriages, Maggie implies, have failed to change them. When her father refuses to accept this implication, Maggie assumes the whole responsibility herself. If her father cannot admit to being selfish, "then, father, *I* am." By making such an assertion, she allows him to question her present situation. The proof, Adam Verver argues, that he and Maggie are too much together (if that is what their selfishness amounts to) would be some sign of the Prince's dissatisfaction. Failing to show that, Maggie has no basis for her claim.

But having, as it seems, anticipated this move on her father's part,

Maggie then asserts that her selfishness is not for them but with the Prince. *They* (she and the Prince) are the too-exclusive couple who have shut out the others (including her father) from their affections. It is perhaps a little difficult at this point to see why she makes such an avowal. Had she been able to compel her father to accept the fact of *their* (her and her father's) selfishness, the clear moral would then be that the two couples should distance themselves more from each other. Only later does it become apparent that Maggie's objective in claiming her selfishness with the Prince will be to argue that she has abandoned her father to "the consequences of his marriage." Before arriving at that point, however, she must deal with the questions inevitably raised in declaring she is selfish *for* the Prince. In particular, she must somehow dispose of the implication that the reason for her selfishness is her jealousy of him—which might suggest she has some reason for it (i.e., his affair with Charlotte). She avoids these implications by defining her selfishness for him in a different sense. He is "her motive—in everything." But this equivocal profession does not prevent her father from probing for a possible reason for jealousy, i.e., the Prince's unfaithfulness to her. Whereupon she tells him: "My idea is this, that when you love only a little you're naturally not jealous—or are only jealous also a little, so that it does n't matter. But when you love in a deeper and intenser way, then you're in the very same proportion jealous; your jealousy has intensity and, no doubt, ferocity. When however you love in the most abysmal and unutterable way of all—why then you're beyond everything, and nothing can pull you down" (2:262).

Thus Maggie expresses the insight her recent suffering has given her. Yet it was not that which she had wanted to speak of. Her "selfishness" has been only a pretext for shifting their conversation from her state to his. But sensing the satisfaction her being happy seems to give her father, she then dilates upon the topic. The image of her happiness that Adam Verver conjures up for himself, that of "a creature consciously floating and shining in a warm sea, some element of dazzling sapphire and silver," recalls the other sea that had symbolized in volume 1 the passionate union of the Prince and Charlotte. But if this metaphor of Maggie's happiness is false, it remains significant that in her desire to ease her father's mind she should attempt to create, out of her own deep suffering, an illusion of happiness. It reflects the generosity of her affection for him, while the way in which he receives this attests to the measure of his feeling for her.[12] When he tells her (as if in response), "I guess I've never been jealous," he means perhaps only to remark on his relation to his deceased wife and on the absence

of passion in his own life compared to hers. But she takes him as
wishing to imply that, having married Charlotte for his daughter's sake,
he is really concerned only with Maggie's happiness. To "love in the
most abysmal and unutterable way of all"—that, as Maggie understands it, is how he loves not Charlotte but herself, which in turn
makes him able to bear everything, including Charlotte's infidelity with
the Prince. Maggie takes him, then, as implying that for her sake he
is willing to suffer everything; that he will live in and through her
happiness. After this there can be nothing more to say; nothing more,
at least, than what she tells him: "Oh it's you, father, who are what I
call beyond everything. Nothing can pull *you* down." Here her phrasing makes one wonder whether it was her father she had had in mind
when speaking earlier of loving "in the most abysmal and unutterable
way of all": to love *him* in that way would enable her to transcend any
jealousy of the Prince.

Their conversation now seems to come to an end, as if having reached
its logical outcome. What remains unresolved, however, is that for
which Maggie had risked exposing everything—the fate of her father
and Charlotte. This, then, is one of those moments in the second half
of the novel when everything indeed hangs by a hair. Only Adam
Verver's refusal to accept their mutual pretense of a resolution, his
desire to probe what she had meant by describing herself as "selfish,"
affords her another chance to achieve her aim. His wish to see her
concede that she is not selfish allows her to insist upon it. He then
touches more deeply than ever before on her relation to her husband
and the possibility of his adultery. "But you've just been describing to
me," he protests, "what you'd take, if you had once a good chance,
from your husband." With her quick response, "Oh I'm not talking
about my husband!" she inadvertently compromises herself. Under the
present circumstances, even to mention Charlotte is dangerous, regardless of how she might try to cover it up by describing her "with
high hypocrisy, as paying for his daughter's bliss." If Maggie seeks to
determine Charlotte's fate above all, what she can least bear from her
father at this point is intense questioning about her relations with
Charlotte. Her brilliant solution to her dilemma, of naming her father,
allows her to renew her original claim of selfishness. In naming him,
she transforms the whole meaning of his question of what she would
"take" from someone. With him, obviously, it can only be a matter of
generosity she cannot repay.

From this point on, Maggie can now see her way to the end. That
way will consist of putting her father on the defensive, of focusing on
what *his* life has been without her. In so doing, she herself can come

very close to naming Charlotte and the Prince, to specifying the heart of her dilemma: "Everything that touches you, everything that surrounds you, goes on—by your splendid indifference and your incredible permission—at your expense" (2:267). Her near-intimation of what he might suspect to be the source of her trouble necessarily prompts him to ask further: in what sense, really, has his generosity been burdensome for her? Here Maggie must make her most daring move: she must invoke the term "sacrifice" to demonstrate the utter seriousness of what she says. Only thus can she convince him of her genuine desire to see him alter his situation.

By invoking the term "sacrifice," she allows him to ask the pregnant question, "But to what in the world?" On her answer to it the whole issue rests: "This was the moment in the whole process of their mutual vigilance in which it decidedly *most* hung by a hair that their thin wall might be pierced by the lightest wrong touch. It shook between them, this transparency, with their very breath; it was an exquisite tissue, but stretched on a frame, and would give way the next instant if either so much as breathed too hard. She held her breath, for she knew by his eyes, the light at the heart of which he could n't blind, that he was, by his intention, making sure—sure whether or no her certainty was like his" (2:267–68).

What follows is one of the most remarkable developments in the novel. In the middle of a long passage purporting to give Maggie's thoughts, we find the intrusion of Adam Verver's, wondering if she will break down and name Amerigo. That intrusion represents his presence in her consciousness, seeking to wrest from it an answer to his doubts. For her to name Amerigo would be to imply that she is now constantly with the Prince out of jealousy—which would in turn imply his affair with Charlotte. When the narrative returns to Maggie, however, we know she will successfully resist his attempt to make her confess. From now on, she can once more throw the burden of emphasis back upon him and his situation.[13] When she finally answers that she sacrifices him "simply to everything and to every one," that she takes "the consequences of his marriage as perfectly natural," it is only to remind him of his having married for her sake and of his having, as a result, no real marriage for himself. He can now take it from her that it is her genuine desire to see him improve his situation, and this without her having had at any point to reveal the source of her trouble, which would have meant making him suffer. When he suggests the possibility of his moving to American City with Charlotte, she receives a glimpse of the ultimate result of all her efforts.

But there remains one final phase of the drama, one last affirmation to make. Her father had proposed moving to American City on the understanding that this was her wish. When he queries her about her "belief" in him, it is as if for final confirmation of his plan. At the same time her answer stands as a pledge of her affection. To his oblique query she can now, as the measure of his sacrifice looms in larger and larger perspective, respond: "I believe in you more than any one." More than in Amerigo, just as he, on his side, can also "believe" in her more than in Charlotte, more than in anyone else. This moment, then, represents the final avowal of the one affection in *The Golden Bowl* that knows no limits, an affection willing in the final analysis to sacrifice even itself. It stands as a solemn testimony to the high cost of the pursuit of form in human existence, and is also, in retrospect, the understanding upon which the novel's ultimate attainment of form in the human sense is firmly based.

If the great "night-piece" that develops out of the bridge party at Fawns presents Maggie as playwright, its sequel reveals an even greater artificer: Adam Verver. This "little meditative man in the straw hat kept coming into view with his indescribable air of weaving his spell, weaving it off there by himself. In whatever quarter of the horizon the appearances were scanned he was to be noticed as absorbed in this occupation; and Maggie was to become aware of two or three extraordinary occasions of receiving from him the hint that he measured the impression he produced" (2:284–85). When weaving his spell he is invariably "off there by himself." Once, finding him napping in the Principino's room, Maggie thinks of "the unfathomable heart folded in the constant flawless freshness of the white waistcoat" (2:305). Unfathomable in being at once human yet strangely pitiless: Maggie fails to understand why it does not respond to Charlotte's suffering. In its indifference it assumes an almost Godlike aspect: to move so as to shape the form of human life without, seemingly, any regard for the cost in terms of feeling or emotion—this would be to affirm a remorseless aestheticism, one that transcends human suffering in its vision of a higher justice for which the moral consciousness becomes one with an apprehension of form.

Thus Charlotte is described as "doomed" to a fate she does not yet know, at which she can only fearfully guess—her final, physical separation from the Prince which will send her to American City with Adam Verver. That "little quiet gentleman who mostly wore, as he moved alone across the field of vision, a straw hat, a white waistcoat and a blue necktie, keeping a cigar in his teeth and his hands in his pockets, and who oftener than not presented a somewhat meditative

back while he slowly measured the perspectives of the park and brood-
ingly counted (it might have appeared) his steps" (2:283–84) becomes
for Maggie, on account of his "unfathomable heart," somewhat opaque.[14]
The detailed description of his physical appearance suggests how un-
knowable everything behind it has become. Most unfathomable of all,
perhaps, is his awareness of his effect on Charlotte. As Maggie gazes
at him down the length of the great gallery at Fawns, however, watching him take in all the assembled formal symmetries of his collection,
she might have been no more than "an earnest young woman with a
Baedeker" and he "a vague gentleman to whom even Baedekers were
unknown" (2:285–86).

On these inspections Charlotte almost invariably appears, hanging
behind him at a distance of one or two cases. And indeed, in the elab-
orate game at which he is an adept, "one of the highest," she is in fact
always a few steps behind in her perceptions. Her failure to keep up
is typified as a form of enslavement: "and the likeness of their connexion would n't have been wrongly figured if he had been thought
of as holding in one of his pocketed hands the end of a long silken
halter looped round her beautiful neck" (2:287). Here as elsewhere
the narrative unfailingly remarks on Charlotte's physical beauty. Even
as her mind is smothered under developments she fails to understand,
she retains her high value as an aesthetic object. Yet the opposition
between that value and her suffering brings James finally to his deepest
questioning of the aims of aestheticism.

Reduced to the role of *cicerone* in the absence of any more important function (above all for the Prince), she conscientiously performs
her duties for the visitors at Fawns: "Her words, addressed to the
largest publicity, rang for some minutes through the place, every one
as quiet to listen as if it had been a church ablaze with tapers and she
were taking her part in some hymn of praise" (2:290). The "hymn of
praise" evokes a religious aura whose source is the sacredness of art.
Charlotte's imagined participation in the hymn suggests that she too
now conforms her life, her feelings, and her desires to the worship of
art. With prescribed rituals of appreciation, life becomes assimilated
to art through the expression of emotion in appropriate forms. But if
the hymn of praise gives form to an emotion, it also restricts it within
the limits of form. Similarly, Charlotte's life and emotions are now
constrained within a ritual whose form is determined by Adam Verver.

Such constraints necessarily produce tensions. Amid a world of
beautiful forms and images, the vases of *vieux Saxe* with their "ba-
roque" ornamentation, there remains an irreconcilable realm of human
suffering and pain. Constricted by the form of "appreciation," it seeks

finally to rise above the limits of form in order to find emotional release:

> So the high voice quavered, aiming truly at effects far over the heads of gaping neighbours; so the speaker, piling it up, sticking at nothing, as less interested judges might have said, seemed to justify the faith with which she was honoured. Maggie meanwhile at the window knew the strangest thing to be happening: she had turned suddenly to crying, or was at least on the point of it—the lighted square before her all blurred and dim. The high voice went on; its quaver was doubtless for conscious ears only, but there were verily thirty seconds during which it sounded, for our young woman, like the shriek of a soul in pain. (2:291–92)

Thus Charlotte becomes nothing more than a voice, and this "objectification" of her signifies both her assimilation to a purely aesthetic element and the loss of everything that had defined her humanness. The high voice quavers with the strain of the demands it makes upon itself; like that of a consummate artist, it "aims truly at effects far over the heads of gaping neighbours." Witnessing its efforts, however, Maggie cannot but be conscious of what it suffers as it attempts to deny its own nature.

As she realizes Charlotte's situation, Maggie experiences a sudden access of emotion. The "lighted square before her" becomes "all blurred and dim," as if to indicate a dissolution of the sense of aesthetic form, its surrender to sympathetic awareness. That sense had been firm, but it collapses in recognizing the human cost of sustaining form in our existence. If the "hymn of praise" represents the highest form of appreciation, the breakdown of the voice attempting to perform it reveals the emotion sacrificed to this attempt. What before had been a vague apprehension of Charlotte's suffering suddenly intensifies with the "shriek of a soul in pain": in the look Maggie exchanges with her father there is a mute question as to whether the cost of their attempt to recover form by restoring their marriages has been too great, and whether they have failed sufficiently to measure the feelings subsumed in this process. If we are to count the cost of form in terms of Charlotte's suffering, for a crucial moment that suffering indeed appears too much.

The movement by which Maggie returns to affirming her original purpose is one the narrative can perhaps only partly indicate. What it involves is, among other things, her sense of her father's relation to his wife and everything it implies. By the subtlest conceivable modulation, the narrative then passes into the realization that even emotion, even a feeling so primitive as pain, must also be weighed in the balance. The reason for the shift in Maggie's thoughts from Charlotte to the Prince seems, at first, not completely clear. We may explain it by a passage from a letter James once wrote to Edith Wharton apropos of her marriage problems and a possible divorce. In it he counsels her to "only sit tight yourself *and go through the movements of life.* That keeps up our connection with life—I mean of the immediate and apparent life; behind which, all the while, the deeper and darker and the unapparent, in which things *really* happen to us, learns, under that hygiene, to stay in its place. . . . Live it all through, every inch of it—out of it something valuable will come" (*Letters* 4:495). The recognition of something even more fundamental than emotion—life itself, the life impulse, what James had called "the deeper and darker and the unapparent" life—is what finally brings Maggie back to her original purpose. The substance of her recognition is that that life persists even when certain emotions die. Thus she imagines the Prince not as having ceased to live but as undergoing a period of emotional gestation that will result in the emergence of different attitudes. Her vision of his metamorphosis suggests in turn the possibility of yet another life for Charlotte and her father, as well as for the Prince and herself. On the promise of that new life, the aspiration toward form in her existence must finally base itself.

> [She] then felt the slow surge of a vision that at the end of another minute or two had floated her across the room to where her father stood looking at a picture, an early Florentine sacred subject, that he had given her on her marriage. He might have been in silence taking his last leave of it; it was a work for which she knew he entertained an unqualified esteem. The tenderness represented for her by his sacrifice of such a treasure had become to her sense a part of the whole infusion, of the immortal expression; the beauty of his sentiment looked out at her always, from the beauty of the rest, as if the frame made positively a window for his spiritual face: she might have said to herself at this moment that in leaving the thing behind him, held as in her clasping arms, he was doing the most possible toward leaving her a part of his palpable self. (2:359)

For both Maggie and her father, as well as for the Prince and Charlotte, the scene of their farewell can suggest something like a performance of the last sacred offices. For this occasion there should not be the intensity of emotion which accompanies awareness of an impending crisis. That crisis, like the peripeteia of a drama, has been met and resolved, and there remains now only a sense of finality, of things having come to their appropriate end. This sense of an ending has in effect been present ever since Maggie's second fateful conversation with her father at Fawns, when he decides to return to America. Nowhere, however, does it loom larger than here, in the quietness of a last farewell that is also the moment of most intimate nearness between father and daughter. One recalls, as do the protagonists themselves, the incidents that have brought them to this outcome: the decision on Adam Verver's part to marry so as to make Maggie "right" in her marriage, the discovery on Maggie's part of the Prince's adultery with Charlotte which begins as a strange new awareness of her changed relation to him and ends with the antiquary's disclosures, and then the long drawn-out quest to restore the marriages to their original state, accompanied by Maggie's uncertainty about her father's knowledge of the affair and about the Prince's true intentions.

It is appropriate that the communion of father and daughter should be summed up in a picture, since in it are expressed everything she means to him and, even more importantly, he to her. Through it their awarenesses merge, and it endures as a testament to their communion of consciousness. Even before, we are given the "slow surge of a vision" that after a minute or two brings her across the room to where her father stands looking at the picture. We have of course encountered numerous earlier references both to Maggie's and to Charlotte's vision, especially of one little man in a straw hat and white waistcoat who stands off by himself weaving his spell. But in the present case vision assumes an added meaning. Earlier, the appearance of Adam Verver within the field of Maggie's or Charlotte's gaze had emphasized the material figure as the personality behind it became unfathomable or opaque. Then the material aspect had defined the limits of knowledge. But the "slow surge" of vision that now occurs suggests an indwelling emotion that is the deepest expression of the life within us seeking some answering awareness from those whom it embraces in its affection. That Maggie's "vision" consists even more of affection than perception is confirmed by the manner in which it "floats" her across the room to her father. The sustaining power of this vision— how many times has it "seen Maggie through" the difficulties of trying to save him (as she believes) from a knowledge of his wife's adultery? Even now it does something more than merely "see her through," culminating in a clear perception of what matters to her most, now and always. We do not know whether her gaze finally rests upon her father or the painting. In the deepest sense it does not matter: the one is so easily identifiable with the other. Nor does she now see just the little man with the "unfathomable heart" folded in the "flawless fresh-ness" of his white waistcoat. If anything, that heart is only too fath-omable as it draws her to him in its closest embrace. The vision through which she now sees him is one she will always keep, expressive as it is of her whole relation to her father and of everything he has meant to her.

Absorbed in his own thoughts, Adam Verver contemplates the painting he had given his daughter on her marriage, an "early Flor-entine sacred subject." Nowhere else does the narrative mention this work, and the omission is suggestive. In forming a pendant to the celebrated and highly visible golden bowl Charlotte had attempted to offer the Prince as her gift for *his* marriage, the painting possesses an effect similar to that of the book Maggie carries out to Charlotte in the summer house, the first volume of a novel of which Charlotte had inadvertently taken the second. "*This* is the beginning," she tells her; "you've got the wrong volume and I've brought you out the right." But the painting Maggie's father gives her forms a perfect complement to the bowl not only because of its artistic flawlessness but also because of the sentiment it conveys from donor to receiver.[15] Whereas the bowl by its hidden crack might symbolize the "flaw" in the Prince's marriage to Maggie (the hiddenness of the flaw implying that if the Prince ac-cepts the bowl he accepts Charlotte as a presence in his marriage), the perfection of the painting reflects the completeness of Adam Verver's sacrifice for his daughter. As a surrender of what he cherishes most, his gift symbolizes his giving of himself.

For James, like others of his generation—most notably Bernard Berenson—the charm of early Florentine painting, the pristine clarity of the quattrocento, exert a special appeal. In his *Italian Painters of the Renaissance*, Berenson had sought to emphasize the linear definition of Tuscan painters as well as what he termed the "tactile quality" of artists like Giotto.[16] Even before him, Pater had illuminated the special beauties of Botticelli, creating a vogue for the period preceding the High Renaissance. Clarity and light: these qualities so characteristic of the quattrocento could also exemplify the nature of Adam Verver's relationship to his daughter. If turbidity suggests confused or ambig-uous affections, pristine clarity can only imply an unqualified love that gives everything it has to its object.

The painting Maggie's father gives her is described as depicting a sacred subject. Symbolically it points to the sacred quality of art, but also to that of marriage (on account of the occasion of the gift).[17] The fusion of the sanctity of the one with that of the other becomes ex-pressive of art's relationship to life—art, which gives form to our existence, as something sacred in itself; marriage, as the highest possible form, hence sacred on that account. The sacredness of marriage lies in the form it gives to our deepest emotions. We have seen how the adulterous love of the Prince and Charlotte exhausts itself by dwelling upon the person of its object. In marriage, on the other hand, Maggie and the Prince are meant to give themselves not only to each other but above all to their *relation* to each other, to the form this relation takes (marriage) and to the ideal that it inspires, of an enduring communion of thought and emotion. Here what confers sanctity must consist of something other than simply affections. For James these are but the substance of life, the measure of our engagement in our existence. But when they assume a permanent form (such as marriage), that form achieves a transcendence of time which symbolically expresses our eternal relation to another.

For Maggie, the emotional sacrifice symbolized by her father's gift receives enduring form through the painting itself: "the tenderness represented for her by his sacrifice of such a treasure had become to her sense a part of the whole infusion, of the immortal expression. . . ." The infusion of her father's emotion becomes a part of the infusion that is art's own emotion. Thus what had belonged to life passes into the realm of art. Through its act of sacrifice, embodied in the gift of a painting, Adam Verver's affection for his daughter achieves an immortal expression consecrated by the immortal expression that art itself represents. Her recognition of her father's affection, in turn, transforms Maggie's perception of the painting: "the beauty of his sentiment looked out at her always, from the beauty of the rest, as if the frame made positively a window for his spiritual face. . . ." It seems almost as if Adam Verver were looking at her, but in fact it is Maggie who sees her father's face through a kind of spiritual insight. And indeed at this moment the painting rises to the level of a *vera icon,* the true image of the face of Christ said to have been preserved by Veronica, which is as a likeness of Adam Verver's "spiritual face." The effect of this reminiscence, endowing the expression of the painting with a spiritual significance, attests once more to the sacredness of form. To leave this picture behind him, "held as in her clasping arms," is for Maggie as if her father were doing "the most possible toward leaving her a part of his palpable self": through her perception of the painting he is made real to her, and that reality is what she will always preserve. Yet the reality of her perception has its source in a pictorial image whose reality is not one of likeness but rather of form.

That form, however, now represents for Maggie something more than a visual impression. Like her marriage with respect to her relation to the Prince, it gives enduring expression to her relationship with her father. And, just as marriage can become a source of new emotion by symbolically realizing her relation to the Prince, so the painting becomes equally a source of emotion by symbolizing her relationship to her father. And if it does so it will have fulfilled the highest aim of art, which is not to create forms separate from those of life but rather to subsume life into itself. Like the restoration of her marriage which is Adam Verver's ultimate gift to his daughter, it will have achieved a consecration of existence through form: the luminous expression of an ideal in which existence finds both its end and a source of perpetual renewal.

8

THE MUSIC OF TIME

1

"Longtemps, je me suis couché de bonne heure." [For a long time I went to bed at an early hour.] "Longtemps": evocation of past moments, an interval of past time.[1] This interval is implicitly set off from the present: during a certain period of time I went to bed at an early hour, but not anymore. Thus the period indicated by "longtemps" belongs wholly to the past. Yet the space separating it from the present is an indefinite one: we do not know exactly when that period ceased, only that it does not continue into the present. Thus it is no longer connected with the "I" in any tangible sense. The only connection with it now is through memory. And yet, some sort of connection must exist—if only because the "I" can still speak of this period.

In recalling it, however, what memory recognizes above all is a sense of duration. Such duration consists less of specific moments or impressions than of an experience of time itself, the passing of days or years. It reflects, then, our most basic perception of time. Perception of this kind remains without specific content—no distinct images, no sense of precise relation between past and present; hence the impossibility of arriving at any clear sense of time.

Perhaps this has something to do, in turn, with the narrator's loss of temporal awareness: "Parfois, à peine ma bougie éteinte, mes yeux se fermaient si vite que je n'avais pas le temps de me dire: 'Je m'endors.'" [Sometimes, my candle barely extinguished, my eyes would close themselves so quickly that I would not have the time to say to myself: "I'm falling asleep."] Here what is experienced occurs so quickly as to exceed the capacity to register it. But if the narrator is unaware of his falling asleep, the result is a temporal discrepancy between his consciousness of time (which ends with the last moment he is aware of before falling asleep) and actual time.[2]

This discrepancy produces a disorientation of the self: "Et, une demi-

heure après, la pensée qu'il était temps de chercher le sommeil m'éveillait;
je voulais poser le volume que je croyais avoir encore dans les mains
et souffler ma lumière. . . ." [And, half an hour later, the thought
that it was time to go to sleep would awaken me; I would want to
put away the volume that I believed I still had in my hands and blow
out my light.] The thought that it is time to go to sleep has, of course,
no meaning with respect to the narrator, who has already been asleep
for the past half-hour. What it signifies instead is the temporal discrepancy that has taken place. Since the narrator is unaware of the half-
hour that has elapsed since his falling asleep, his thoughts concern
themselves with his last waking moment. The thought of that moment
suggests to him that it is time to sleep. But in order to sleep, he must
make certain preparations (putting away his book, blowing out the
light). Ironically, these preparations for sleeping wake him up. Thus
the narrator wakes because his assertion that it is time to sleep is incorrect: it is incorrect both because a half-hour has already elapsed
since the appropriate time, and because he is already asleep. But if the
narrator's assertion of its being time to sleep is incorrect, this is only
because he himself, by falling asleep, has escaped from the realm of
time, which is that of consciousness. In so doing, however, he loses
his sense of self, to which his recognition (that it is time to sleep) no
longer applies. As a result his "self" or "I," which continues to exist
during the half-hour when he loses all awareness of it, now finds itself
dissociated from his present consciousness.

This dissociation of self from consciousness makes possible an imaginative identification with something else:

> je n'avais pas cessé en dormant de faire des réflexions sur ce que
> je venais de lire, mais ces réflexions avaient pris un tour un peu
> particulier; il me semblait que j'étais moi-même ce dont parlait
> l'ouvrage: une église, un quatuor, la rivalité de François Ier et de
> Charles Quint.

> [I had not ceased in sleeping to reflect upon what I had just been
> reading, but these reflections had taken a somewhat peculiar turn;
> it seemed to me that I was myself that of which the work spoke:
> a church, a quartet, the rivalry of François I and Charles V.]

Here the dissociation of self from consciousness, with its consequent
disruption of normal experience, becomes a prelude to imaginative creation. Insofar as the narrator could not possibly be a church, a quartet,
or the rivalry of François I and Charles V, his feeling of being these
reflects the creative work of a mind that imagines the experience of

other existences. By basing his dreams upon the act of reading (rather than an actual encounter with any of these objects), the narrative emphasizes the imaginative aspect of his activity.

We have seen how that activity begins with freedom from normal constraints of space and time. It thus becomes possible to experience impressions in a different fashion from that of our everyday waking hours. Instead of being subjected to the tyranny of external circumstances, the mind can now transform its impressions, imparting to them a subjective coloring. But if in dreaming the self tends to reflect on its own situation, perhaps we might see in the narrator's dream of a church, a quartet, and the rivalry of François I and Charles V some attempt to alter that situation. It had consisted, we recall, of his being caught in a discrepancy between his consciousness of time and actual time. This discrepancy in turn resulted in a disorientation of the "I" and even a loss of the sense of self. In its attempt to confront the ensuing chaos, the self searches for some means of establishing its true relation to the external world—which means: to time. But the inability of consciousness to grasp the passage of time after the narrator falls asleep, and the resulting discrepancy between what consciousness asserts (that it is time to sleep) and the actual state of the self, belong to a chaos which is not unlike that of experience. Thus the struggle of the self to impose order upon the chaos of experience becomes a quest for its true relation to time—which means its true relation to its own experiences. That quest is, ultimately, nothing less than the quest for a self symbolically lost at the very opening of the novel through its dissociation from consciousness. But in order to comprehend its true relation to time, the self must first arrive at an apprehension of the true nature of time. This apprehension, in turn, consists of a perception of the relation between those different moments that make up time. In the narrator's three dream motifs it becomes possible to discern some attempt to embody such a perception symbolically. These motifs anticipate the form of Proust's *Recherche,* which is in effect a quest for that perception.

At first, perhaps, only the disparity between these motifs seems evident—a material edifice, a musical form consisting of a temporal sequence, and a historical moment that presents the conflicting passions of two great monarchs. Yet the narrative maintains, "it seemed to me I was myself that of which the work spoke."[3] What does this mean? Given the differences between the three motifs, and a dream consciousness which liberates from ordinary limits of space and time, the assertion can only imply three radically different experiences. But what would the nature of each be like?

If we begin with the church, we notice immediately a certain lack of specificity. "Une église" might signify the kind of edifice the narrator remembers from his childhood in Combray (the same church where he later sees the Duchesse de Guermantes) or the ancient Romanesque structure at Balbec that he yearns so much to visit and that proves so disappointing at first sight. But we also know from various sources how intimately the "église" motif is connected for Proust with Gothic architecture, and of how (in a letter to Jean de Gaigneron) he had specifically expressed a desire to name the various sections of his work after the different parts of a Gothic cathedral.[4] In *Le Temps retrouvé*, he even compares the structure of his novel on several occasions to that of a church or cathedral. From this standpoint the "église" might aptly typify the architectural principle within a work of art.[5] As such it can ultimately symbolize the form of the *Recherche* itself. Thus in the first of his three motifs the narrator already prefigures the work he will undertake at the end of the novel. But the "église" also anticipates the crucial episode of the Martinville towers, whose real meaning the narrator grasps only much later.

But if the "église" represents in some sense the architectural idea exemplified in a Gothic cathedral, what might the experience of being such an edifice consist of? How could the narrator possess this kind of consciousness? If the "église" motif can be taken to symbolize the *Recherche,* in becoming an "église" the narrator identifies himself in effect with the work of memory which forms the substance of the *Recherche*. That identification implies, in turn, a fundamental resemblance between the nature of Proust's novel and that of a Gothic cathedral.

To imagine actually being a Gothic cathedral implies attempting to grasp the thought embodied in its structure, above all the rationale behind its architectural scheme. That scheme consists of fusing the most massive of substances with the splendor of a glass vibrant with color. If the windows seem almost overwhelming at times, their brilliance is nevertheless assimilated into a structure that combines the austere purity of geometrical patterns with a dynamic equilibrium of rhythms and stresses within one all-embracing idea. Thus sensuousness is absorbed into form. By being incorporated into a larger structure, the windows acquire a greater meaning than any resulting simply from the brilliance of their color. This meaning is based upon apprehending their relation to all the other parts of a cathedral. At the same time, light vivifies architectural form, as the cathedral becomes a means of connecting the impression of one window with that of another. But because impressions touch directly upon our emotions, to unify them is to assimilate emotion into form.

If the radiance of a window may be compared with that of an individual impression in the *Recherche,* the architectural idea that subsumes the window into a larger scheme would then correspond to the form of the novel. But the form of this novel comes into existence only through a process that transforms the nature of an impression from lived experience into something like form. Through memory, what one experiences is the emotion of a specific moment in time. Such experiences can lead in turn to an apprehension similar to that of form in Gothic. It comes from a realization of how one impression might be juxtaposed with another to create a formal effect. In similar fashion, the memory of a moment's emotion can be combined with other impressions to produce a sense of form. But with this perception comes a recognition that all the moments of our existence possess an ideal relation to each other. Thus the process whereby we experience our emotions becomes ultimately the means by which they become formally expressive. In becoming form, however, they transcend their nature as passion or suffering. The "église" symbolizes the possibility of this transcendence through form.

Among musical forms, the quartet possesses a special character. Whereas other forms may involve excessive duplication of instrumental voices and hence a loss of intimate colloquy between the different players, while solo works fail to offer enough parts for more complex harmonies, the quartet achieves something close to an ideal balance.[6] Its form enables each instrument to announce a new theme in the course of a work. Moreover, the score's texture allows for subtle transformation of an idea when taken up by one instrument or another. Even without thematic variations, the repetition of a theme in a different key can easily transform its emotional significance. In the *Recherche,* similarly, repetition of the same action by different characters (Swann and the narrator, Swann and Charlus, Charlus and Mlle de Vinteuil) can exhibit diverse modulations of a single theme. And in *Le Temps retrouvé* specifically, the transformation through time of an "idea" (embodied in one or another of the principal personae) is exemplified in their altered appearance at the Princesse de Guermantes's matinée. But the interplay of different voices in a quartet also produces a harmony: the first violin characteristically announces a theme which is then seconded by the viola, with the cello occasionally employed for a *contrapposto* effect. In the *Recherche* a similar interplay of "voices" occurs— as in the juxtaposition of Swann and the narrator. The narrator "repeats" Swann's experience in love, but at a certain distance in time comparable to the interval between a theme's announcement ("Un amour de Swann") and its reiteration. A *contrapposto* effect, correspondingly, appears in Charlus's relationship with Morel, through its contrast with Swann's experiences and those of the narrator.

Finally, there is the temporal aspect of music. In *Du côté de chez Swann* Proust touches upon it indirectly as Swann has Odette and others play over and over for him the phrase he loves from the Vinteuil sonata. We have seen how the "église" had symbolized the possibility of preserving a moment by recognizing its ideal relation to other moments. But that ideal relation fails to acknowledge the existence of these moments in time. Through music we come to an awareness of time. Our awareness originates with our desire to hold on to a specific melodic phrase whose beauty moves us. The impossibility of doing so (which leads in Swann's case to wanting to have it replayed) forces us to feel the temporal quality of the phrase, the fact that we are able to apprehend it only through time. In realizing the temporal quality of a particular phrase, however, we experience an apprehension of time itself, which consists of the feeling of an ineluctable succession of moments. Nevertheless, the mind still hopes to recapture the phrase it had heard earlier. Its quest for that phrase leads it to submit to the temporal movement of the piece. When the phrase finally reappears (often unexpectedly), it compels us to recognize how we ourselves (in concentrating our hopes on its reappearance) have come to identify with that phrase. But by realizing our identification with that phrase, we then arrive—through a sense of its place within a movement—at a consciousness of our own existence in time.

In his dreamlike state, the narrator imagines himself actually *becoming* a quartet. This would imply the possibility of experiencing a piece in its entire thematic development. Under such circumstances, what the mind apprehends is the idea of a sequence governing the arrangement of notes which form that piece. If a musical sequence consists of notes arranged in a specific order, our experience of that sequence results in the sense of a particular succession in time. To feel this succession, then, leads to seeing each note simply as part of an arrangement whose essence is the movement from one note to the next. The feeling of that movement, in turn, produces the experience in music of time.

For the *Recherche* it signifies the possibility of apprehending each moment of our existence as an experience of the nature of time itself. As a result the narrator transcends his earlier recognition of form in life, which had been based upon a desire to transcend time. In experiencing time within each moment, he perceives his entire existence as composing an ideal sequence, like that of music. Thus his perception ultimately transforms rather than negating our sense of time.

If the quartet alters time by transforming it into a musical sequence, however, it also suggests a rationale for the third motif, the rivalry between François I and Charles V. Unlike the two preceding motifs, the third refers to a particular historical moment. Since the narrator specifically declares, "it seemed to me I was myself that of which the work spoke," one might well wish to ask: how can an individual possibly *be* a rivalry? Clearly the assertion implies some modification of normal consciousness. Yet to identify oneself with a rivalry (rather than with either figure) requires somehow becoming history itself rather than simply an individual consciousness existing in historical time. Thus we might describe the passions of François I and Charles V as historical—they occur at a specific moment of the past. Nevertheless, the emotion of that moment consists of something more than just these individual passions. By coming into conflict, they create a feeling of rivalry, the sense of a resisting, opposing passion that one seeks to overcome, with the irritating excitement of the actual conflict. But all of this belongs to what we might call the emotion of a past moment, as opposed to merely an individual's past emotion. To speak of being the rivalry of François I and Charles V, then, implies experiencing not just some aspect of a past moment but rather that moment itself.

This experience of a historical moment differs from our experience of music. What it offers is not so much a sense of sequence but the recovery of an actual moment. We have seen how the perception of an ideal relation between various moments of our existence achieves a transcendence of time. But that perception fails to recognize how time forms the medium of our existence. From this standpoint music offers higher possibilities: unlike architecture, it transforms rather than transcending our experience of time. But even music cannot recover our experience of a past moment. It fails to give us the happiness that comes from reliving its emotion. To do so is to become aware of that emotion's eternal existence. But time apprehended in this fashion differs from our normal experience of it: to relive a past moment is really to experience its emotion in its purest form, dissociated from all the circumstances that originally gave rise to it.

Thus the quest for happiness in the *Recherche* depends upon the possibility of recovering past time. We find this quest symbolically expressed in the narrator's search for Albertine, who as "la fugitive" becomes the elusive object of desire fleeing from him through space and time. But it is time that poses the greatest problem: how can he really know what she did, felt, and thought at a given moment of their life together? His attempt to recover the past culminates in his experience in the courtyard of the Hôtel de Guermantes, where the sensation of uneven paving stones inspires a vivid remembrance of Venice. Like the historical motif (the rivalry between François I and Charles V) which anticipates it, it indicates the possibility of recovering a past moment. But this recovery of the past signifies something more (and something other) than a source of pleasure from one's memory of Venice. Ultimately it represents the possibility of recapturing the emotion of a past moment. Applied to the whole of the narrator's life, it would imply being able to re-experience all the past moments of his existence—not, however, as actual moments but rather as moments of pure emotion capable of being arranged in a formal sequence like that of music. Yet the sequence of emotions yields something more than music: a feeling that retains the emotion of each moment even as it perceives its relation to others in time. It is the consciousness, in effect, of life transformed into art.

2

In listening to the works of César Franck heard most often by Proust (the Quartet in D Major, the Piano Quintet in F Minor, the Violin Sonata in A Major), one notices instances in which a theme introduced early in a work reappears unexpectedly much later. If its initial announcement had seemed to convey a sense of promise, the theme's reappearance inevitably recalls that earlier emotion. With regard to our existence, such a theme becomes a leitmotiv, reminding us of past moments filled with anticipations of things to come.

The celebrated episode of the towers of Martinville presents a similar phenomenon.[7] Significantly, the narrator begins his account with a confession of his literary failure: "Combien depuis ce jour, dans mes promenades du côté de Guermantes, il me parut plus affligeant encore qu'auparavant de n'avoir pas de dispositions pour les lettres, et de devoir renoncer à être jamais un écrivain célèbre!" (1:176). [How often since this day, in my walks along the Guermantes way, did it seem to me more distressing than before not to have any propensity for literature, and to have to give up the hope of ever becoming a famous author!] His glimpse of the Duchesse de Guermantes in the church of Combray intensifies the youthful Marcel's suffering at the thought of not having a talent for literature. But if seeing her causes him distress, it also hints at a sense of plenitude within his impression. In an indirect fashion, then, it anticipates his future vocation: "Combien de-

puis ce jour. . . ." Thus his impression corresponds to other moments of his life—specifically, moments of recognition. In his walks
along the Guermantes way he is undoubtedly reminded of his encounter with the duchesse and of the impression she had made upon
him. Subsequently the memory of that encounter assumes the function
of a leitmotiv. By recalling his impression, the narrator is able to transcend time by bringing the present into ideal relation with a moment
from the past. Yet the relation remains undeveloped—a result of his
inability to articulate his impression.

Nevertheless, there remains the feeling of a mysterious meaning within
particular impressions:

> Alors, bien en dehors de toutes ces préoccupations littéraires et
> ne s'y rattachant en rien, tout d'un coup un toit, un reflet de
> soleil sur une pierre, l'odeur d'un chemin me faisaient arrêter par
> un plaisir particulier qu'ils me donnaient, et aussi parce qu'ils
> avaient l'air de cacher au-delà de ce que je voyais, quelque chose
> qu'ils invitaient à venir prendre et que malgré mes efforts je n'ar-
> rivais pas à découvrir. (1:176).

> [Then, quite apart from all these literary preoccupations and in
> no way connecting itself with them, suddenly a roof, a gleam of
> sunlight on a stone, the scent of a path would make me stop
> because of the singular pleasure they would give me, and also
> because they had the air of concealing, beyond what I could see,
> something they invited me to come and take, and which despite
> my efforts I never managed to discover.]

The appeal of such sensations implies something more than sensuous pleasure. In itself that pleasure would be incapable of awakening
a sense of symbolic significance. But the sight of a roof offers a suggestion of form, while the gleam of sunlight on a stone conveys warmth
as well as a visible radiance, imparting a felt intensity to consciousness.
In a similar fashion the scent of a path can evoke vividly the emotion
of a past moment.

Yet even this does not suffice to account for the attraction of such
experiences, their "air of concealing, beyond what I could see, something they invited me to come and take." Of that ineffable "something" the narrator goes on to say:

> Comme je sentais que cela se trouvait en eux, je restais là, im-
> mobile, à regarder, à respirer, à tâcher d'aller avec ma pensée au-
> delà de l'image ou de l'odeur. Et s'il me fallait rattraper mon
> grand-père, poursuivre ma route, je cherchais à les retrouver, en

fermant les yeux; je m'attachais à me rappeler exactement la ligne du toit, la nuance de la pierre qui, sans que je pusse comprendre pourquoi, m'avaient semble pleines, prêtes à s'entrouvrir, à me livrer ce dont elles n'étaient qu'un couvercle. Certes ce n'était pas des impressions de ce genre qui pouvaient me rendre l'espérance que j'avais perdue de pouvoir être un jour écrivain et poète, car elles étaient toujours liées à un objet particulier dépourvu de valeur intellectuelle et ne se rapportant à aucune vérité abstraite. Mais du moins elles me donnaient un plaisir irraisonné, l'illusion d'une sorte de fécondité et par là me distrayaient de l'ennui, du sentiment de mon impuissance que j'avais éprouvés chaque fois que j'avais cherché un sujet philosophique pour une grande oeuvre littéraire. (1:176–77)

[Since I felt that this something was to be found in them, I would stand there motionless, looking, inhaling, attempting to go beyond the image or the odor in my thought. And if I had to catch up with my grandfather, or to continue on my way, I would try to recapture them by closing my eyes; I would apply myself to recalling exactly the line of the roof, the precise color of the stone, which, without my being able to understand why, had seemed to me full, ready to open, to deliver to me that for which they were only a lid or cover. Certainly it was not impressions of this sort which could restore to me the hope I had lost of becoming one day an author and poet, since they were invariably associated with a specific object devoid of intellectual value and not relating to any abstract truth. But at least they gave me an unreasoning pleasure, the illusion of a kind of creativeness, and thereby distracted me from ennui, from the sense of my impotence which I had felt each time I had sought a philosophical subject for a great literary work.]

That an impression should appear to invite or beckon to the narrator marks a significant personification. We are told these impressions had the "air of concealing" something they "invited me to come and take." But if the impression conceals something, what it conceals cannot be itself. Instead it becomes an intermediary between the narrator and a higher meaning he is in search of.[8] As such it acquires the function of a spiritual presence within his life. Its act of concealment seems almost a deliberate provocation. In this fashion its actions manifest a definite intention hidden from the narrator. Precisely by being concealed, however, that intention appears as part of a higher plan or scheme. But its existence implies a specific *telos* within the narrator's life, hence a standpoint from which the whole of it can be viewed outside time. From that standpoint each moment can be seen to possess a relation to every other. Since the viewpoint from which they are perceived lies outside time, this relation must be "spatial" rather than temporal. Such a relation raises in turn the possibility of an architectonic arrangement of all the moments of the narrator's existence. Thus what the personification ultimately embodies is an intuition of form in his existence.

We have seen how his impressions had suggested to the narrator something "beyond what I could see" and which in spite of his efforts he had "never managed to discover." Subsequently, he goes on to observe that this "something" he is in search of appears to be contained within his impressions ("que cela se trouvait en eux"). By experiencing them as fully as possible, he attempts "to go beyond the image or the odor by means of my thought." They themselves seem by their nature to encourage his attempt, insofar as they appear "ready to open themselves up, to deliver that for which they were only a lid or cover." From these indications it is clear that the actual impression does not offer any immediate revelation of what the narrator is looking for. Nor, on the other hand, does its meaning lie in itself. Yet the narrator can speak of what he is in search of as being contained *within* it. Moreover, the experience of it seems in some fashion significant—hence his effort "to look, to inhale," as much as possible. But if what he seeks transcends the realm of phenomena, how can he possibly arrive at it through experience?[9]

In an earlier draft for *Le Temps retrouvé* (*L'Adoration perpétuelle*) Proust had explored this question even more fully. There the narrator declares: "c'est le petit trait que l'image, l'impression d'une chose avait marqué en relief en nous, auquel il faut arriver, s'attacher scrupuleusement, en faire sortir la signification" (*Matinée chez la princesse de Guermantes*, p. 166). [It is the little mark which the image, the impression of a thing has indicated in relief within us to which one must come, attach oneself scrupulously, in order to elicit the significance.] This "little mark" that an impression makes upon us is in some sense its effect. Invariably the image appears to contain something other than itself ("Toujours cette image qui recèle [quelque chose] d'autre qu'elle"); we feel that "elle a un fond que nous ne voyons pas" (ibid.) [it possesses a depth or bottom we do not see]. Similarly, in the "Carnet" of 1908 Proust can speak of the "consistance" or "épaisseur" (thickness) of impressions (*Le Carnet de 1908*, p. 124). But the "fond" or depth of the impression seems "semblable à quelque chose que sa vue a ébranlé en nous-même, si bien qu'en cherchant en nous, peut'être pourrions-nous le trouver" (*Matinée*, p. 166) [similar to something that its perception has stirred up within us, so that in searching within ourselves we can perhaps find it]. As in the Martinville episode, this impression or image is felt as "nothing more than a cover" (*couvercle*) (*Matinée*, p. 167). And, in a remark that will appear in the final version of *Le Temps retrouvé*, the narrator can speak of such impressions as musical airs that haunt us with a desire to recognize and recall them, as if we somehow knew them—yet without in fact ever having heard them.

The haunting quality of these impressions forces the narrator to make an even more intense effort to comprehend them:

> J'ai bien senti en touchant par la pensée cette image qui est dans mon cerveau, que sous elle il y a quelque chose, mais quoi? Je promène de nouveau ma pensée dans mon cerveau comme une sonde, je cherche le point précis de l'image où j'ai senti quelque chose, jusqu'à ce que je l'aie retrouvé, ma pensée s'est heurtée à quelque chose qui l'arrêtait à un peu de matière, je veux dire de pensée encore inconnue en moi. . . . (*Matinée*, p. 168)

> [I clearly felt in touching through thought this image which was in my brain, that beneath it there was something, but what? I guided my thought again within my brain like a probe, searching for the precise point of the image at which I had felt something until I had found it again; my thought struck against something which stopped it at a little bit of matter, which is to say, at a thought still unknown to me. . . .]

What is this "little bit of matter" ("un peu de matière") that the narrator's thought strikes against in seeking to fathom his impression? Without actually being external, it conveys nevertheless the effect of something external—in other words, of something outside the realm of thought. This something within the image cannot be assimilated to thought, fails to dissolve within the subjective medium of consciousness. Hence the sensation of striking against it: it is what we cannot reduce to the feeling of our own subjectivity. Thus it counts as something *objective*. It is what resists the desire of consciousness to dominate. Yet this something is contained *within* the impression. Consequently it cannot belong to the external world—not, at least, to the realm of phenomena, which arguably might be said to exist only as perceived by consciousness. Nor, however, can this something within the impression belong to the external world, since then it could not form part of the impression, whose medium is subjective. This something, then, can only be the felt perception of something objective (an external world) *within* a subjective impression: the effect of the real upon consciousness. It consists of a recognition of something external to the self. As such it carries the stamp of its authenticity ("la griffe de son authenticité"). For we do not imagine something external and opaque: we must feel its opacity, experience its resistance to subjectivity, in order to arrive at the sensation of something objective.

But if something within an impression seems objective, it also lies outside of time. In our experience, time is invariably associated with consciousness. We apprehend it through the transience of our impressions. What resists that transience, then, must exist outside of time. Thus the sensation of something objective within an impression bears the stamp of the real through its transcendence of time, the apprehension it gives us of an eternal or perduring element in things. This eternal element elicits what the narrator calls "the joy of reality recaptured" ("la joie de [la] réalité retrouvée") (*Matinée,* p. 169). Such joy springs from the recognition of something within our impressions that triumphs over time. Because of its association with our impressions, however, this something (which we call "reality") can be recaptured through memory. And that in turn allows us to believe that we too, through our apprehension of it, might somehow share in its transcendence of time.

Simultaneously the narrator makes another, equally important recognition. Earlier he had referred to the something within an image as an "obstacle fécond" (fecund obstacle) (*Matinée,* p. 168). Its fecundity lies in its capacity to produce the recognition of a creative faculty within himself. This something within the impression corresponds, as he had noticed, to something within us, so that "in searching within ourselves we can perhaps find it." Subsequently he equates the "little bit of matter" with "a thought still unknown to me." Thus the material quality of the something within his impression is identical to that of thought, but of a thought which is literally described as "unknown *in* me" ("inconnue en moi")—unknown and yet at the same time existent within the self. This thought (which haunts him like a seemingly familiar musical air) is nothing other than the recognition of something objective in things—in other words, of their eternal aspect. But with the recognition of that eternism comes a perception of thought's capacity to deal with something that transcends time. In recovering its impressions, thought becomes capable of grasping something eternal and, consequently, of rising to perceptions with an eternal truth. To possess these, however, implies thought's being in some sense eternal itself. Hence the feeling of fecundity, of power, in the apprehension of a timeless element within our impressions.

The narrator indicates that his impressions had seemed to him "full" (*pleines*), not on account of the objects perceived—a roof, or sunlight gleaming on a stone—but because of something within these impressions. Hence it is unnecessary for him to see the actual objects again: he has only to shut his eyes and try to recover them ("chercher à les retrouver"). What he "recovers" is, of course, not the objects but his own impressions. Specifically, he attempts to recall the exact line of a roof, the precise color of a stone he had seen. Why should these be important to him? Clearly, one can speak of such details as expressive. What they evoke is a "fullness" of meaning which results from the experience of assimilating certain impressions.

This "fullness" assumes the form of what the narrator calls an "illusion of creativeness" ("illusion de fécondité"), which he also describes as an "unreasoning pleasure" ("plaisir irraisonné") and elsewhere as a "singular pleasure" ("plaisir particulier"). Here one should perhaps take "illusion" not in the true/false sense but rather as signifying the kind of creative illusion exemplified in dreams and fantasies, or the reverie that appears earlier in the "overture." The illusion the narrator now enters into results from the fullness of his impressions being transformed into a feeling of creativeness within himself. If this fullness reflects an intensified awareness of perception, the same awareness can lead to realizing his own creative capacity, by seeing his ability to transform an impression into a higher insight concerning consciousness itself. Simultaneously, the narrator also receives his first glimpse of how he might later recover past impressions and thereby bridge the abyss of time.

The realization of his inherent creative capacity gives the narrator an "unreasoning pleasure"—"unreasoning" because, as he observes later, "it was certainly not impressions of this sort" that would restore to him his hope of becoming a writer, since "they were invariably connected with a specific object devoid of intellectual value and not relating to any abstract truth." Here the text is, of course, ironic: precisely by recalling these impressions, the narrator later comes to realize his vocation as a writer.[10] Nevertheless, from his earlier perspective, it is impossible to really grasp their future meaning. Thus a moment of experience becomes genuinely proleptic of a moment of memory: it anticipates that moment when the mind will manage to relate its different experiences to each other, and thus create a work of art. By relating them, it will create a temporal architecture that connects its experiences through intellectual perception. It will then finally arrive at those "abstract truths" the narrator now despairs of. But even the present passage already offers a glimpse of that later recognition which will illuminate the whole of the *Recherche*. Thus in its proleptic relation between present experience and future comprehension, the narrative reflects the inherent structure of time.

The episode in which the narrator sees the church towers of Martinville and Vieuxvicq from a novel perspective indicates the form of this temporal architecture. Toward the end of one afternoon, Marcel and his parents prolong their walk far beyond its usual time. Fortunately they encounter a neighbor, Doctor Percepied, who offers them a ride home in his carriage. In the course of their ride Marcel receives his memorable glimpse of the church towers:

> Au tournant d'un chemin j'éprouvai tout à coup ce plaisir spécial qui ne ressemblait à aucun autre, à apercevoir les deux clochers de Martinville, sur lesquels donnait le soleil couchant et que le mouvement de notre voiture et les lacets du chemin avaient l'air de faire changer de place, puis celui de Vieuxvicq qui, séparé d'eux par une colline et une vallée, et situé sur un plateau plus élevé dans le lointain, semblait pourtant tout voisin d'eux. (1:177–78)

> [At a bend in the road I experienced all at once this special pleasure which was unlike any other, of seeing the two church towers of Martinville, upon which shone the setting sun and which the movement of our carriage and the windings of the road had the air of making shift in position, then [the church tower] of Vieuxvicq which, separated from them by a hill and a valley, and situated on a more elevated plain in the distance, seemed nevertheless right beside them.]

The novel perspective produces a distinct impression upon the youthful Marcel:

> En constatant, en notant la forme de leur flèche, le déplacement de leurs lignes, l'ensoleillement de leur surface, je sentais que je n'allais pas au bout de mon impression, que quelque chose était derrière ce mouvement, derrière cette clarté, quelque chose qu'ils semblaient contenir et dérober à la fois. (1:178)

> [In registering, in noticing the form of their spires, the displacement of their lines, the illumination of their surfaces by sunlight, I felt I was not getting to the bottom of my impression, that

something lay behind this movement, behind this clearness, something they seemed at once to contain and conceal.]

These towers appear at such a distance that the narrator is surprised to find himself suddenly in front of the Martinville church. Nor, he confesses, did he know why he had felt pleasure in seeing the towers at that distance. But instead of consigning his experience to the same limbo as numerous similar impressions, he compels himself to reflect upon it until it yields something of its mysterious import:

> Bientôt leurs lignes et leurs surfaces ensoleillées, comme si elles avaient été une sorte d'écorce, se déchirèrent, un peu de ce qui m'était caché en elles m'apparut, j'eus une pensée qui n'existait pas pour moi l'instant avant, qui se formula en mots dans ma tête, et le plaisir que m'avait fait tout à l'heure éprouver leur vue s'en trouva tellement accru que, pris d'une sorte d'ivresse, je ne pus plus penser à autre chose. À ce moment et comme nous étions déjà loin de Martinville en tournant la tête je les aperçus de nouveau, tout noirs cette fois, car le soleil était déjà couché. Par moments les tournants du chemin me les dérobaient, puis ils se montrèrent une dernière fois et enfin je ne les vis plus. (1:178)

> [Soon their lines and their sunlit surfaces, as if they had been a sort of rind, peeled away, a little of what had been concealed from me in them appeared to me, and I had a thought which had not existed for me the instant before, which formulated itself into words in my head, and the pleasure which the sight of them had just caused me to experience was so much intensified that, overcome by a sort of intoxication, I could no longer think of anything else. At this moment, and as we were already far from Martinville, in turning my head I caught sight of them again, completely black this time, because the sun had already set. From time to time the turns of the road would conceal them from me, then they showed themselves for a last time, and finally I could see them no more.]

From a symbolic standpoint, the carriage ride represents in effect the movement of time. As the carriage hurtles forward, it offers the narrator at each instant a slightly different view of the towers. Each instant thus corresponds to a specific impression, hence a specific "experience." By noticing the towers' constantly changing appearance, the narrator becomes aware of his own shifting position—which is to say, his movement through time. By seeing external objects, then, he experiences the passing of time. In *Le Temps retrouvé* when he sees Swann,

Charlus, and others from his youthful past transformed by age, he comes to realize how in a human sense the passage of time leads ultimately to death, the extinguishing of consciousness and, consequently, all sense of time.

Because of the peculiar nature of our experience of time, what is clearly visible at one moment can cease to be so the next. In the narrator's carriage ride, the windings of the road result in quite different perceptions of the towers depending upon the precise angle of a turn. The distance from which one views an object can also affect one's perception. A greater distance will have a softening effect, tempering the imperfections of an edifice as well as allowing its essential features to emerge more clearly. Similarly, the relation between two objects can often be seen more clearly at a distance. In the present scene the distance from which the narrator observes the towers of Martinville and Vieuxvicq corresponds symbolically to that of time. This temporal distance produces a softening effect upon our impressions similar to that which modifies Marcel's view of the church towers. Only through such temporal distance does it become possible for him to discern a relation between different moments of his existence, just as his distance from the towers had made possible the juxtaposition between those of Martinville and Vieuxvicq. Thus the scene anticipates the moment when the narrator will recognize the inherent form of his life and hence the possibility of assimilating it into art.

This recognition consists of perceiving the relation between one moment of his life and another. As a relation it is "architectonic" in its juxtaposition of two moments widely separated in time. Their juxtaposition, in turn, is made possible by the nature of such moments. We have seen how they become equated with particular experiences, corresponding to the various "views" the narrator receives of Martinville and Vieuxvicq: in each instance we feel various impressions associated with a specific emotion. But our apprehension of a moment differs from actually experiencing a moment in terms of our consciousness of time. In our everyday existence we feel the constant flow from each moment to the next. In that respect there is no "stasis" within a moment: our sense of individual moments disappears. In our apprehension of a moment, however, we lose our feeling of the flow of time. By no longer existing within the moment, we become capable of perceiving each moment as an individual, objective entity. As a result, our apprehension becomes similar to the narrator's perception of the towers. Though constantly changing, that perception inevitably presents a single image at any given moment. It thereby achieves a definite stasis outside of time. Similarly, our apprehension of a moment also consists of an image permeated by emotion. Through memory it becomes detachable from the moment in which it occurs. It then becomes capable of being juxtaposed with similar impressions in an "architectonic" relation transcending time.

In the narrator's perception of the towers of Martinville and Vieuxvicq, this transcendence of time is symbolically expressed as a transcendence of space: the tower of Vieuxvicq, separated by a hill and a valley from those of Martinville, now appears immediately beside them as if all the intervening distance had vanished. In transcending space, the juxtaposition of these towers ultimately transcends time—the "time," materially speaking, necessary for the narrator to traverse the distance from one church to the other. That distance corresponds to the temporal distance between his impressions of the two churches. In connecting these impressions, he transcends the temporal distance between them to attain a perception of their "ideal" relation to each other.

What occurs as he does so is an elision of those lived moments that must otherwise intervene between the narrator's perception of one church and the other. In our everyday existence, that intervening space will be filled by passions, suffering, innumerable experiences that deaden our aesthetic consciousness. Thus Swann finds his capacity for aesthetic perception dulled by what he suffers on account of his love for Odette. Only when he no longer loves her does he become capable of taking up once more his long-planned essay on Vermeer. In a similar fashion, with his momentary glimpse of the three towers together, the narrator rises above all the moments of dullness, wasted passion, and suffering in his life to perceive the ideal relations that make up a work of art.

The transcendence of time represented by a juxtaposition of church towers produces an apotheosis of consciousness. Its transformation is symbolically expressed through the motif of "ensoleillement": a sunset illumination of the towers.[11] When the apprehension of a given moment enables the mind to perceive the ideal relations between its experiences, it then recognizes what we have called the eternism of its apprehension. If an impression is transitory, the apprehension of it on the other hand is timeless. At moments of intense awareness the mind actually experiences its apprehensions. But the experience of an apprehension differs fundamentally from the experience of a moment. Because the apprehension is timeless, experiencing it leads to a perception that is not merely negative (the absence of time) but rather the feeling of a moment's inexpressible fullness. Here the mind transcends time not merely through some form of intellection but through an actual experience. This experience in turn creates an apotheosis of consciousness. Since the very conditions through which we perceive are inescapably temporal, a change in our experience of time must also transform the way we perceive—and hence consciousness itself.

The emotion that accompanies a transcendence of time endows consciousness with a luminous aura. Hence the "ensoleillement," the sunlit radiance of the towers: a symbolic expression of the inner radiance which results from realizing how that transcendence occurs through the experience of an apprehension. Thus the mind discovers the object of its quest within itself. Its recognition gives it a special pleasure, in seeing how it can thereby create its own happiness. Previously the self had sought happiness in external things, above all the love of others (the narrator's mother, later Gilberte). But the knowledge that it need not seek out the other, that it can find its happiness by creating it through an act of mind, irradiates the self with a feeling of its own creative power similar to the "illusion de fécondité" described earlier. To go beyond the impression of an image or an odor, then, becomes equivalent to going beyond the experience of a moment to a form of pure consciousness. Thus the apprehension that captures the essence of a moment becomes also the means of ultimately transcending it.

The subsequent description of the narrator's experience by a youthful Marcel reveals in some sense the limitations of "literature"—specifically its power to recapture an impression. Clearly the young Marcel's account is quite "literary." For this reason, it fails to render his actual impression. By personifying the appearance of the towers, for instance, his description neglects to notice his own experience in perceiving them. Accordingly, there is no mention of his exact sensations nor of their effect on him. What is omitted is the felt experience of phenomena, an experience whose apprehension transcends time. By disregarding what actually happens to him, the youthful Marcel refuses to enter into the whole question of time and its relation to experience. Consequently, a genuine transcendence of time through lived experience becomes impossible. What occurs instead is only an apparent transcendence: by equating his impression with a figural symbolism, the young Marcel attempts to preserve it by elevating it to the realm of formal motifs. In the process, however, he distorts his impression. Since that impression is essentially temporal, in equating it with an image or motif he abolishes its temporal aspect. Thus the description of his impression ceases to represent experience, becoming instead a mere "transposition" of it.

By personifying his impression, the youthful Marcel attempts to ascribe to it an immediate meaning. The failure of his attempt is revealing. In equating his impression with various motifs, he seeks to

embody its significance within something that is itself expressive. Thus
the meaning of the original impression is made to depend upon that
of a personification. Yet this personification might not be any more
meaningful than what it personifies. The "transposition" also over-
looks the fact that the original impression had not disclosed any particular meaning, offering instead only a more general experience of
significance. Here the form of the experience is suggestive. Were each
of the motifs (i.e., each of the towers) individually expressive of something, what they express would consist of a specific meaning which
would then be grasped by the narrator. But if the narrator fails to
discover a specific meaning in the individual motifs, this can only suggest that their meaning lies in their relation to each other. That relation, in turn, makes possible the "architectonic" arrangement of his
experiences.

The formation of this architectonic arrangement defines the movement of Proust's whole novel. But the movement of the *Recherche* is
exemplified even within the present episode, since what it offers is, in
effect, two "impressions" of the same scene, brought into architectonic
relation with each other. By juxtaposing these two impressions the
narrative illuminates both: each acquires new significance through its
relation to the other. In attempting to formulate the meaning of Marcel's impression, the youthful account anticipates a quest that will gov-
ern the entire *Recherche,* while the later version reveals the means by
which the narrator finally arrives at an insight enabling him to perceive
the relation between different moments of his existence. Without the
earlier account, the significance of his later insight would remain unclear, while absence of this insight leaves his earlier search for meaning
unfulfilled. By juxtaposing his two impressions, the narrative reveals
an inherent architectonic structure in time, through which a later moment elucidates an earlier one. But in forming part of that structure,
each moment manifests the assimilation of life to form.

We have seen how Marcel's earlier description had sought to ascribe
meaning to an impression through personification. It begins with a
glimpse of the church towers of Martinville from a distance: "Seuls,
s'élevant du niveau de la plaine et comme perdus en rase campagne,
montaient vers le ciel les deux clochers de Martinville" (1:179). [Alone,
elevating themselves from the level of the plain and as if lost in the
expanse of open country, the two church towers of Martinville rose
toward the sky.] We know from the narrator's remarks on Stendhal
in *La Prisonnière* how altitude becomes associated for Proust with spirituality. But if a "feeling of altitude" is equated with spirituality, the

movement toward a greater height implies spiritual aspiration. In the present passage it manifests itself in a delicate personification of the towers of Martinville ("s'élevant du niveau de la plaine," "montaient vers le ciel"). Ultimately personification becomes symbolism, by endowing the towers with something like a consciousness of their own act:

> Bientôt nous en vîmes trois: venant se placer en face d'eux par une volte hardie, un clocher retardataire, celui de Vieuxvicq, les avait rejoints. Les minutes passaient, nous allions vite et pourtant les trois clochers étaient toujours au loin devant nous, comme trois oiseaux posés sur la plaine, immobiles et qu'on distingue au soleil. (1:179)

> [Soon we saw three: placing itself opposite them by a bold leap, a dilatory church tower, that of Vieuxvicq, had joined them. The minutes passed, we were traveling quickly, and yet the three towers were always a long way in front of us, like three birds perched upon the plain, motionless and conspicuous in the sunlight.]

Compared with the narrator's later "impression," his juxtaposition of the towers in this youthful version yields no aesthetic pleasure. Here the illusion that makes the three towers seem to stand next to each other is attributed not to a shift in perspective but to a personified will in the tower of Vieuxvicq, which by a "bold leap" joins the others. Whereas the later juxtaposition results from a creative perception connecting different experiences, the personification that ascribes "will" to a tower displays no recognition of the creative capacity within itself. Consequently there can be no moment of illumination (*ensoleillement*), no moment in which awareness of the eternism of an impression floods the visible object with its own radiance. This moment of consecration occurs when the mind recognizes its own capacity to transform its impression into something eternal. For the youthful Marcel, that moment never arrives: the sunlight which illuminates the spires of Martinville is perceived only *after* the tower of Vieuxvicq has "withdrawn" from its magical juxtaposition with the others.

Thus the illumination of the towers becomes simply an aspect of their personification: "Puis le clocher de Vieuxvicq s'écarta, prit ses distances, et les clochers de Martinville restèrent seuls, éclairés par la lumière du couchant que même à cette distance, sur leurs pentes, je voyais jouer et sourire" (1:179). [Then the tower of Vieuxvicq withdrew, took up its distance, and the towers of Martinville remained alone, illuminated by the light of the setting sun which even at that distance I could see playing and smiling on their sloping sides.] Here emphasis remains upon the towers rather than on the sunlight that transfigures them: the radiance (*ensoleillement*) is absent from a youthful description which appears unconscious of the inherent splendor of experience.

But perhaps the muted quality of the earlier account, its lack of an epiphany, comes from subordinating its motifs to the lyrical evocation of "three maidens" of a legend, to whom Marcel compares the three towers:

> Ils me faisaient penser aussi aux trois jeunes filles d'une légende, abandonnées dans une solitude où tombait déjà l'obscurité; et tandis que nous nous éloignions au galop, je les vis timidement chercher leur chemin et après quelques gauches trébuchements de leurs nobles silhouettes, se serrer les uns contre les autres, glisser l'un derrière l'autre, ne plus faire sur le ciel encore rose qu'une seule forme noire, charmante et résignée, et s'effacer dans la nuit. (1:179–80)

> [They made me think too of three maidens in a legend, abandoned in a solitary place where darkness had begun to fall; and as we distanced ourselves from them at a gallop, I saw them timidly seeking their way and, after a few awkward, stumbling movements of their noble silhouettes, drawing close to one another, gliding behind one another, forming against the still-rosy sky no more than a single dark shape, charming and resigned, and vanishing into the night.]

Everything now becomes a matter of mood and tone, as color assumes the form of a chromatic harmony of black against the fading rose tint of twilight. The harmony deepens with the failing light, even as a musical harmony deepens by prolonging the sounds composing it. With the gradual merging of the silhouettes, moreover, Proust evokes the musical effect of a resolution of dissonances as the "trébuchements" blend at last into a single impression. The final effacement of the figures moves even closer to the nature of music in being a development that unfolds progressively through time. Thus Marcel's youthful description, though "retardataire" in crucial respects compared to his later version, already begins to explore the problem that will ultimately be left to music: how to express our apprehension of the passing of time as representing the essential condition of our existence.

3

Sometime around the middle of World War I Proust appears to have attended a concert at the Théâtre de l'Odéon. A group of young musicians known as the Poulet Quartet had performed that night with the composer Gabriel Fauré at the piano. Impressed by the playing of the quartet (especially that of the violist, Amable Massis), Proust had asked Fauré to introduce him to the quartet members after the concert. Subsequently he wrote to Massis, inviting him to come to see him at boulevard Haussmann. A first interview led to several others. Soon after the war, Proust expressed a desire to have the quartet perform César Franck's quartet for him at his new apartment in rue Hamelin. The musicians signified their willingness in principle, and after some conferences to secure the best possible conditions for the performance, arrived on the appointed night. The quartet was played in Proust's salon, with the musicians placed in the middle of the room and Proust lying down on a long reclining chair, listening with his eyes closed. When they had finished, he asked them politely if they would be willing to play a certain portion of the work again. They complied; when they were done, he thanked them warmly and accompanied them out into the night—presumably in order to ask further questions about the work.[12]

The anecdote contains numerous elements characteristic of the *Recherche:* the work heard at a public concert which gives rise to a spiritual awakening in the listener (Swann hearing the Vinteuil sonata for the first time), the solicitation of private hearings (Charlus having Beethoven's late quartets played for himself), the inspiration of music for literature, and, finally, the imperious politeness that insists on having a piece performed over and over again so as to grasp the secret of its effect, the mysterious appeal of its theme—which, because of the nature of the music, can at first only be experienced without being understood (Swann attempting to analyze the theme from the Andante of the Vinteuil sonata, and later, having Odette play it for him over and over again). In some sense, all these instances point to the relationship between music and time. Because of its temporal nature, a work of music cannot be apprehended all at once in its entirety. Instead we assimilate it in and through time. Thus our experience of it becomes like that of our actual existence, since each "moment" of a piece, like time itself, cannot be arrested or preserved (hence the desire to hear a work privately, or even repeatedly, as a means of retaining it better). The experience of music reproduces our experience of time.

To grasp the essence of that experience becomes tantamount, then, to understanding time and correspondingly the nature of our existence.

We have seen how the "église" motif gives rise to perception of an architectonic relation between different moments. Such relations, however, exist outside of time, and hence fail to touch upon our actual lives. In order to become more meaningful, art must somehow express our experience of time. But this experience of time occurs in its purest form in music.[13] For Proust, each musical theme or phrase embodies a particular emotion. In hearing a musical work we experience a sequence of emotions. But since the same emotions make up our existence, we arrive through listening at a sense of our own life as a sequence of moments of suffering and passion. In the process, we become aware of a higher meaning than any within our emotions. It springs from a recognition that the moments in which they occur form a sequence expressive of an inner movement that governs the succession of those emotions. Thus we perceive the meaning of emotion not in its intensity or passion but in the idea of pure sequence it evokes.[14] Transposed, this idea becomes the intuition that all the moments of our existence might form an ideal sequence and in so doing convey some higher meaning which we ourselves, in living and suffering each individual moment as it occurs in time, are prevented from grasping. Through music, however, we receive a glimpse of it.

The treatment of music in the *Recherche* begins with Swann's introduction to the Vinteuil sonata.[15] Swann's first impression is of a sensuous chaos: "D'abord, il n'avait goûté que la qualité matérielle des sons sécrétés par les instruments" (1:205). [At first he had perceived only the material quality of the sounds secreted by the instruments.][16] Nothing assumes yet any definite form. Even so, the impression yields a particular pleasure:

> Et ç'avait déjà été un grand plaisir quand, au-dessous de la petite ligne du violon, mince, resistante, dense et directrice, il avait vu tout d'un coup chercher à s'élever en un clapotement liquide, la masse de la partie de piano, multiforme, indivise, plane et entrechoquée comme la mauve agitation des flots que charme et bémolise le clair de lune. (1:205)

> [And it had already been a great pleasure when, below the delicate line of the violin, thin, resistant, dense and directing, he had suddenly perceived the mass of the piano part seeking to elevate itself in a liquid wash of sound, multiform, indivisible, smooth yet clashing like the mauve agitation of waves charmed and transformed into flat notes by the moonlight.]

Earlier the "overture" had commenced with a similar chaos of the senses. As a result of falling asleep, the narrator experiences impressions which are both vivid and confusing. Yet the chaotic ferment of sleep had been creative, yielding the three motifs governing the subsequent development of the *Recherche*. Here the chaos with which Swann's impressions begin presents a similar creative ferment. The impressions themselves are confused and contradictory: the violin line is at once "thin" and "delicate" (*petite*), yet "resistant, dense and directing," while the "mass" of the piano part appears both "multiform" and "indivisible," "smooth" yet "clashing." But even here there are already signs of an effort to interpret these phenomena. Thus the narrative attempts to ascribe a volition to the different instruments: the violin line is "directing," while the piano part "attempts to elevate itself" in a liquid wash of sound. And perhaps this creative ferment is what gives rise ultimately to the element of synesthesia at the end of the passage, comparing the surge of keyboard sound to the "mauve agitation of waves charmed and transformed into flat notes by the moonlight." The "mauve agitation of waves" introduces an element of color, while the transformation of these waves into flat notes (i.e., "flats" as opposed to "sharps") reverses the movement from the visual back to the tonal. The irresoluteness of the movement reflects the confusion of Swann's impressions, but the synesthesia is indicative of a desire on his part to relate one set of phenomena to another and thus impart form to what he perceives.

At this moment the perception of something like a theme first occurs:

Mais à un moment donné, sans pouvoir nettement distinguer un contour, donner un nom à ce qui lui plaisait, charmé tout d'un coup, il avait cherché à recueillir la phrase ou l'harmonie—il ne savait lui-même—qui passait et qui lui avait ouvert plus largement l'âme, comme certaines odeurs de roses circulant dans l'air humide du soir ont la propriété de dilater nos narines. Peut-être est-ce parce qu'il ne savait pas la musique qu'il avait pu éprouver une impression aussi confuse, une de ces impressions qui sont peut-être pourtant les seules purement musicales, inétendues, entièrement originales, irréductibles à tout autre ordre d'impressions. Une impression de ce genre, pendant un instant, est pour ainsi dire *sine materia*. (1:205–6)

[But at a given moment, without being able to distinguish clearly a contour or to give a name to what had pleased him, charmed all of a sudden, he had sought to capture the phrase or harmony—he himself did not know which—that was passing and had opened up his soul more largely, as certain odors of roses circulating in the humid evening air have the property of dilating our nostrils. Perhaps it was because he did not know music that he was able to feel an impression so confused, one of those impressions that are perhaps nevertheless the only purely musical ones, without extension, entirely original, irreducible to any other order of impressions. An impression of this sort, for an instant, is so to speak *sine materia.*]

What emerges most clearly so far is that music consists above all of impressions. Thus Swann finds himself unable to distinguish what he hears as either phrase or harmony because he perceives it simply as musical sound. All we know is how it affects him: like "certain odors of roses circulating in the humid evening air." He receives from it an almost physical sensation, which only emphasizes the resemblance between his present musical impression and various sensory or material phenomena. "Perhaps," the narrator suggests, "it was because he did not know music that he could feel an impression so confused." Yet immediately afterward such impressions are qualified as the only ones of a "purely musical" kind. Had Swann been a musician, in other words, he would no doubt have seen the music in terms of phrases and harmonies, of thematic development—but this would be to reduce it to a schema of spatial relations which no longer embodies the essence of music. That essence, as we have seen, consists of what we experience in hearing it. Hence it cannot be assimilated to any other order of impressions, including the sense of spatial form that comes from a technical knowledge of music. The impression one receives is also "without extension" (*inétendues*) and *sine materia*. It exists within the mind alone. Nevertheless it remains simply an impression—what the mind experiences on hearing certain sounds in a specific sequence.

But if hearing music signifies a particular form of experience, the mind naturally seeks some way to retain it:

Sans doute les notes que nous entendons alors, tendent déjà, selon leur hauteur et leur quantité, à couvrir devant nous yeux des surfaces de dimensions variées, à tracer des arabesques, à nous donner des sensations de largeur, de ténuité, de stabilité, de caprice. Mais les notes sont évanouies avant que ces sensations soient assez formées en nous pour ne pas être submergées par celles qu'éveillent déjà les notes suivantes ou même simultanées. Et cette impression continuerait à envelopper de sa liquidité et de son "fondu" les motifs qui par instants en émergent, à peine discernables, pour plonger aussitôt et disparaître, connus seulement par le plaisir particulier qu'ils donnent, impossibles à décrire, à se rappeler, à nommer, ineffables—si la mémoire, comme un ouvrier qui travaille à établir des fondations durables au milieu des flots, en fabriquant pour nous des fac-similés de ces phrases fugitives, ne nous permettait de les comparer à celles qui leur succèdent et de les différencier. (1:206)

[Doubtless the notes we then hear tend already, according to their pitch and quantity, to cover before our eyes surfaces of varying dimensions, to trace arabesques, to give us sensations of breadth, tenuity, stability, caprice. But the notes have disappeared before these sensations become sufficiently formed in us not to be submerged by those already awakened by succeeding or even simultaneous notes. And this impression would continue to envelop in its liquidity and its "blending" the motifs that momentarily emerge, barely discernible, to plunge as quickly and disappear, known only by the special pleasure they give, impossible to describe, to recall, to name, ineffable—if memory, like a laborer who works to lay down durable foundations in the midst of the waves, by fabricating for us facsimiles of these fugitive phrases, did not permit us to compare them with those that follow and to differentiate them.]

Like other external phenomena, the notes we hear produce certain impressions in us ("arabesques," but also sensations of breadth, tenuity, stability, caprice). These impressions, in turn, form experiences. But, like all experiences, they are evanescent: no sooner does a sensation occur than it is "submerged" by those that succeed it. And thus we encounter in the realm of music the same problem we have already found in life: how to preserve the experience of a particular moment from the constant passage of time. Unlike the architectonic structure evoked earlier, music reproduces in its sequence our experience of time, in which motifs do not normally rise above the temporal flow (or if so, only briefly). In attempting to preserve them the mind confronts the problem of temporality. Because of its nature, music precludes the possibility of retaining the experience of an individual moment. Instead the listener is compelled to recognize time itself as the essence of music. In so doing, he or she no longer contends with the "liquidity" or "blending" (*fondu*) of impressions, their tendency to dissolve into the temporal sequence. By acknowledging that tendency, the listener comes to realize how our experience of time offers a medium for our apprehension of music. But the experience of time in music becomes meaningful only if we can discern some distinction or resemblance between one moment and another. Without such discrimination, it becomes impossible to retain anything of those moments. But all our perceptions—and consequently any possibility of meaning—depend in turn upon memory.

By drawing up a rapid "schema" of a musical work, memory makes possible the discernment of a pattern:

> Ainsi à peine la sensation délicieuse que Swann avait ressentie était-elle expirée, que sa mémoire lui en avait fourni séance tenante une transcription sommaire et provisoire, mais sur laquelle il avait jeté les yeux tandis que le morceau continuait, si bien que, quand la même impression était tout d'un coup revenue, elle n'était déjà plus insaisissable. Il s'en représentait l'étendue, les groupements symétriques, la graphie, la valeur expressive; il avait devant lui cette chose qui n'est plus de la musique pure, qui est du dessin, de l'architecture, de la pensée, et qui permet de se rappeler la musique. Cette fois il avait distingué nettement une phrase s'élevant pendant quelques instants au-dessus des ondes sonores. Elle lui avait proposé aussitôt des voluptés particulières, dont il n'avait jamais eu l'idée avant de l'entendre, dont il sentait que rien autre qu'elle ne pourrait les lui faire connaître, et il avait éprouvé pour elle comme un amour inconnu. (1:206)

> [Thus, scarcely had the delicious sensation Swann experienced died away than his memory had furnished him on the spot with a transcription, summary and provisional, but upon which he had been able to cast a glance while the piece continued, so that when the same impression returned all of a sudden it was no longer ungraspable. He represented to himself its extent, symmetrical groupings, notation, and expressive value; he had before him this thing which was no longer pure music, which was drawing, architecture, thought, and which permits one to recall the music. This time he had clearly distinguished a phrase elevating itself for a few seconds above the sonorous waves. It had at once proposed to him particular pleasures which he had never had a conception of before hearing it, which he felt nothing other than the phrase could have made known to him, and he felt for it something like an unknown form of love.]

It hardly matters that the "transcription" is only "summary and provisional." Nor does memory seek to capture our actual sensations. To do so would mean reliving the same moment, which is impossible. By seeking to transcribe rather than re-create its experience, memory acknowledges this impossibility. In making use of a "transcription" it attempts to circumvent the transience of individual moments. Because our experiences occur in time, we cannot retain them: the nature of each experience lies precisely in being superseded by another. But were we wholly absorbed in our experiences, it would be impossible to save anything from them: each moment would consist entirely of our experience of that moment, without the possibility of recalling or comparing it with anything else. To avoid being drawn into the abyss of pure experience, the mind must represent its moments in another form. Hence the "extent, the symmetrical groupings, the notation, the expressive value" that Swann ascribes to his impressions of the Vinteuil sonata. Music thus becomes "drawing, architecture, thought"—whatever makes possible a remembrance of music by transforming it into something other than pure experience. By preserving a "transcription" memory can then re-create our actual experience of a musical work in different terms based on that transcription. In this fashion the mind attempts to overcome the problem posed by the transience of our impressions.

What the transcription of an experience makes possible is the recognition of a sensation when it recurs. Recognition of a sensation's recurrence gives form to our experience of time by establishing a relation between different moments. Unlike the architectonic relation of the Martinville episode, however, the relation that arises through such recognition results directly from a temporal experience. Whereas the earlier architectonic perception had implied a transcendence of time, the present recognition occurs precisely because of the temporal sequence of our perceptions. As a result, we perceive the second sensation as a recurrence of the first.[17] Thus the relation between the two sensations is a profoundly temporal one. It consists of a perception of the nature of time itself, and the presence within it of something like form. Here the recognition of a relation assumes a deeper significance. Because it is created out of the very process by which we experience time, it represents an apprehension of the essential nature of time. But it also signifies the mind's capacity to triumph over the fleeting or transient quality of our experiences. In recognizing the recurrence of a sensation, the mind arrives at a perception that in some sense perdures—hence one transcending the duration of the experiences themselves.

In being based upon these experiences, the transcendence of time embodied in Swann's recognition possesses a different quality from that of Marcel's architectonic perception at Martinville. Whereas the form of Marcel's perception depends upon a denial of time (equivalent to a denial of the distance between the towers of Martinville and Vieuxvicq), the form in Swann's recognition of a relation between his sensations corresponds to an intrinsic form in our experience of time. Unlike the earlier architectonic perception, this recognition is in fact part of the temporal sequence of our experiences. As a perception of the recurrence of a sensation, it occurs only when the actual sensation recurs. We "experience" it, then, at the same moment as the actual sensation. But in addition the recognition itself, as a perception of *recurrence,* specifically concerns the relation of one experience to another in time. Thus we perceive recurrence only through our experience of time. It is as if some moment of our life were to be repeated, allowing us not only to recapture our original sensation (thereby transcending time by recovering what was lost) but also to perceive the relation of that moment to others and hence the nature of our whole existence as a temporal sequence.

But if our experience of the passage of time manifests an inherent form, this in turn implies the presence of form in our existence, which consists in large part of our awareness of time. By making such an experience possible, music presents an analogy to our existence.[18] It thus becomes endowed with symbolic significance. Recognizing a phrase from the Vinteuil sonata, Swann experiences a renewal of his original impression of it. "Elevating itself for a few seconds above the sonorous waves," this phrase possesses for him a mysterious and irresistible appeal. It inspires a recognition of form within the work that symbolically becomes, through the relation of music to life, a perception of form or sequence and hence of meaning within his whole existence. If that insight discloses the prospect of "particular pleasures" ("des voluptés particulières"), however, these pleasures (like Baudelaire's "volupté") will be aesthetic rather than sensual. The "unknown form of love" ("un amour inconnu") Swann now feels arises from a sense of spiritual awakening. Through his recognition of form in music, he receives a glimpse of something like the meaning of time, which consists of our arriving at a perception of form in our actual existence.

At present, nevertheless, that perception remains concealed from him. For Swann it appears contained somehow within the mysterious phrase that had transformed his awareness. Like Marcel's impressions earlier, this phrase now assumes, by means of a delicate personification, a suggestive air:

D'un rythme lent elle le dirigeait ici d'abord, puis là, puis ailleurs, vers un bonheur noble, inintelligible et précis. Et tout d'un coup, au point où elle était arrivée et d'où il se préparait à la suivre,

après une pause d'un instant, brusquement elle changeait de direction et d'un mouvement nouveau, plus rapide, menu, melan-
colique, incessant et doux, elle l'entraînait avec elle vers des perspectives inconnues. Puis elle disparut. Il souhaita passionnément
la revoir une troisième fois. Et elle reparut en effet mais sans lui
parler plus clairement, en lui causant même une volupté moins
profonde. Mais rentré chez lui il eut besoin d'elle, il était comme
un homme dans la vie de qui une passante qu'il a aperçue un
moment vient de faire entrer l'image d'une beauté nouvelle qui
donne à sa propre sensibilité une valeur plus grande, sans qu'il
sache seulement s'il pourra revoir jamais celle qu'il aime déjà et
dont il ignore jusqu'au nom. (1:207)

[With a slow rhythm it directed him first here, then there, then
somewhere else, toward a noble, unintelligible and precise happiness. Then all of a sudden, from the point at which it had
arrived and from which he was preparing to follow it, after an
instant's pause, it abruptly changed direction, and with a new
movement, more rapid, slender, melancholy, incessant and sweet,
it drew him along with it toward unknown perspectives. Then
it disappeared. He longed passionately to see it a third time. And
it reappeared in effect, but without speaking to him more clearly,
causing him even a pleasure less profound. But, having returned
home, he had need of it: he was like a man into whose life a
woman passing by, whom he has seen for a moment, has just
introduced the image of a new beauty that gives to his own sensibility a greater value, without his even knowing if he can ever
see again the one whom he already loves and of whom he does
not know even the name.]

As with Marcel's earlier impressions, the "personification" of a motif results from its manifesting something like will or volition. Thus
the phrase "directs" Swann's movements toward a specific goal. But
just as he is about to reach it, the phrase "abruptly" changes its course.
Since in doing so it has no apparent rationale, one tends to ascribe
the change to something like an individual will. In drawing him along
toward "unknown perspectives" it appears without either plan or purpose. And its subsequent abrupt disappearance seems purely capri-
cious. By leading him first to one point, then another, however, the
phrase progressively increases the fascination it exerts over him. Finally, by a movement well known in the analysis of desire, it intensifies
his longing to possess it to a culminating point through its disappearance. The personification then comes to its climax with an allusion

to Baudelaire's "À une passante," the symbolic figure who transforms
the poet's consciousness by embodying a fleeting glimpse of the beautiful.

In this fashion, by almost imperceptible degrees, the description of
a musical sequence modulates into an evocation of the subsequent history of Swann's love for Odette, and later the narrator's for Albertine.
Like the phrase from the Vinteuil sonata, each of these women becomes in turn the elusive object of desire, "la fugitive," who reveals
to the protagonist an image of the beautiful that transforms his consciousness of existence. What the narrative seeks to present here however is not primarily a foreshadowing of subsequent developments.
Swann of course has no knowledge of what is to come, but more
significantly even the narrator's awareness remains muted—as if recognition of the resemblance between Swann's quest for the elusive
phrase and the later loves of Swann and the narrator must be deferred
until the moment these passions are actually felt. In that sense the
process of recognition in the *Recherche* conforms to its experience of
time. But the silent shift from description of the Vinteuil sonata to
the analysis of desire suggests that the inner movement which governs
all the moments of our existence is in effect like that of music: a sequence of emotions expressive of form. Thus everything Swann or the
narrator will later discover in love finds its meaning not in their emotions but in the sequence into which they fall. Perception of that sequence makes it possible to transcend the suffering caused by these
emotions. Through its perception the mind arrives ultimately at an
apprehension of the nature of time, and hence of our existence. By
discovering form even within our experience of time, we become aware
of the sequence of our moments as symbolically expressive. Yet the
meaning of such moments lies finally not in a transcendence of time
but rather in experiencing it. And this meaning is itself a creation of
time.

4

Toward the end of the *Recherche* we notice how scenes occur with
increasing frequency at night.[19] Night: the hours when darkness ob-
scures everything with its fine mist, making objects that had previously
seemed quite clear difficult even to see. Thus night becomes a time of
confusion, when impressions formed during the day are strangely re-
versed as things present hitherto-unnoticed aspects, with appearances
dissolving in an uncertain half-light. In *Le Temps retrouvé* the period
following the narrator's return to Paris after many years in a sanato-

rium opens with a scene at night. Events now seem to move at an accelerated pace: the narrator has lost touch with the passage of time.[20] Ultimately there is the sense of an ending, with its visible signs of aging and death. A certain scene recurs: the narrator meets someone for the last time at twilight or at night. When he next hears of them, it is from someone else who announces their death.

But if the confusion of nighttime parallels that of the "overture" in some respects, it carries nevertheless a quite different meaning. The failure to keep up with the pace of time, like the failure to apprehend what is taking place, indicates a decline in the capacities of consciousness. We see this in *Le Temps retrouvé* in a scene in which the narrator, feeling thirsty, enters a hotel which Saint-Loup appears to be leaving—the same hotel where, on the same night, the narrator also discovers Charlus engaged in sadomasochistic practices. But he cannot be sure whether the departing figure was really Saint-Loup, and the meaning of what he subsequently overhears in the hotel remains obscure to him as well. Its obscurity seems to result from a failure to comprehend, as if the darkness that prevents him from seeing Saint-Loup clearly were expressive of some inner twilight in which the mind no longer recognizes what it once knew. In another sense, the narrator also fails to "recognize" Charlus, who appears in an unexpected role. The whole scene acquires a phantasmagoric quality, as of some dream in which certain aspects of a person are revealed in particularly lurid fashion while others remain hidden in darkness. The declining condition of consciousness is indicated by the shock the narrator receives from seeing Saint-Loup and later Charlus—a shock caused by the mind's inability to assimilate what it perceives, so that its perceptions become exaggerated or distorted. Thus the narrator's encounter with Charlus is glaringly exposed, while his glimpse of Saint-Loup slips away into the realm of the half-seen.

But even what is exposed cannot, because of its very nature, be clearly seen: the narrator "metaphorizes" his perception of Charlus, scourged, bloody, and covered with bruises (showing that what the narrator sees is not occurring for the first time), by comparing him to the mythical Prometheus—and in so doing distances himself from what he cannot bear. Above all, the mind's inability to assimilate its impressions is expressed through the experience of obscurity—of hearing conversations one doesn't understand (where the reasons for one's not understanding remain unclear), or seeing figures or faces one cannot distinguish, without knowing why. But that is precisely what the experience of obscurity consists of: our not knowing why something should be obscure. Here the sense of obscurity anticipates death, which marks the final extinction of consciousness. At that point the mind ceases even to ask why something should be obscure.

In one of her letters to the narrator after leaving him, Albertine also anticipates this ultimate moment:

> Je suis très touchée que vous ayez gardé un bon souvenir de notre dernière promenade. Croyez que de mon côté je n'oublierai pas cette promenade deux fois crépusculaire (puisque la nuit venait et que nous allions nous quitter) et qu'elle ne s'effacera de mon esprit qu'avec la nuit complète. (3:468)

> [I am very touched that you should have kept a happy memory of our last drive. Believe that for my part I shall not forget this doubly crepuscular drive (since night was falling and we were about to part) and that it will not be effaced from my mind until the night is complete.]

The narrator immediately doubts the sincerity of her sentiment—which only emphasizes its thematic importance. "That you should have kept a happy memory" ("que vous ayez gardé un bon souvenir")—how important it is, in retrospect, that the narrator should preserve this episode in his memory, since in fact he will never see Albertine again. Her words imply the distance between them: what he possesses now is no longer Albertine herself but only his remembrance of her. Nor does she consider the possibility of returning to him. Hence the wish, and perhaps even the desire, that he should possess her in another way, through memory.[21] The drive is described as "doubly crepuscular" because night is imminent and the lovers about to part from each other. What does this mean? What else but that the time after their separation must be construed as a kind of night? Yet we know from what follows that night is associated with death. Hence separation too becomes a form of death. But death "effaces" everything: as Albertine tells the narrator, the memory of their last drive will not be "effaced" from her mind until night becomes complete. In a similar if less drastic fashion, their separation also "effaces" the memory of Albertine for the narrator.

The form such effacement assumes is that of oblivion or forgetfulness—"l'oubli" in the Proustian sense. Like death, forgetfulness represents an inescapable condition of our existence. Thus we find ourselves in the constant process of losing those we love to oblivion.[22] In *La Fugitive*, Albertine's desertion of the narrator typifies its material equivalent. It symbolizes the tendency of all experience toward its own ultimate self-effacement. Since each moment yields a new experience, we cannot normally retain past moments in the form of experiences. But that is precisely the problem: we cannot continue to experience a past moment. To do so, of course, would make it impossible to assimilate its successor. But in fact each moment brings with it new phenomena, which in turn necessarily result in new experiences. Thus the past moment becomes a memory, which marks the beginning of its self-effacement. In no longer experiencing it, we cease to feel an immediate response to it, thereby diminishing the intensity of its presence. But in sensing the transient quality of all moments, the self seeks to retain its past, as a means of preserving the pleasure of each moment. Hence the narrator's passionate desire to recover Albertine after her departure.

This desire to possess Albertine can help explain both the narrator's earlier emotion and his attempt to recapture it now. Previously, desire had been associated with her physical presence, which by itself had sufficed to induce in him the emotion he had sought. When she deserts him, the feeling that presses upon him most strongly is his almost physical need of her: he finds it difficult to go to sleep without her, everything in his room reminds him of her as he recalls the habits of their life together. His inability to recover her only symbolizes more expressively the impossibility of recapturing the literal past. To be sure, the ultimate form of this would be to experience the same physical sensations he had felt before. But that is precisely what cannot be done: to do so would involve nothing less than recreating all the conditions of the past, including what he himself was at that time. Thus our physical sensations form the most elusive aspect of our past. Of the narrator's various love relationships (Mme de Guermantes, Gilberte, Albertine), it is no accident that the one with Albertine should cause him to feel most strongly the tendency of the past toward oblivion, since this relationship—more than any of the others—had been based upon physical attraction. As the object of his desire, Albertine becomes "la fugitive" following her separation from him and even more so after her death. Her absence creates a void that must somehow be filled, dependent as the narrator has become upon her physical presence. In pursuing her, he pursues in reality his lost self, the emotion Albertine embodies for him.

After her death this pursuit takes place through time instead of space.[23] In his obsession with her secret thoughts and emotions, his compulsive desire to know about her clandestine sexual relations with others, the narrator seeks to recover his own past self through her. The impossibility of obtaining reliable information from her during her life with him, coupled with his physical need of her, had induced earlier a satisfaction of desire through sexual love. Now, unable to possess her physically, he attempts to possess her emotionally. Hence his jealousy of Andrée and others close to her. Yet this jealousy assumes a peculiar form (including among other things a desire for Andrée's presence, as a reminder of Albertine). More revealing is the narrator's wish to tell Albertine what he believes he now knows of her sexual liaisons after his conversations with Andrée. To know what Albertine had sought to deny him (knowledge of her affairs) can convey a feeling of possession. Yet that feeling becomes real only through the "experience" of possession—what he would feel by seeing Albertine's response to his telling her what he now knows. Her response would give reality to what he knows by showing the effect his knowledge has on her. And the reality of his knowledge of her implies the reality of his possession of her. Yet his quest for her ends in failure because of the unknowability of the other: after all his investigations, the narrator realizes at last the impossibility of knowing the "real" Albertine. And without knowing her it is impossible emotionally to possess her.[24]

Here we encounter again the fundamental problem of recovering a past emotion. To experience that emotion once more—as opposed to merely "remembering" it—implies confronting the object that had caused the original emotion.[25] In physical or psychological terms, then, the object of the narrator's quest remains the same.[26] One might say that his problem results from the impossibility of recovering an external other (whether as physical presence or self) from whom he has been separated through time. But what does this really mean, if not that he is separated from the object through *himself,* through what he has experienced after last encountering that object—since, from a Proustian perspective, time is nothing more than a succession of experiences? And if such is the case, the object one seeks must also be contained within oneself, within the impression of a past moment that one seeks to recover. Thus the recovery of that moment would also bring about a recovery of the object now "lost" in time.

Hence the chance sensation caused by two uneven pavement stones in the courtyard of the Guermantes hôtel suffices to elevate the narrator to a consciousness transcending time, his doubts about his capacity for literary creation, ultimately his fear of death.[27] As a result he experiences the same happiness afforded earlier by a view of trees seen in a drive about Balbec, the sight of the church towers of Martinville, the taste of a madeleine dipped in tea, and many other sensations of which the last works of the composer Vinteuil had seemed to represent a kind of synthesis.[28] His impression now is of intense azure, a refreshing coolness, and dazzling light: Venice. Just as the taste of a madeleine had revived for him his childhood at Combray, so the sensation of uneven pavement stones unexpectedly reawakens his experience of Venice.

The recovery of a past moment of his life fills the narrator with a profound happiness. At first this happiness had seemed to consist solely of the pleasure produced by certain sensations. Because they are so intense, they prevent him temporarily from even identifying the moment at which they originally occurred. Only gradually does he come to recognize them as part of his impression of Venice, as he sees how the sensation of uneven pavement stones had reawakened his memory of the flagstones in the baptistry of St. Mark's. Yet the source of his happiness lies in something more than the pleasure of re-experiencing past sensations. If his experience at the present moment is no less transient than that of an earlier one, the happiness of recovering a past moment must consist of something deeper. In that sense, the quest for Albertine had been misguided: what the narrator had sought could not have been obtained simply from the sensations which had originally given him pleasure. Hence the "enigma of happiness" that he feels the present moment proposing to him. If one can derive pleasure from sensation only by experiencing it, this implies being subject to the transient quality of the moment—as well as the impossibility of preserving its pleasure.

In describing the recovery of a past moment in Venice the narrator observes that the happiness (*félicité*) he felt was the same as that inspired by the reawakening of his childhood impressions of Combray through tasting a madeleine. The difference, "purely material," was merely "in the images evoked." In both instances, a chance sensation had made possible his recovery of an earlier moment. In re-experiencing it, the narrator feels once more all the sensations he had felt before.[29] Consequently the present moment seems identical to his original experience. But if it is actually possible to recover all our past sensations, that recovery implies a transcendence of time: what vanishes at this crucial point is the whole subsequent interval separating a given moment of the past from the present. If time consists of all the experiences contained in each moment, a moment becomes part of the past only when other experiences intervene between it and our present consciousness. In so doing they create that distance between ourselves and our earlier experiences which we refer to as time. Since each experience is connected with those that follow it, to relive a given moment necessitates passing over our experiences of all the intervening moments. Hence the difficulty of re-experiencing a specific moment of the past. To recover the experience of it would mean in effect to annul time, the interval between that moment and the present. With-out such an interval there can be no sense of past time but only an eternal present.

Thus the narrator's experience affirms that the essence of time is not the irrevocable slipping away of each individual moment. Instead there is something deeper even than our feeling of the passage of time. The possibility of re-experiencing a past moment of our life implies the existence of an eternal element in time. In rediscovering our earlier impressions, we are conscious of their existing in some sense outside of time.[30] Clearly they cannot really disappear—otherwise we could not experience them again. Yet in re-experiencing them, we are equally aware of recovering them, which suggests their gradual effacement during the moments we had ceased to feel them. Hence the strange, blissful consciousness that fills us in recapturing a past moment: the disappearance of our sense of time, a luminous awareness of the etern-ism of our impressions, the feeling that we ourselves no longer exist in time. And thus the absence for the narrator of any fear of death, a fear that originates with our awareness of the passing of time.

But re-experiencing an earlier moment implies a danger of con-sciousness's falling into an "abyss" in which it suffers once more all the tensions of the original moment. Unlike mere recollection, the reminiscences of the "mémoire involuntaire" include the specific sen-sations of each moment. These result from the effect of external phe-nomena upon us. Through our own past experiences, we feel the pres-sure of various things: people, places, situations. We need only relive our own past emotions with sufficient intensity, for such things to become real to us once more: the intensity of an emotion which was originally a response to them attests to their reality. And if, experi-encing that intensity again, we come to feel their reality, we risk be-coming subject to the anguish or passion or desire they originally caused us. To do so however would be to re-enter the realm of time.

Nevertheless, the recovery of a past moment had filled the narrator with a mysterious happiness. What he experiences now are no longer external phenomena but his own sensations of them. As a result he does not feel the concern such phenomena had originally caused him. What remains are his own sensations, which themselves assume the role of phenomena. Were the narrator to experience only his past sen-sations, they might produce a different response from before, because of subsequent changes in himself. But these sensations had been con-nected earlier with specific emotions. In experiencing his sensations again the narrator also feels his own past emotions. Thus everything in his original impression of the moment is renewable, except for the external conditions that had made it possible.

What is imperishable in each moment of the past, however, is not sensation but the emotion associated with it. When the narrator re-experiences the intoxicating azure, refreshing coolness, and dazzling light that embody his impression of Venice, what he finds in them is not so much a pleasurable sensation but the emotion that had informed his impression. What he now possesses, nevertheless, is something other than the exact feeling of the original moment. And, through an absence of the concerns affecting that original moment, his new experience comes closer to a state of pure emotion than anything described earlier. Thus it avoids the "abyss" of consciousness that arises from experiencing the past as present.

Originally, the emotion that permeates a moment occurs through our concern with external phenomena. In recovering that emotion without its attendant concerns the narrator is able to perceive the beauty of a past moment.[31] This beauty is nothing other than that of our emotion. For the narrator, feeling an earlier emotion once more induces a transcendent happiness. Yet the original emotion need not have been specifically happy. What enables it to inspire happiness now is simply its being pure emotion.[32] As pure emotion it allows the self to experience a different kind of sensation from anything it might have felt at the original moment. What the self now feels is the *sensation of an emotion*. This sensation consists of experiencing an emotion as though it were something material: it then excites a sensation in us. But since what excites sensation is itself already an emotion, in experiencing it we feel something besides that emotion—the sense, namely, of a plenitude of emotion that comes from experiencing pure emotion. But the experience of pure emotion is nothing other than happiness: the emotion of experiencing pure emotion. From this standpoint the narrator's quest for happiness could conceivably end here, with the discovery of happiness as the experience of pure emotion.

That it does not indicates a transformation of the past moment which occurs when the narrator re-experiences it.[33] We have seen earlier how the moment had affected him as proposing an "enigma of happiness." Its proposal implies the existence of something beyond the happiness he now feels in pure emotion. His glimpse of a transcendent or higher significance begins with a new experience of a past moment. As a result the sensations of that moment are no longer felt as sensations. Perhaps the essence of sensation consists of something like an awareness of our own experiences. In feeling a sensation, we become conscious of the effect of some external phenomenon. The effects of such phenomena occur, of course, within ourselves. Yes we tend to think of those effects as external, assimilating them to the phenomena that cause them. By regarding them as external, in turn, we cease to believe in the possibility of possessing them: instead we ascribe them to external things which we ourselves then attempt to confront or possess. But if these sensations occur within ourselves, they remain capable of being apprehended at any moment. When we apprehend such sensations through something like involuntary memory, we experience them without the external phenomena that originally produced them. As a result, we become conscious of our own apprehension of them. In experiencing our apprehension, we arrive at a feeling of pure consciousness, in which our only sensation is that of our own awareness of an impression.

This apprehension of pure consciousness defines what the narrator refers to as "un peu de temps à l'état pur" (3:872) [a little bit of time in the pure state]. We have seen how the moments of our everyday existence are governed by our feeling of time, which results from our experience of various sensations. Since each sensation occupies a specific duration, it produces the sense of a finite interval of time. But were it possible to experience not the sensation but our awareness of it, we would then feel something like pure time. This experience of our own awareness has no temporal element in it: it exists outside of time. But because the feeling of time results from the experience of a sensation, any experience of that experience would then be one of the very essence of time—the experience, in other words, of our sensation of time, yielding us an apprehension of time itself. Time itself, or time in the pure state, consists then of our experiencing our own consciousness in the act of experiencing a particular sensation. The experience of that sensation creates time, but we realize the essence of time only when we are able to apprehend the process by which time comes into existence. In obtaining a glimpse of that process, however, we also realize how we ourselves are responsible for the creation of time, and how we thereby contain within ourselves the possibility of transcending it.

In recovering the emotion of a past moment, the narrator comes to realize the true meaning of his experience of time. Earlier, when all his impressions had seemed to him merely random or accidental, a chance perception of the towers of Martinville juxtaposed with that of Vieuxvicq had symbolically revealed an "architectonic" relation between two moments transcending the temporal nature of our existence. Later, through hearing the works of the composer Vinteuil (as

Swann had done earlier), the narrator is able to appreciate the beauty
in our experience of time. But it remains for him to recover his earlier
impression of Venice through the sensation of uneven pavement stones
in the courtyard of the Guermantes hôtel in order to perceive the
meaning each moment might have in itself. That meaning will consist
not simply of its relation to other moments, nor of the feeling of time
it yields when experienced as part of a sequence, but rather of the
perception we receive of how even the impressions and sensations of
each moment are themselves part of a sequence which (unlike that of
music) possesses an eternal or perduring existence.

Since each moment consists essentially of an emotion produced by
various sensations, a sequence of moments becomes in effect a sequence of emotions. Were it possible to experience such a sequence,
the result would be equivalent to experiencing the narrator's entire
existence. Yet in one important respect this sequence differs from the
narrator's actual existence. Whereas in his life the emotion of each moment yields to its successor, the apprehension of a sequence implies
the possibility of experiencing each moment's emotion without losing
its predecessor. Only in this fashion does it become possible to experience the emotions of different moments as forming a sequence. As
a result of that experience, these moments assume an expressive significance which surpasses even that of music. Transposed, it reveals
the beauty of each moment of the narrator's existence.

The possibility of re-experiencing a past moment reveals that its
impression must exist in some sense outside of time. If what was experienced at that moment can be re-experienced now, the content of
this impression must consist of something extratemporal. In order for
it to exist, however, it must be experienced by a self. And if the impression is extratemporal, the self that experiences it in both past and present moments must also transcend time. The recognition of that self
had filled the narrator with an ineffable happiness. Yet such happiness
remains fleeting, insofar as this recognition of a self transcending time
is fugitive: it occurs solely with the illumination of the "mémoire involontaire." But if recognition of an implicit self depends upon re-
experiencing a past impression, a self exists in effect only at the moment of re-experiencing its impression. Thus the impression, rather
than the self, figures as most intimately associated with what the narrator calls "l'essence des choses"—the essence of things.

In itself, this essence must consist of something beyond the realm
of phenomena. By attempting to fathom an impression to the bottom
(the process Proust refers to earlier as "sondage") we become aware
of its existence. But because of the subjective nature of consciousness,

our only knowledge of it remains locked within our impressions. An impression consists of sensation and emotion. If sensation gives to our apprehension of something that which the narrator had called "the idea of existence," only the emotion of a past moment can on the other hand preserve our knowledge of this realm's existence.

By itself, sensation cannot perdure in memory. Only its association with an emotion enables us to retain it. Thus the narrator's involuntary memory of Venice presents an inseparable fusion of pleasure, desire, and sensation: a spatial sense of the piazza in relation to the basilica, of the embankment adjacent to the piazza, of the canal next to the embankment, and of the impulse, mixed with and arising from all these views, for a ride on the water. In similar fashion, the involuntary reminiscence of Balbec had combined an early morning view of the sea with the scent of the narrator's bedroom, the sensation of a breeze, a desire for lunch, and a hesitation between various excursion possibilities. Invariably emotion forms a nexus for these physical sensations. Perception, meanwhile, does not remain inert: it immediately leads on to desire, which then becomes subtly interfused with perception itself so that any recollection of our impressions becomes necessarily colored by the emotions that permeate them. What we ultimately seek to recover is the relation of a past moment to our present self, by relating a past moment through emotion to our past self. If memory preserves our impressions only through their relation to the self, however, it seems equally clear from the narrator's experience with the "mémoire involuntaire" that one cannot recover the self directly; it exists essentially as a medium for impressions. Hence emotion becomes our means, through recovery of a past moment, of finally recovering a past self.

The possibility of recovering the impression of even a single moment from one's past implies the possibility, at least, of recapturing all the others. Together these impressions form in effect a sequence of emotions similar to that of music. But the sequence of emotions that defines the narrator's past differs in at least one important respect from a work of music. Whereas in music the notes that make up a phrase can only express an emotion, what the involuntary remembrance of a past moment offers us is that emotion itself. Moreover, the expression of emotion in a musical sequence is purely symbolic, being without those remembered sensations and impressions which, as Proust says, give to our apprehension of something the sense of existence. Without those concomitant sensations and impressions which relate an emotion to a specific moment of our past by making it the embodiment of our response to some particular person or scene, such an emotion can have no meaning for the self: it possesses only an imaginative relation to the movement of our actual existence.

For this reason it had been a mistake for Swann to discern in the Vinteuil sonata only a personal meaning. The one he attempts to ascribe to it is something it cannot, by its very nature, have: since it cannot embody the actual experiences of love and jealousy, the innumerable rendezvous with Odette, the glimpses and half-glimpses of her possible unfaithfulnesses, the scent of lilacs that he always associates with her, the particular "Botticellian" look of her face, and countless other things, it cannot really represent for him the actual meaning of this past epoch of his life (however mistakenly he may believe in its doing so), since that meaning must lie in his impressions of all these things and the emotions contained within those impressions. But if meaning is then contained within the moments themselves, we perceive it only in retrospect. Our experience is like that which the narrator describes whereby certain remembered impressions seem to solicit our attention, as if they contained some hidden truth we were trying to discover, where the effort we make is like that of trying to recall some musical phrase that comes back to us though we have never heard it before and would have to force ourselves to listen to it and transcribe it (3:878). That phrase or tune becomes a kind of leitmotiv of our existence. It expresses a meaning that lies not in itself but in the sequence of emotions that make up our lives. And in that sense it, like music itself, leads to something beyond music: an apprehension of the possible significance contained within the recognition of a sequence in these emotions that is the underlying "theme" of time in our existence.

When we try to recall a musical phrase that comes back to us even though we have never heard it before, we attempt to recognize something we know in a deeper sense despite our not having experienced it. With regard to our impressions, this recognition consists of the feeling that what we are now experiencing possesses a relation to something else, something we are now trying to "recognize." But if to recognize something implies establishing its relation to something we previously knew, how can we have a recognition when we do not even know what we were supposed to have a previous knowledge of? What remains with us nevertheless is the feeling of a relation between our experiences and something we believe we know. This relation itself, then, is what we "recognize."

The feeling of such a relation suggests that there is a correspondence between the experience of a given moment and something we assume (since we are unable to place it among our actual experiences) to have a kind of ideal or transcendent existence. But this correspondence between a given moment and something ideal tends in turn to "spatialize" that moment.[34] Since what is ideal possesses a perduring quality, it obviously cannot be subject to the passage of time. For a given moment to have a relation to something ideal implies that that moment too must have its perduring aspect. If so, however, its existence becomes more "spatial" than temporal: it not only has definite limits (as opposed to our experience of time, in which one moment passes imperceptibly into the next) but its permanence enables it to have fixed relations with other subjects. Thus through its association with an ideal realm, the moment now becomes something permanent and objective.

In searching for the hidden truth behind a particular impression, the narrator compares his efforts specifically to those we make in trying to recall a musical phrase. The nature of such a phrase suggests the idea of a sequence. To be able to recall that phrase, then, would mean perceiving the sequence that governs the moments of the narrator's own existence. But he cannot recall the phrase, which is tantamount to saying he does not perceive the sequence. At the same time, the narrator seems to suggest there is something unbearable about knowing this phrase, that we would have to force ourselves in order to listen to and transcribe it. If the phrase symbolizes the sequence behind all our past moments, to know it would then be to know that all the pleasures of these moments, as well as all their suffering and passion, are not meaningful in themselves: that they exist only on account of the sequence they embody, which dictates both their occurrence and their arrangement. Yet since the sequence consists not of musical notes but of our actual experiences, to know they form an ideal sequence does not ultimately nullify their individual significance. Instead it allows us to know that our passions are meaningful in a deeper sense, since as part of an ideal sequence they transcend time. But perhaps their deepest meaning lies in their sequence. Thus when we recognize an experience as possessing a hidden significance, we perceive it as belonging to such a sequence. What the formation of that sequence by our experiences suggests is that all our emotions have their own supreme reason for being, a reason which is more than simply pleasure or passion. But if our emotions have their reason for being, then our life too, whose sequence they form, must also have its reason for existence. Hence the meaning of our life comes to be in its sequence—which is to say: its occurrence in time.

We have seen how the source of a feeling of mysterious significance in our impressions had remained hidden from the narrator. If he possesses the intuition that his experiences form an ideal sequence, that sequence itself remains nevertheless beyond the reach of intelligence. Thus the ideal sequence consisting of his experiences is one he comes to know only through its occurrence in time. The significance of its occurrence in time is what he now seeks to express through the creation of a work of art.[35] Only by creating a structure that allows him to represent that ideal sequence in its temporal form will it become possible for him to affirm his apprehension of its significance.

Because the source of his experiences remains hidden from him, however, the meaning of those experiences must always suffer from a certain lack or absence, one which could have been filled only by an apprehension of their source. One might describe this as the lack of a sense of divine presence. For Proust it implies the necessity of attempting to realize, through art, the meaning contained in that feeling of presence. Through the depiction of his experiences, the narrator seeks to fulfill the function of presence, which is that of creation. Only by creating his life within a work of art can he attain what was given to him in his epiphanic experiences of the towers of Martinville or of the trees of Balbec: the sense of creation, of ushering into existence that which becomes meaningful through its occurrence in time. In re-creating the moments of his past life, the narrator causes the emotions of those moments to exist again. But their coming into existence again is not simply their resurrection from the past: on account of the narrative structure that is the *Recherche,* they must enter once more into the realm of time. Yet the time into which they now enter differs in a crucial respect from that of their original occurrence. Whereas that earlier time had been merely a medium through which the narrator's experiences had come to him, the time in which they now occur offers the closest approximation to a transcendent ideal sequence that art is capable of.

We have seen how the reconciliation of emotion with form had posed the fundamental problem of the Aesthetic quest. In passing into form, our experiences cease to be what they were: the sensations and impressions of our actual existence. But if the intellectualization of our sensations renders them incapable of offering us the vivid and moving appeal of our human experiences, it makes possible on the other hand an apprehension of something that transcends our suffering and our passion. And if the quest for such transcendence is a necessary outcome of what began as a quest for the beauty of our sensations, one must perhaps seek the reason for that outcome in the nature of sensation itself. Yet the quest for transcendence has a further implication, insofar as it seeks the source of meaning in something possessing an ideal or eternal existence. In so doing, it aspires to the highest possible fulfillment of any attempt to assimilate life to form.

NOTES

PRELUDE

1. For my opening passage, see Ruskin's *Stones of Venice, Works* 10:82. Of Ruskin on St. Mark's façade John Rosenberg observes: "It is Venice seen through the eyes of an esthete with a great gift for word-painting"; *The Darkening Glass: A Portrait of Ruskin's Genius* (New York: Columbia University Press, 1961), p. 91. In my analysis I attempt to show, however, the symbolism of various motifs. In a letter to his father (February 18, 1852) Ruskin remarks: "To give Turneresque descriptions of the thing would not have needed ten days' study—or residence" (*Ruskin's Letters from Venice,* p. 185). On the context of Ruskin's remark (and, more generally, his father's influence on *Stones*) see Robert Hewison, "Notes on the Construction of *The Stones of Venice*" in Robert Rhodes and Del Ivan Janik, eds., *Studies in Ruskin* (Athens: Ohio University Press, 1982), pp. 131–52. My reading of Ruskin on St. Mark's façade draws upon his own method of "reading" architecture: "Reading, as Ruskin exemplifies it in *Stones,* is the interpretation of figures whose probable meaning is arrived at through comparison with related figures in other texts or works of art and reference to nature and to relevant scriptural passages" (Elizabeth Helsinger, *Ruskin and the Art of the Beholder* [Cambridge: Harvard University Press, 1982], p. 201).

For other discussions of Ruskin's description of St. Mark's, see Richard Stein, *The Ritual of Interpretation* (Cambridge: Harvard University Press, 1975), pp. 91–93, and Paul L. Sawyer, *Ruskin's Poetic Argument: The Design of the Major Works* (Ithaca: Cornell University Press, 1985), pp. 107–8, and, on Ruskin's method in *Stones,* pp. 92–93. On the special significance of Venice for Ruskin, see John Dixon Hunt, *The Wider Sea: A Life of John Ruskin* (New York: Viking Press, 1982), pp. 195–200.

In his diaries Ruskin declares: "It [Venice] is the Paradise of cities. . . . This and Chamouni are my two bournes of earth" (*Diaries* 1:183).

2. Thus the shift in Ruskin's religious attitudes from roughly 1846 or 1848 to 1858 colors without essentially altering this awareness. On Ruskin's shift from Evangelical to humanist belief, see Rosenberg, *The Darkening Glass,* pp. 22–41, esp. pp. 31–32. Similarly, George Landow points out Ruskin's delight in explicating symbolism even after his loss of faith (*The Aesthetic and Critical*

Theories of John Ruskin [Princeton: Princeton University Press, 1971], p. 445). Thus in *Fors* Ruskin continues to affirm a kind of Romantic symbolism. Of Giotto's "Caritas" he writes: "Giotto is quite literal in his meaning, as well as figurative" (*Works* 27:130). On Ruskin and Romantic symbolism, see Robert Hewison, *John Ruskin: The Argument of the Eye* (Princeton: Princeton University Press, 1976), pp. 72–73. According to Landow, allegory (the symbolical Grotesque) can even function in Ruskin as a replacement for his loss of faith (Landow, *Aesthetic and Critical Theories*, pp. 456–57).

3. On Ruskinian "seeing," see Sawyer, *Ruskin's Poetic Argument*, pp. 37–40. On the relation in Ruskin between seeing and artistic creation, see George Landow, "Ruskin, Holman Hunt, and Going to Nature to See for Oneself," in Rhodes and Janik, *Studies in Ruskin*, pp. 60–84.

4. On Ruskin's relation of order to beauty, see Landow, *Aesthetic and Critical Theories*, pp. 115–19.

5. On Ruskin's theory of "Typical Beauty" in general, see Landow, *Aesthetic and Critical Theories*, pp. 110–46. Elsewhere, Landow finds its source in Ruskin's theology (p. 168). See also on this point Hewison, *John Ruskin: The Argument of the Eye*, pp. 55–59. For the influence of Evangelicalism specifically, see Landow, *Aesthetic and Critical Theories*, pp. 334–56.

6. See on this subject Richard Dellamora, "A Victorian Optic: Translucent Landscape in Coleridge, Ruskin, and Browning," *Prose Studies* (1980), 3:271–86, and Sawyer, *Ruskin's Poetic Argument*, pp. 94–97. In a letter of October 18, 1837 (i.e., during Ruskin's student years at Oxford) Margaret Ruskin speaks of one of his friends as "an admirer of Shelley Coleridge and all Johns special favourites" (*Ruskin Family Letters* 2:482).

7. Cf. Landow, *Aesthetic and Critical Theories*, p. 253: "Ruskin's Evangelical emphasis upon man's fallen nature, therefore, demanded that he create a theory of beauty as divine order; for just as the sinner could be saved from his innate depravity only by continuous acts of divine grace, so too the individual's perception of beauty could be saved from trivializing subjectivity only by the continuous presence of God. In other words, the aesthetic theories of the second volume of *Modern Painters*, like Evangelical conceptions of the role of God in individual salvation, require the presence of an immanent God."

8. On the "treasure" motif in Ruskin, see Sawyer, *Ruskin's Poetic Argument*, pp. 30–31 and 175–76.

9. Thus *Fors Clavigera*: "Not one word of any book is readable by you except so far as your mind is one with its author's, and not merely his words like your words, but his thoughts like your thoughts" (*Works* 27:459).

10. Cf. Ruskin's definition in *Fors* of the principal literary genres in terms of feeling: "Dramatic poetry is the expression by the poet of other people's feelings, his own not being told. Lyric poetry is the expression by the poet of his own feelings. Epic poetry is the account given by the poet of other people's external circumstances, and of events happening to them, with only such expression either of their feelings, or his own, as he thinks may be conveniently added" (*Works* 27:628). See also the definition of poetry in *Praeterita*: "The

arrangement, by imagination, of noble motive for noble emotion" (*Works* 35:483).

11. See the commentary on this passage in Helsinger, *Ruskin and the Art of the Beholder*, pp. 132–33. In a letter to Charles Eliot Norton, Ruskin writes: "There is not a tree of Turners which is not rooted in ruins;—there is no sunset of his, which does not set on the accomplished fate of the elder nations" (*Correspondence*, p. 352).

12. On color as purifying element, see Landow, *Aesthetic and Critical Theories*, pp. 143–44.

13. On the "organic" in works of art, see *Modern Painters:* "In work which is not composed, there may be many beautiful things, but they do not help each other. They at the best only stand beside, and more usually compete with and destroy, each other. They may be connected artificially in many ways, but the test of there being no invention is, that if one of them be taken away, the others are no worse than before. But in true composition, if one be taken away, all the rest are helpless and valueless" (*Works* 7:209).

14. On Ruskin's theory of "Vital Beauty," see Landow, *Aesthetic and Critical Theories*, pp. 146–79, esp. 162–66 on Vital Beauty and the happiness resulting from an organism's sense of life, along with the difficulty of intuiting that happiness. In *John Ruskin: The Argument of the Eye,* Robert Hewison postulates a link between natural theology and Ruskin's Vital Beauty: "Natural theology sanctifies vital beauty; Evangelical typology sanctifies typical beauty" (p. 58). But Vital Beauty involves the experience or sentience of life within creatures themselves: natural theology, the external perception of creation by human beings.

15. On the symbolism of dawn or sunrise specifically see Ruskin's *Queen of the Air* (*Works* 19:302–3).

16. Thus Ruskin's distinction between "human myths" and "natural myths"— both forms of symbolism. See *The Queen of the Air* (*Works* 19:361). With regard to "human myths," moreover, Ruskin in *Fors* anticipates the "iconology" of Erwin Panofsky and others: "A symbol is scarcely ever invented just when it is needed. Some already recognized and accepted form or thing becomes symbolic at a particular time" (*Works* 27:405).

17. See on this point Hewison's *John Ruskin: The Argument of the Eye,* pp. 77–79.

18. Cf. the description of Venice in Ruskin's diaries: "For there the fancies of men have suffered the Sea Change of half a score centuries; there their minds have met from the east and west, and the currents of a hundred nations have whirled and eddied in the narrow vortex, ever with new glory rising from the foam; and the Stern Pisan and the Dreamy Greek and the restless Arab, the languid Ottomite and the strong Teuton; there the patience of early Christianity and the enthusiasm of mediaeval superstition, and the fire of ancient and the rationalism of recent infidelity, have all had their work, and all their time" (*Diaries* 2:453).

19. On Ruskin's theory of color, see Landow, *Aesthetic and Critical Theories*, pp. 426–27, 429–31, 438–39.

20. See Ruskin's remark in *Modern Painters* 5: "Note, with respect to this matter, that the peculiar innovation of Turner was the perfection of the colour chord by means of *scarlet*. Other painters had rendered the golden tones, and the blue tones, of sky; Titian especially the last, in perfectness. But none had dared to paint, none seem to have seen, the scarlet and purple" (*Works* 7:413). On Ruskin's lifelong defense of Turner, see Rosenberg, *The Darkening Glass,* pp. 9–13, 17–18, and, on its early phase specifically, Van Akin Burd, "Ruskin's Defense of Turner: The Imitative Phase," *Philological Quarterly* (1958), 37(4):465–83.

On hearing of Turner's death, Ruskin described the artist in a letter to his father as "my earthly Master." And elsewhere, speaking of Turner's works: "for they are to me Nature and art in one" (*Ruskin's Letters from Venice,* pp. 111, 145). For Ruskin's assessment of Turner vis-à-vis his predecessors, see Patrick Conner, "Ruskin and the 'Ancient Masters' in *Modern Painters,*" in Robert Hewison, ed., *New Approaches to Ruskin* (London: Routledge and Kegan Paul, 1981), pp. 17–32. In an 1845 letter from Italy, Ruskin claims to discern in Turner the influence of Tintoretto (*Ruskin in Italy,* p.223).

21. "And as the sunlight, undivided, is the type of the wisdom and righteousness of God, so divided, and softened into colour by means of the firmamental ministry, fitted to every need of man, as to every delight, and becoming one chief source of human beauty, by being made part of the flesh of man; —thus divided, the sunlight is the type of the wisdom of God, becoming sanctification and redemption. Various in work—various in beauty—various in power" (*Works* 7:418). See also Turner's deathbed remark: "The Sun is God" (quoted by Ruskin in *Fors, Works* 28:147). On the symbolism of the sun in late Turner and Ruskin's interpretation of it, see Helsinger, *Ruskin and the Art of the Beholder,* pp. 241–45, identifying sunlight with the artist's vision rather than with the light of a sanctified nature. But it seems to me that in the conclusion of *Modern Painters* 5 it is necessary to take into account Ruskin's relation of light to the natural symbolism of color, which would make nature the ultimate source of that symbolism.

22. See on this subject John Dixon Hunt, *The Pre-Raphaelite Imagination 1848–1900* (Lincoln: University of Nebraska Press, 1968), pp. 82–83.

23. For another reading of "Bridal Birth," see Stein, *The Ritual of Interpretation,* pp. 190–92.

24. To a certain extent Rossetti's "realism" here corresponds to the Pre-Raphaelite Brotherhood's emphasis on going back to nature. For a summary of PRB principles see William Holman Hunt, *Pre-Raphaelitism and the Pre-Raphaelite Brotherhood,* esp. pp. 84–91, 107, 112, 130–38.

25. In a letter to Coventry Patmore, Rossetti compares one of his own paintings (*The Passover*) to others by Herbert and Millais, "in which the symbolism is not really inherent in the fact, but merely suggested or suggestible, and having had the fact made to fit it" (*Letters* 1:276). On the problems arising from Rossetti's over-emphasis upon material aspects of a scene (hence failing to suggest sufficiently a spiritual meaning), see John Dixon Hunt, *The Pre-Raphaelite Imagination,* pp. 144–45. On Rossetti's symbolism in general,

see Stein, *The Ritual of Interpretation*, pp. 170–71, 180–81 and Jerome Buckley, *The Victorian Temper* (Cambridge: Harvard University Press, 1951), pp. 165–69.

26. As Barbara Charlesworth (Gelpi) finely observes: "The moment of most sensuous perception is at the same time a moment of spiritual insight, perhaps of vision" (*Dark Passages: The Decadent Consciousness in Victorian Literature* [Madison: University of Wisconsin Press, 1965], p. 9). Houston Baker also notices Rossetti's use of "sensuous, personal experience" in his *House of Life:* see "The Poet's Progress: Rossetti's *The House of Life,*" *Victorian Poetry* (1970), pp. 1–14. See also Stein, *The Ritual of Interpretation,* pp. 125–26 and 204, 207.

Graham Hough's comment on Rossetti's paintings of the Annunciation seems equally apposite: "When Rossetti paints the Annunciation he is not depicting one of the mysteries of the Christian faith in any theological sense. But he is not merely painting it as he might paint a theme from Keats; he is depicting something that has really been a content of his own soul—a sense of awe, of humility and of revelation, in which many of the emotions that attach to the Christian mystery are included" (*The Last Romantics* [London: Duckworth, 1949], pp. 53–54). In his journal of the PRB, William Michael Rossetti notes Dante's *Ecce Ancilla Domini* as changed from Latin to English "to guard against the imputation of popery"(Fredeman, ed., *The P.R.B. Journal,* p. 99).

In a letter to James Smetham (December 10, 1865), Rossetti himself writes: "I had better tell you frankly at once that I have no such faith as you have. Its default in me does not arise from want of natural impulse to believe, nor of reflection whether what I should alone call belief in a full sense is possible to me" (*Letters* 2:582). On Rossetti's religious views, see William Michael Rossetti, *Dante Gabriel Rossetti: His Family-Letters with a Memoir* 1:114 and David Sonstroem, *Rossetti and the Fair Lady* (Middletown, Conn.: Wesleyan University Press, 1970), pp. 20, 28. See also Arthur Symons's description of the Symbolist movement: "for in speaking to us so intimately, so solemnly, as only religion had hitherto spoken to us, it becomes itself a kind of religion, with all the duties and responsibilities of the sacred ritual" (*The Symbolist Movement in Literature,* pp. 8–9).

27. See the similar experience of Edmund Gosse as described in *Father and Son,* pp. 342–44. The climax of Gosse's "conversion" to secularism occurs with his perception of the beauty and charm of the visible world: "Then a little breeze sprang up, and the branches danced. Sounds began to rise from the road beneath me. Presently the colour deepened, the evening came on. From far below there rose to me the chatter of the boys returning home." On *Father and Son* see Jerome Buckley, *The Turning Key* (Cambridge: Harvard University Press, 1984), pp. 103–8 and Linda Peterson, *Victorian Autobiography* (New Haven: Yale University Press, 1986), chap. 6.

28. Cf. Newman's *Apologia Pro Vita Sua:* "For myself, it was not logic that carried me on; as well might one say that the quicksilver in the barometer changes the weather. It is the concrete being that reasons; pass a number of

years, and I find my mind in a new place; how? the whole man moves; paper logic is but the record of it" (p. 155).

29. For another instance of such transposition, see Gautier's "Sainte Casilda" (from *España*): "Pour l'oeuvre des bourreaux la vierge découverte / Montre sur sa poitrine, albâtre éblouissant, / A la place des seins, deux ronds couleur de sang, / Distillant un rubis par chaque veine ouverte" (*Poésies complètes* 2:259). At first glance one might see this merely as an example of Gautier's well-known tendency to transform nature into art. But the figure of Saint Casilda is itself already a painted one, which transposes the erotic to the lapidary. A similar "lapidary" aesthetic, sublimating emotion to the gemlike or crystalline, appears in Théodore de Banville's "Décor," with its identification of "stalactites" as "larmes gelées" (frozen tears) (*Les Stalactites,* p. 116).

30. On the precedence of art over nature in Gautier (whereby nature is seen only in relation to art) see Gabriel Brunet, "Théophile Gautier, poète," *Mercure de France* (October 15, 1922), pp. 289–332, esp. 308–10, and Michel Crouzet, "Gautier et le problème de 'créer,' " *Revue d'Histoire littéraire de la France* (July–August 1972), pp. 659–87, esp. 670–71. For some instances in Gautier's own works see the opening of *Albertus* with its depiction of a Flemish town "tel que les peint Teniers" (*Émaux et Camées,* p. 153) and the following poems from *España*: "A Madrid," "Sur le Prométhée du musée de Madrid," "Ribeira," "Deux tableaux de Valdès Léal," and "A Zurbaran" (*Poésies complètes* 2:270, 272, 304–8, 309–11). A similar attitude appears in Théodore de Banville: "Pour Mademoiselle" (inspired by Fanny Ellsler) describes ballet dancers in terms of bas-reliefs (*Les Stalactites,* 280–81). On the "artificiality" of art for Gautier, see also Jean Pommier, "A propos des 'Emaux et Camées': notes et impressions," *Revue universitaire* (March–April 1943), pp. 49–53 and (May–June 1943), pp. 101–6, and Georges Poulet, *Trois essais de mythologie romantique* (Paris: Corti, 1966), pp. 111–12. Finally, on the aesthetic of *Émaux et Camées* specifically as anti-Romantic, see Serge Fauchereau, *Théophile Gautier* (Paris: Denoël, 1972), pp. 90–95.

31. See especially Gautier's equation in his preface of art with pleasure: "Au lieu de faire un prix Monthyon pour la récompense de la vertu, j'aimerais mieux donner, comme Sardanapale, ce grand philosophe que l'on a si mal compris, une forte prime á celui qui inventerait un nouveau plaisir; car la jouissance me paraît le but de la vie, et la seule chose utile au monde" (*Mademoiselle de Maupin,* p. 24). On Gautier's preface see inter alia René Jasinski, *Les Années romantiques de Th. Gautier* (Paris: Vuibert, 1929), pp. 169–217, and Adolphe Boschot, *Théophile Gautier* (Paris: Desclée de Brouwer, 1933), pp. 138–45; on the formula "l'art pour l'art" specifically, see Jasinski, pp. 210–12, and Boschot, pp. 346–52.

32. For a possible source of Gautier's "Symphonie en blanc majeur" see Théodore de Banville's "La Symphonie de la Neige" in *Les Stalactites,* esp. p. 353, ll.13–16.

33. On the motif of whiteness in Gautier, see Michel Crouzet, "Gautier et le problème de 'créer,' " pp. 666–67. On the frequency of whiteness in

general as a motif in the Decadence, see Holbrook Jackson, *The Eighteen Nineties* (London: Grant Richards, 1913), pp. 169–72.

34. On the aesthetic theories of Whistler in relation to aestheticism, see Hough, *The Last Romantics,* pp. 175–87. See also Wilde's "Mr. Whistler's Ten O'Clock" in Wilde, *Miscellanies,* pp. 63–67.

35. In "The Portrait of Mr. W. H.," Wilde describes all art as "being to a certain degree a mode of acting, an attempt to realise one's own personality on some imaginative plane out of reach of the trammelling accidents and limitations of real life" (*Lord Arthur Savile's Crime,* p. 147). Cf. Max Beerbohm's "A Defence of Cosmetics": "Drama is the presentment of the soul in action" (*The Yellow Book,* p. 7).

36. Symons, *The Symbolist Movement in Literature,* p. 139. On the influence of *La Faustin* upon *À Rebours,* see Robert Baldick, *The Life of J. -K. Huysmans* (Oxford: Clarendon Press, 1955), pp. 28, 83.

37. On Huysmans's "aesthetic of ennui" see Helen Trudgian, *L'Esthétique de J. -K. Huysmans* (Paris, 1934; rpt. Geneva: Slatkine, 1970), chap. 9.

38. Cf. Aubrey Beardsley's *Venus and Tannhäuser,* which applies the same aesthetic to erotica, speaking of the "irritation of loveliness that can never be entirely comprehended, or ever enjoyed to the utmost" (*The Story of Venus and Tannhäuser,* p. 30). Thus Holbrook Jackson's apt characterization of *Venus and Tannhäuser* as "an *À Rebours* of sexuality" (*The Eighteen Nineties,* p. 75). On Beardsley see Annette Lavers, "'Aubrey Beardsley, Man of Letters,'" in *Romantic Mythologies,* ed. Ian Fletcher (London: Routledge and Kegan Paul, 1967), pp. 243–70 and, on *Venus and Tannhäuser* specifically, pp. 261–62.

39. On the vogue of late Latin authors in Aestheticism, see Linda Dowling, *Language and Decadence in the Victorian Fin de Siècle* (Princeton: Princeton University Press, 1986), pp. 151–53.

40. On the influence of Edmond de Goncourt's *La Maison d'un artiste* upon des Esseintes's collection of aesthetic objects, see Charles Maingon, *L'Univers artistique de J. -K. Huysmans* (Paris: Nizet, 1977), pp. 63–65.

41. On the cult of the artificial in Huysmans and des Esseintes, see Pierre Cogny, *J. -K. Huysmans à la recherche de l'unité* (Paris: Nizet, 1953), pp. 81–84. See also Max Beerbohm in "A Defence of Cosmetics": "Nay, but it is useless to protest. Artifice must queen it once more in the town. . . . For behold! The Victorian era comes to its end and the day of sancta simplicitas is quite ended. The old signs are here and the portents to warn the seer of life that we are ripe for a new epoch of artifice" (*The Yellow Book,* p. 1).

42. See Arthur Symons on Pater: "With this conscious ordering of things, it became a last sophistication to aim at an effect in style which should bring the touch of unpremeditation, which we seem to find in nature, into a faultlessly combined arrangement of art" (*Studies in Two Literatures,* p. 185). Thus des Esseintes takes Pater's program one step further.

43. On des Esseintes's quest, see Cogny, *J. -K. Huysmans à la recherche de l'unité,* pp. 75–77. Cogny sees des Esseintes, however, simply as seeking "l'évasion hors du réel," overlooking the intrinsic logic of the quest itself.

44. Perhaps this explains Huysmans's partiality to the faculty of sight, as the medium allowing for the most rapid assimilation of impressions. Hence the emphasis in his art criticism upon the pleasures of sensation afforded by various pictorial elements. It leads him to criticize even the Impressionists for failing to render fully the experience of seeing various phenomena (*OC* 6:104–5). At the same time it can prompt his praise of Renoir (*OC* 6:204), as well as his eulogy of Pissarro, who seems to him to embody the fundamental aspirations of the new movement in painting (*OC* 6:257). On Huysmans's art criticism, see Baldick, *The Life of J. -K. Huysmans,* chap. 8 and Trudgian, *L'Esthétique de J. -K. Huysmans,* chap. 4.

45. On Huysmans's ambivalent Christianity in *À Rebours,* see Cogny, *J. -K. Huysmans à la recherche de l'unité,* pp. 104–5.

46. Thus Huysmans's tribute to the painter Félicien Rops in *Certains:* "Il a restitué à la Luxure si niaisement confinée dans l'anecdote, si bassement matérialisée par certaines gens, sa mystérieuse omnipotence; il l'a religieusement replacée dans le cadre infernal où elle se meut et, par cela même, il n'a pas créé des oeuvres obscènes et positives, mais bien des oeuvres catholiques, des oeuvres enflammées et terribles" (*OC* 10:105).

47. Baldick notes, however, that "even when his conversion was an accomplished fact, he [Huysmans] was still unable to explain how he had come to write that spontaneous and impassioned prayer of des Esseintes" (*The Life of J. -K. Huysmans,* p. 87).

48. See, for example Leconte de Lisle, *Oeuvres* 1:63–66 ("Hypatie"), 1:212, ll. 721–34, and 1:273–87 ("Hypatie et Cyrille"), esp. p. 284, ll. 284–94.

49. Ibid., p. 53, l. 21. See Lionel Johnson's remarkably similar poem "Harvest" (*Poetical Works,* pp. 119–20).

50. One notices this even in Swinburne's best passages. See for instance, *Atalanta in Calydon, Complete Works* 7:321, 335–36.

51. Perhaps Swinburne's ultimate failure results in part from unresolved emotional contradictions in his work. See Barbara Charlesworth (Gelpi), *Dark Passages,* pp. 19–35 and Graham Hough, *The Last Romantics,* p. 192.

52. Of course, the exclusion of Swinburne necessarily raises questions concerning the definition of aestheticism as a movement. See on this subject Linda Dowling's bibliography, *Aestheticism and Decadence* (New York: Garland, 1977), with numerous relevant entries as well as her own remarks, pp. xiii–xiv and xiv–xxiii. Even the more limited period of the nineties remains difficult to classify: see on this subject Helmut Gerber's "The Nineties: Beginning, End, or Transition?" in Richard Ellmann, ed., *Edwardians and Late Victorians* (New York: Columbia University Press, 1960). Some synoptic studies—for example, R.V. Johnson's brief survey, *Aestheticism* (London: Methuen, 1969)— seem to me too restrictive in their definitions (e.g., his separation of aestheticism as a "view of art" from "a view of life" and "a practical tendency in literature and the arts" [p. 12]—which precludes the possibility of assimilating life to art in a larger synthesis). Others, such as Edmund Wilson's *Axel's Castle* (New York: Scribner's, 1931), envision the period too broadly in describing it simply as a "counterpart to the Romantic reaction of the end of the century

before" (p. 10), subordinating it, under the rubric of Symbolism, to an over-simplifed Modernism.

53. On the versification of "Chanson d'automne" and its effects, see Jacques-Henry Bornecque, *Les Poèmes Saturniens de Paul Verlaine,* rev. ed. (Paris: Nizet, 1967), pp. 119–20.

54. Of the mood of this poem Pierre Martino astutely remarks: "Il est triste, mais il jouit de sa tristesse; il l'aime" (*Verlaine,* rev. ed. [Paris: Boivin, 1951], p. 54. Similarly, Antoine Adam remarks that in *Poèmes saturniens* Verlaine's essential preoccupation is not with expressing a felt anguish but with the aesthetic quality of his verse. See Adam's *Verlaine,* 2d ed. (Paris: Hatier, 1961), p. 73.

55. In his *Lumières sur les Fêtes Galantes de Paul Verlaine,* rev. ed. (Paris: Nizet, 1969), Jacques-Henry Bornecque observes: "Cette complexe élégance de la forme veut refléter l'élégance subtile du bonheur" (pp. 93–4). On the ethos of the *Fêtes galantes,* see also Antoine Adam, *Verlaine,* pp. 86–87. It seems particularly revealing that the typical Watteau landscape which inspires Verlaine in the *Fêtes galantes* should have been described earlier by both Arsène Houssaye and the Goncourts as suggestive of "paradise"—like the "paradis sur terre" evoked by Flaubert in *L'Éducation sentimentale.* For Houssaye and the Goncourts, see Bornecque, pp. 31–32. Similarly, Pierre Martino notes the phrase "fêtes galantes" used by the Goncourts in describing Watteau's paintings (*Verlaine,* p. 66). Verlaine's description of François Coppée's *Les Intimités* characterizes his own contemporaneous *Fêtes galantes* perfectly: "ces vers exquis, extrêmement raffinés sans apparence d'effort et même avec une délicate affectation de laisser-aller élégiaque, que raille par instants une légère note d'ironie triste" (Verlaine, *Oeuvres en prose complètes,* p. 629).

56. For another view, see R. P. Blackmur's comments on this scene in his *Henry Adams,* ed. Veronica Makowsky (New York: Harcourt Brace Jovanovich, 1980), p. 43.

57. On the relation between the death of Adams's sister and the conceptual chapters of *The Education,* see Robert Sayre, *The Examined Self: Benjamin Franklin, Henry Adams, Henry James* (Princeton: Princeton University Press, 1964), pp. 114–15, and, on the role of shocks and confusion within *The Education* in general, pp. 104, 111. For more recent, briefer examinations of *The Education* within the autobiographical genre, see Paul Jay, *Being in the Text* (Ithaca: Cornell University Press, 1984), pp. 153–60, and Jerome Buckley, *The Turning Key* (Cambridge: Harvard University Press, 1984), pp. 108–13. Where Jay's work sees in *The Education* a "general tendency to run from comfortable order to uncomfortable chaos" (p. 157), however, it fails, I think, to take sufficiently into account the movement toward order in the later theoretical chapters *after* "Chaos" and "Failure."

58. Ernest Samuels records the following from Adams's marginalia in his copy of John B. Stallo's *Concepts and Theories of Modern Physics:* "Singular that the result of eliminating metaphysics should always be to become more metaphysical. Force becomes merely a mode of thought . . . " (*Henry Adams: The Major Phase* [Cambridge: Harvard University Press, 1964], p. 385). I view

this assimilation of force to thought as the decisive turning point of *The Education*. For other views of the work's structure, see Samuels, pp. 350–51 (comparing *The Education* to Carlyle's *Sartor Resartus*) and Sayre, *The Examined Self*, p. 127 (regarding the definition of self by autobiography as the decisive act in that autobiography).

59. See John Carlos Rowe, *Henry Adams and Henry James: The Emergence of a Modern Consciousness* (Ithaca: Cornell University Press, 1976), pp. 124–26.

60. See Rowe, *Henry Adams and Henry James*, pp. 38–39, on the perception of relation as the defining act of consciousness in both James and Adams.

61. Significant in this respect is the possible early influence of J. S. Mill's *Positive Philosophy of Auguste Comte:* "Foresight of phenomena and power over them depend on knowledge of their sequences, and not upon any notion we may have formed respecting their origin or inmost nature" quoted in Ernest Samuels, *The Young Henry Adams* [Cambridge: Harvard University Press, 1948], p. 134).

62. Thus in his critique of Adams's "dynamic theory" *qua* theory (*Henry Adams: The Major Phase*, p. 387), Samuels fails perhaps to take its relation to the autobiographical self sufficiently into account.

63. On the subject of Adams's borrowings from Viollet-le-Duc on the Chartres windows, see Robert Mane, *Henry Adams on the Road to Chartres* (Cambridge: Harvard University Press, 1971), pp. 149–50. For Adams on the Chartres windows more generally, see pp. 141–52. Mane's summary assessment: "This feeling for color which Adams, with all the intensity he is able to summon, tries to revive not only in himself but in his reader is his most personal contribution to the study of Chartres" (p. 149). Mane subsequently attempts to link Adams's appreciation of the windows to an English Romantic tradition that includes Keats and Shelley. But although these figures anticipate Aesthetic tendencies, surely Adams's treatment, with its appeal to the sensuousness of color, belongs to a later phase of Aestheticism. On the Chartres windows, see also J. C. Levenson, *The Mind and Art of Henry Adams* (1957; rpt. Stanford: Stanford University Press, 1968), pp. 264–68.

64. In *Henry Adams on the Road to Chartres*, pp. 69–70, Mane points to John La Farge as a particular influence upon Adams's idea of the primacy of color in painting (i.e., affirming Delacroix against Ingres).

65. For this reason I find it disappointing that in his discussion of Adams's aestheticism (*Henry Adams on the Road to Chartres*, pp. 231–44) Robert Mane feels compelled to conclude: "For, although Adams' pursuit was primarily aesthetic, he himself never really posed as an aesthete, that is, to use the simplest dictionary definition, as 'one professing devotion to the beautiful'" (p. 239). Although Mane also discusses the specific affinities between Adams and various Aesthetic writers (e.g., Ruskin and Pater), it seems to me possible to place Adams more decisively within a larger Aesthetic tradition. On Adams's relation to Pater, Ruskin, Newman, and Arnold, and, specifically, his resistance to nineteenth-century medievalism, see Levenson, *The Mind and Art of Henry Adams*, pp. 248–51.

1. "HARMONIE DU SOIR"

1. Jean Pommier has traced this line ("chaque fleur s'évapore ainsi qu'un encensoir") to Victor Hugo's *Les Voix Intérieures*. See Pommier's *La Mystique de Baudelaire* (Paris: Les Belles Lettres, 1932), p. 17. On Baudelaire and Hugo more generally, see Léon Cellier, *Baudelaire et Hugo* (Paris: Corti, 1970). In a letter to Paul de Saint-Victor (November 23, 1855), Baudelaire asks to borrow some volumes of Hugo's poems (*Correspondance* 1:324). For some of Baudelaires's letters to Hugo, see *Correspondance* 1:81–82 and 1:596–99. Also of interest is his letter to the *Figaro* on Hugo and *la jeune France* (*Correspondance* 1:500–1).

2. In Baudelaire's *Le Spleen de Paris* 18 ("L'Invitation au voyage") flowers and reverie are associated with each other (*OC* 1:303). Jean-Paul Sartre aptly describes the self-reflexive quality of Baudelairean consciousness in his *Baudelaire* (Paris: Gallimard, 1947), p. 203.

3. Thus the invocation to night and twilight in *Le Spleen de Paris* 22 ("Le Crépuscule du soir"), whose "fête intérieure" (that of the imagination) celebrates its "délivrance" from daytime "angoisse" and its freedom for the pleasures of reverie (*OC* 1:312). But the "lueurs roses" seem thematically related to "Le soleil s'est noyé dans son sang qui se fige": perhaps one might see them as symbolic of the affections, which resist the encroachment of a night (death) that at last extinguishes them. On the theme of night in Baudelaire, see Gérald Antoine, "La nuit chez Baudelaire," *Revue d'Histoire Littéraire de la France* (April–June 1967), pp. 151–77. On the "poetics" of twilight cf. Théodore de Banville's preface to *Les Stalactites*: "En effet, il ne serait pas plus sensé d'exclure le demi-jour de la poésie, qu'il ne serait raisonnable de le souhaiter absent de la nature; et il est nécessaire, pour laisser certains objets poétiques dans le crépuscule qui les enveloppe et dans l'atmosphère qui les baigne, de recourir aux artifices de la négligence." And subsequently: "C'est surtout quand il s'agit d'appliquer des vers à de la musique qu'on sent vivement cette bizarre et délicate nécessité, et surtout encore lorsqu'il faut exprimer en poésie certain ordre de sensations et de sentiments qu'on pourrait appeler musicaux" (p. 102).

4. On Baudelaire's theory of colors and the affinities between color and music, see Pommier, *La Mystique de Baudelaire*, pp. 4–10. On this topic Baudelaire reveals especially the influence of E.T.A. Hoffmann. See Rosemary Lloyd, *Baudelaire et Hoffmann: Affinités et Influences* (Cambridge, Eng.: Cambridge University Press, 1979).

5. On the concept of the aura, see Walter Benjamin, *Charles Baudelaire: A Lyric Poet in the Era of High Capitalism,* tr. Harry Zohn (London: NLB, 1973), pp. 145–52, which defines "aura" as "the associations which, in the home of the *mémoire involuntaire,* tend to cluster around the object of a perception" (p. 145). On the "magical" sense of the aura in Baudelaire, see Georges Blin, *Le Sadisme de Baudelaire* (Paris: Corti, 1948), p. 99.

6. Cf. Jean Prévost's comment: "For Baudelaire, an odor or fragrance [*le parfum*] is above all the means of evoking memories" (*Baudelaire: Essai sur la création et l'inspiration poétiques* [Paris: Mercure de France, 1953], p. 180.

On the role of "parfums" in Baudelaire, see Prévost, pp. 180–84, and Lloyd James Austin, *L'Univers poétique de Baudelaire* (Paris: Mercure de France, 1956), pp. 220–35.

7. On synesthesia in Baudelaire, see Pommier, *La Mystique de Baudelaire,* pp. 4–6, 10–15.

8. On Baudelaire's concept of beauty, see Marc Eigeldinger, *Le Platonisme de Baudelaire* (Neuchâtel: La Baconnière, 1951), pp. 19–25. Eigeldinger emphasizes especially the unattainability of beauty—which seems particularly significant here as Baudelaire associates that beauty with the sky or heavens (*le ciel*).

9. On "le coeur" in Baudelaire, see Lloyd James Austin, *L'Univers poétique de Baudelaire,* pp. 186–87.

10. See on this topic Benjamin Fondane, *Baudelaire et l'expérience du gouffre* (Paris: Seghers, 1947).

11. See Jean Prévost on Baudelaire's "sadisme littéraire" in his *Baudelaire,* esp. pp. 220–21; more comprehensively, Georges Blin, *Le Sadisme de Baudelaire,* esp. pp. 36–47 on "autosadism" or the fusion of sadism with masochism in Baudelaire, and, more recently, Leo Bersani, *Baudelaire and Freud* (Berkeley: University of California Press, 1977), chap. 7.

12. Jean Pommier suggests another source for Baudelaire's striking image in a poem from the original edition of Banville's *Les Cariatides:* "[Venus] a mis sa lèvre chaude à ce sang qui se fige." See his *Dans les chemins de Baudelaire* (Paris: Corti, 1945), p. 199.

13. On "Le Soleil" see F. W. Leakey, *Baudelaire and Nature* (Manchester: Manchester University Press, 1969), pp. 13–14, 106–8; and Ross Chambers, "Baudelaire et l'espace poétique: à propos du 'Soleil,' " in *Le Lieu et la formule: Hommage à Marc Eigeldinger* (Neuchâtel: La Baconnière, 1978), pp. 111–20. On the "sunset" motif in Baudelaire, see Leakey, pp. 267–79, and Marc Eigeldinger, "La Symbolique solaire dans la poésie de Baudelaire," *Revue d'Histoire Littéraire de la France* (April–June 1967), pp. 133–50.

14. On Baudelairean allegory, see Nathaniel Wing, "The Danaides Vessel: On Reading Baudelaire's Allegories" in his *Limits of Narrative* (Cambridge: Cambridge University Press, 1986), pp. 8–18, which perceptively describes the "play" with allegory in Baudelaire. On Baudelaire's symbolism, see Pommier, *La Mystique de Baudelaire,* pp. 22–23, 72–74; Austin, *L'Univers poétique de Baudelaire,* pp. 162–84; Leakey, *Baudelaire and Nature,* pp. 173–250. In their efforts to assimilate Baudelaire to Romantic symbolism, however, both Pommier and Austin fail, I think, to recognize sufficiently how the subjective nature of Baudelairean symbolism (for which see esp. Austin, p. 172), by emphasizing the mind's creative role, leads to something distinctly more aesthetic than spiritual (unlike the Romantic symbol). But see Leakey, p. 182, on the "supernatural" (*surnaturel*) state of mind as involving vivid impressions and their symbolic significances. Subsequently he emphasizes the subjective nature of the "surnaturel" for Baudelaire (p. 185) but then goes on to equate it with "our (wholly secular) modern 'surreal' " (ibid.). Yet surely there is a difference: the Baudelairean "surnaturel" involves a heightened state of sen-

sibility in which perceptions of an external world are colored by subjective emotions, whereas the modern "surreal" develops simply out of fantasy or associationism, as an affirmation of artistic creativity. In her *Baudelaire: Les Fleurs du Mal* (London: Arnold, 1960), Alison Fairlie speaks of Baudelaire's "surnaturalisme" as consisting of "the use of objects in the material, the 'natural' world as symbols which evoke something other than their physical appearance: in fact, non-naturalistic or suggestive art" (p. 16). But for Baudelaire, the "surnaturel" would seem to imply something more: a sense of *aura*, of the sacred, resulting from the transfigured state of the consciousness that perceives.

15. In this context one might speak of what Charles Asselineau once called Baudelaire's "religion de la forme" (*Baudelaire et Asselineau,* ed. Jacques Crépet and Claude Pichois [Paris: Nizet, 1953], p. 85). And here we find the significance of all the well-known attestations of Baudelaire's "dandyisme" (Asselineau, p. 99; Banville, *Mes souvenirs,* p. 84). They manifest the desire for a perfection of self which is the equivalent of a transformation of life into form. As Barbey d'Aurevilly remarks in his *Du Dandysme et de George Brummell,* "Le Dandysme est toute une manière d'être . . ." (*Oeuvres romanesques complètes* 2:673). And subsequently, speaking of Beau Brummell: "Il était un grand artiste à sa manière; seulement son art n'était pas spécial, ne s'exerçait pas dans un temps donné. C'était sa vie même . . ." (ibid., p. 693). On Baudelaire's "dandyisme" see Margaret Gilman, *Baudelaire the Critic* (New York: Columbia University Press, 1943), pp. 157–59 and Ellen Moers, *The Dandy: Brummell to Beerbohm* (New York: Viking, 1960), chap. 12.

16. On the function of memory in Baudelaire, see Ross Chambers, "Mémoire et mélancolie," in his *Mélancolie et opposition: Les debuts du modernisme en France* (Paris: Corti, 1987), pp. 167–86, esp. 171–72 and 177–80, on memory as "fertile" or inspired by a *manque*, a lack or absence.

17. For a "secular" view of "le spirituel" in Baudelaire, see Sartre's *Baudelaire,* pp. 199–204. For a more religious perspective, however, see Charles du Bos's remarkable "Méditations sur la vie de Baudelaire" in his *Approximations* (Paris: Plon, 1922), esp. pp. 203–10; Marcel Ruff, *Baudelaire* (Paris: Hatier, 1966), pp. 98–101; Prévost, *Baudelaire,* pp. 58–60; and Pierre Emmanuel, *Baudelaire: The Paradox of Redemptive Satanism,* tr. Robert T. Cargo (University: University of Alabama Press, 1970), esp. pp. 164–74. But compare, on the other hand, the remarks in Claude Pichois, *Baudelaire,* pp. 251–52. The recollections of Ernest Prarond on this subject are significant, if inconclusive: see Pichois, pp. 30–31. See also Baudelaire's own pronouncements in his letters on pantheism and "l'analogie universelle" (*Correspondance* 1:207, 248, 336–37). In his *Sadisme de Baudelaire,* pp. 84–90, Georges Blin discusses Baudelaire's belief in the "magical" efficacy of religious ritual and prayer. The whole question of the nature of Baudelairean spiritualism is of the utmost importance for the interpretation of the *Fleurs du mal*. See Ruff, pp. 105–7; Pichois, pp. 204–5, 206–9; Fairlie, *Baudelaire: Les Fleurs du Mal,* pp. 10–12, 33–34; more recently, Bersani, *Baudelaire and Freud,* pp. 16–22; and Ross Chambers, "Un despotisme 'oriental,'" in his *Mélancolie et opposition,* pp.

131–66, esp. 158–60. Chambers argues that for Baudelaire "spleen" and "idéal" are but two "modes poétiques" originating from the same "oriental" despotism, the "acte despotique" that invariably appropriates or assimilates the other. But one must, I think, see these two Baudelairean modes as simultaneously engaged in a dialectical interaction in which each produces or elicits the other by way of reaction or response.

2. "DE LA COULEUR"

1. For an overview of Baudelaire's theory of color, see André Ferran, *L'Esthétique de Baudelaire* (Paris: Hachette, 1933), pp. 139–50. Ferran cites the influence of a contemporary theoretical treatise on Baudelaire and Delacroix, Chevreul's *De la loi du contraste simultané des couleurs* (1839). He then goes on to explain how the binary colors, orange (yellow and red), green (yellow and blue), and violet (blue and red), attain their maximum intensity when juxtaposed against the primary color (red, yellow, blue) not included in their own composition: hence, orange and blue, green and red, violet and yellow. For another discussion of Baudelaire's theory of color, see the introduction to David Kelley's critical edition of the *Salon de 1846* (Oxford: Clarendon Press, 1975), pp. 26–31, esp. 30–31 on the relation of color to the subjectivity (temperament) of the painter. On "De la couleur" specifically see also F. W. Leakey, *Baudelaire and Nature* (Manchester: Manchester University Press, 1969), pp. 79–82; Margaret Gilman, *Baudelaire the Critic* (New York: Columbia University Press, 1943), pp. 39–40, 42–44, 52–53; and D. J. Kelley, "Deux aspects du *Salon de 1846* de Baudelaire: la dédicace Aux Bourgeois et la Couleur," *Forum for Modern Language Studies* (1969), 5(4):331–46, esp. 341–45.

2. In his discussion of Delacroix's works in the *Exposition universelle* of 1855, Baudelaire observes: "D'abord il faut remarquer, et c'est très important, que, vu à une distance trop grande pour analyser ou même comprendre le sujet, un tableau de Delacroix a déjà produit sur l'âme une impression riche, heureuse ou mélancolique. On dirait que cette peinture, comme les sorciers et les magnétiseurs, projette sa pensée à distance. Ce singulier phénomène tient à la puissance du coloriste, à l'accord parfait des tons, et à l'harmonie (préétablie dans le cerveau du peintre) entre la couleur et le sujet. Il semble que cette couleur, qu'on me pardonne ces subterfuges de langage pour exprimer des idées fort délicates, pense par elle-même, indépendamment des objets qu'elle habille. Puis ces admirables accords de sa couleur font souvent rêver d'harmonie et de mélodie, et l'impression qu'on emporte de ses tableaux est souvent quasi musicale" (*OC* 2:594–95).

3. Thus Baudelaire, in his essay "L'Oeuvre et la vie d'Eugène Delacroix": "Il vous semble qu'une atmosphere magique a marché vers vous et vous enveloppe. Sombre, délicieuse pourtant, lumineuse, mais tranquille, cette impression, qui prend pour toujours sa place dans votre mémoire, prouve le vrai, le parfait coloriste" (*OC* 2:753). And in his *Salon de 1859,* speaking again of Delacroix: "C'est l'infini dans le fini. C'est le rêve! et je n'entends pas par ce

mot les capharnaums de la nuit, mais la vision produite par une intense méditation, ou, dans les cerveaux moins fertiles, par un excitant artificiel. En un mot, Eugène Delacroix peint surtout *l'âme* dans ses belles heures" (*OC* 2:636–37).

4. Elsewhere in the *Salon de 1846,* Baudelaire defines color slightly differently: "La couleur est composée de masses colorées qui sont faites d'une infinité de tons, dont l'harmonie fait l'unité" (*OC* 2:455). Here, however, he speaks of colors collectively, rather than of an individual tint or hue.

5. In his *Salon de 1859,* Baudelaire recalls Delacroix's remark on this subject: " 'La nature n'est qu'un dictionnaire,' répétait-il fréquemment." To which the critic adds, by way of elucidation: "mais personne n'a jamais considéré le dictionnaire comme une composition dans le sens poétique du mot. Les peintres qui obéissent à l'imagination cherchent dans leur dictionnaire les éléments qui s'accordent à leur conception; encore, en les ajustant avec un certain art, leur donnent-ils une physionomie toute nouvelle" (*OC* 2:624–25). On nature as "dictionary" see Leakey, *Baudelaire and Nature,* pp. 131–32 and, more generally, on Baudelaire's contradictory attitudes toward depicting nature in art, pp. 127–50; on the "anti-Nature" sentiment in Baudelaire's circle, pp. 113–20. On the opposition of both Delacroix and Baudelaire to realism, see Ferran, *L'Esthétique de Baudelaire,* pp. 148–50, and Leakey, *Baudelaire and Nature,* pp. 71–79. Elsewhere Baudelaire observes: "La nature extérieure . . . n'est qu'un amas incohérent de materiaux que l'artiste est invité à associer et à mettre en ordre, un *incitamentum,* un réveil pour les facultés sommeillantes" (*OC* 2:752). In the *Exposition universelle* (1855), moreover, he speaks of the "immense clavier des *correspondances*" [immense keyboard of *correspondences*] (*OC* 2:577)—implying that, like a piano keyboard, these "correspondences" exist to be "played upon," i.e., arranged into various compositional sequences or harmonies.

6. In Baudelaire's *Salon de 1845* there is a reference to this work (*OC* 2:358), as well as in his critique of the *Exposition universelle* of 1855, under the title *Dante et Virgile* (*OC* 2:592). An obscure poem by Baudelaire's close friend Théodore de Banville ("Le Rosier du Luxembourg," apparently unpublished until 1936), suggests something of the importance Delacroix's painting must have had for Baudelaire and others of his circle during their formative years. Banville writes:

"Nous montions au Musée où nous voulions revoir / Les Delacroix, la barque affreuse où le flot noir / Submergeant les damnés de leur [*sic*] eau débordante / Avec de longs sanglots porte Virgile et Dante, / Et ses femmes d'Alger. . . ."

For the text of the poem and a discussion of its circumstances and importance, see Jacques Crépet, *Propos sur Baudelaire,* ed. Claude Pichois (Paris: Mercure de France, 1957), pp. 17–20. Elsewhere Banville notes Baudelaire's possession of Delacroix's series of Hamlet lithographs (*Mes souvenirs,* p. 80). On the affinities between Delacroix's theory of painting and Baudelaire's, see Ferran, *L'Esthétique de Baudelaire,* pp. 145–50, citing passages from Delacroix's *Journal.* For Delacroix's influence on Baudelaire, see Prévost, *Baude-*

laire, pp. 42–47, 108–17 and Margaret Gilman, *Baudelaire the Critic,* pp. 9–14, 35–40. For a discussion of the problems involved in the "Baudelaire and Delacroix" issue, see pp. vii–ix of David Kelley's preface to his edition of the *Salon de 1846.*

7. On Baudelaire's predilection for this particular color combination, see pp. 194–95 of Alison Fairlie, "Aspects of expression in Baudelaire's art criticism" in her *Imagination and Language* (Cambridge: Cambridge University Press, 1981).

3. HISTORY AS A WORK OF ART

1. Thus Burckhardt in his *Weltgeschichtliche Betrachtungen:* "Diese [Geschichtsphilosophie] ist ein Kentaur, eine *contradictio in adjecto;* denn Geschichte, d. h. das Koordinieren ist Nichtphilosophie und Philosophie, d. h. das Subordinieren ist Nichtgeschichte" (*GW* 4:2). And subsequently: "Wir sind aber nicht eingeweiht in die Zwecke der ewigen Weisheit und kennen sie nicht. Dieses kecke Antizipieren eines Weltplanes führt zu Irrtümern, weil es von irrigen Prämissen ausgeht" (ibid.).

2. In his preface to *Die Zeit Constantins des Grossen,* similarly, Burckhardt writes that he "hat überhaupt nicht vorzugsweise für Gelehrte geschrieben, sondern für denkende Leser aller Stände, welche einer Darstellung so weit zu folgen pflegen, als sie entschiedene, abgerundete Bilder zu geben imstande ist" (*GW* 1:ix). He also acknowledges that "seine Behandlungsweise als eine subjektive bestritten werde" (ibid.). In his *Weltgeschichtliche Betrachtungen* he comments: "Unsere Bilder derselben sind meist doch blosse Konstruktionen, wie wir besonders bei Gelegenheit des Staates sehen werden, ja blosse Reflexe von uns selbst" (*GW* 4:4). See also Hayden White, *Metahistory* (Baltimore: Johns Hopkins University Press, 1973), pp. 261–62 on Burckhardt's conception of history-writing as a work of art. White subsequently claims (pp. 262–63) that the only meaning in history for Burckhardt must be a "Contextualist" one, consisting of a relationship between the different events that define a historical period. But this is to neglect the significance which for Burckhardt manifests itself through the *form* of the period—a form defined by the historian's arrangement of that period's events and aspects.

3. In this fashion Burckhardt circumvents the criticism often levelled at his work on account of its "spatialization" of time. See, for instance, Robert Klein's essay on "Burckhardt's *Civilization of the Renaissance* Today": "Finally—and this is probably the most important objection to Burckhardt's chosen framework—the entire period which he calls 'Italian Renaissance,' and which stretches, according to him, from the fall of the Hohenstaufen to the Spanish domination of Italy, is considered as one unit; within these wide boundaries, he ascribes common characteristics to all poetry, to all the religious and political life of Italy" (Klein, *Form and Meaning: Essays on the Renaissance and Modern Art,* tr. Madeline Jay and Leon Wieseltier [New York: Viking, 1979], p. 26). See also on this subject Arnaldo Momigliano, *Essays in Ancient and Modern Historiography* (Middletown, Conn.: Wesleyan University Press, 1977), pp. 297–

99, criticizing what Momigliano terms Burckhardt's "systematic form." For Burckhardt, however, what represents the Renaissance is not so much its individual aspects but rather their relation to each other. In this sense it does not matter whether the treatment of those aspects is atemporal or "spatial": all that matters is how their relations combine to create a form corresponding to the form of Renaissance life itself. For Burckhardt's own schema of such relations, see the reproduction of his initial plan for *Die Kultur* in Werner Kaegi, *Jacob Burckhardt: Eine Biographie* (Basel: Schwabe, 1956), 3:668.

4. For the influence of Michelet's formula upon Burckhardt, see Wallace K. Ferguson, *The Renaissance in Historical Thought* (Boston: Houghton Mifflin, 1948), pp. 176–77, 192. On the tradition of Renaissance historiography before Burckhardt in general see, besides Ferguson, Kaegi, *Jacob Burckhardt*, 3:673–87.

5. Here perhaps more than anywhere else one senses the affirmation of an ideal that rises above what Hayden White describes as Burckhardt's "ironic vision" (*Metahistory*, pp. 233–37, 244–47). In Burckhardt, however, that ideal can only be expressed symbolically.

4. MUSIC AT TWILIGHT

1. On Pater's "The School of Giorgione" see Richard Stein, *The Ritual of Interpretation* (Cambridge: Harvard University Press, 1975), pp. 218–24.

2. Cf. Harold Bloom's description of the "near solipsism of the isolated sensibility, of the naked aesthetic consciousness deprived of everything save its wavering self and the flickering of an evanescent beauty in the world of natural objects, which is part of the universe of death" (from "The Place of Pater: *Marius The Epicurean*" in his *Ringers in the Tower* [Chicago: University of Chicago Press, 1971], p. 189). On the philosophical sources of Pater's scepticism and subjective idealism, see Billie Andrew Inman, "The Intellectual Context of Walter Pater's 'Conclusion,'" in Harold Bloom, ed., *Walter Pater: Modern Critical Views*, (New York: Chelsea House, 1985), esp. pp. 135–41.

3. For Pater's childhood fascination with religious ritual, see Michael Levey, *The Case of Walter Pater* (London: Thames and Hudson, 1978), pp. 46–47. On Pater's aesthetic ideal see Daniel O'Hara: "According to Pater's earliest essays . . . the aesthetic ideal would seem to be a self-conscious quest for that symbolic vision of absolute beauty in which the innocent joy of childhood and the unhappy experience of maturity are reconciled in the idea of the wise creator who can give, on the model of sacred history, whether Greek or Christian, a transcendent imaginative significance to life" (*The Romance of Interpretation: Visionary Criticism from Pater to de Man* [New York: Columbia University Press, 1985], p. 22). See also on this point J. Hillis Miller, "Walter Pater: A Partial Portrait," *Daedalus* (Winter 1976), 105(1):97–113. And, on the "Paterian Temperament," Graham Hough, *The Last Romantics* (London: Duckworth, 1949), pp. 166–74.

Elsewhere Pater elaborates, in a different context, upon the kind of religious secularism implied here, with its consecration of the human as divine. In his *Greek Studies,* the divine is expressed within the human sphere: "The office of the imagination, then, in Greek sculpture, in its handling of divine persons, is thus to condense the impressions of natural things into human form; to retain that early mystical sense of water, or wind, or light, in the moulding of eye and brow; to arrest it, or rather, perhaps, to set it free, there, as human expression" (*Greek Studies,* pp. 32–33).

See also John Addington Symonds's characterization of Renaissance art: "In this way the painters rose above the ancient symbols, and brought heaven down to earth. By drawing Madonna and her son like living human beings, by dramatizing the Christian history, they silently substituted the love of beauty and the interests of actual life for the principles of the Church. The saint or angel became an occasion for the display of physical perfection, and to introduce 'un bel corpo ignudo' into the composition was of more moment to them than to represent the macerations of the Magdalen. Men thus learned to look beyond the relique and the host, and to forget the dogma in the lovely forms which gave it expression" (*Renaissance in Italy: The Age of the Despots,* pp. 18–19).

4. On the relation, similarly, between painting and literature in Pater, see Gerald Monsman, *Walter Pater's Art of Autobiography* (New Haven: Yale Univ. Press, 1980), pp. 37–38.

5. Cf. Pater's *Appreciations:* "If music be the ideal of all art whatever, precisely because in music it is impossible to distinguish the form from the substance or matter, the subject from the expression, then, literature, by finding its specific excellence in the absolute correspondence of the term to its import, will be but fulfilling the condition of all artistic quality in things everywhere, of all good art" (pp. 37–38). On the fusion of form and content in Pater's theory of art, see Hough, *The Last Romantics,* pp. 163–64. And, on the tension between substance and form, Gerald Monsman, *Pater's Portraits: Mythic Pattern in the Fiction of Walter Pater* (Baltimore: Johns Hopkins University Press, 1967), pp. 9–12.

In *The Ritual of Interpretation* Stein asserts: "For what he means by this suggestive formula [i.e., of all art aspiring to the condition of music] is not so much that art should provide a coherent intellectual structure for its own apprehension as that within it different kinds of effects should merge to produce a rich and satisfying confusion" (p. 219). But Pater emphasizes something clear and exact: the "absolute correspondence" between term and import, form and substance—ultimately, between life and art.

6. On Pater's idea of "vision" see Frank Kermode, *The Romantic Image* (London: Routledge and Kegan Paul, 1957), pp. 20–22 and Harold Bloom, *The Ringers in the Tower* (Chicago: University of Chicago Press, 1971), p. 191.

7. See Pater's *Appreciations:* "To treat life in the spirit of art, is to make life a thing in which means and ends are identified: to encourage such treatment, the true moral significance of art and poetry" (p. 62).

8. On the Renaissance as an embodiment of Pater's aesthetic ideal, see

Daniel O'Hara, *The Romance of Interpretation*, pp. 32–33, and Gerald Monsman, *Pater's Portraits*, pp. 12–14.

9. According to Michael Levey, Pater altered this title in later editions in response to Mrs. Mark Pattison's criticism of the work's historical weakness (*The Case of Walter Pater*, pp. 141–42, 144). But Mrs. Pattison's review fails to take into account the imaginative nature of Pater's historical conception.

10. On Pater's idea of history in *The Renaissance* see David J. DeLaura, *Hebrew and Hellene in Victorian England* (Austin: University of Texas Press, 1969), pp. 234–35. DeLaura detects an incompatibility between Pater's historical relativism and a progressive "educational" ideal (à la Lessing). On the nature of Pater's historical interpretation, see also Hough, *The Last Romantics*, p. 159, and Iain Fletcher, *Walter Pater* (London: Longmans, 1959), p. 16.

11. In this respect Pater's enterprise conforms to what he elsewhere observes of Henri-Frédéric Amiel: "he was meant, if people ever are meant for special lines of activity, for the best sort of criticism, the imaginative criticism; that criticism which is itself a kind of construction, or creation, as it penetrates, through the given literary or artistic product, into the mental and inner constitution of the producer, shaping his work" (*Essays from 'The Guardian,'* p. 29).

12. See on this topic Stein, *The Ritual of Interpretation*, pp. 224–34.

13. Cf. his letter to Violet Paget of June 4, 1884 apropos of her *Euphorion:* "It is not *easy* to do what you have done in the essay on 'Portrait Art', for instance—to make, viz. *intellectual theorems* seem like the life's essence of the concrete, sensuous objects, from which they have been abstracted. I always welcome this evidence of intellectual structure in a poetic or imaginative piece of criticism, as I think it a very rare thing, and it is also an effect I have myself endeavoured after, and so come to know its difficulties" (*Letters of Walter Pater*, pp. 53–54).

14. On Pater's idea of the Renaissance and its "reconciliation" with the Middle Ages, see DeLaura, *Hebrew and Hellene*, pp. 237–44.

15. See Pater's apostrophe in his essay on "Raphael" to "the age of the Renaissance": "an age of which we may say, summarily, that it enjoyed itself, and found perhaps its chief enjoyment in the attitude of the scholar, in the enthusiastic acquisition of knowledge for its own sake" (*Miscellaneous Studies*, p. 38). For the influence of Matthew Arnold on Pater, both in this formulation and elsewhere, see DeLaura, *Hebrew and Hellene*, pp. 231–36, 242–43.

5. ART AND LIFE

1. Thus Herbert Sussman observes that even Wilde's criticism (with its characteristic form of the dialogue) consists not so much of objective statement but rather of a subtle interplay between different viewpoints that mirrors "the continuous flux of the inward life." See his "Criticism as Art: Form in Oscar Wilde's Critical Writings," *Studies in Philology* (January 1973), 70:108–22.

2. *Letters of Oscar Wilde*, p. 471. See also the description of the protagonist of "The Young King": "And it seems that from the very first moment of his recognition he had shown signs of that strange passion for beauty that was destined to have so great an influence over his life" (*A House of Pomegranates / The Happy Prince*, p. 5).

For the influence of Pater's *Renaissance* on Wilde during his years at Oxford, see Richard Ellmann, *Oscar Wilde* (New York: Knopf, 1988), pp. 47–48. "Much of it [i.e., *The Renaissance*]," Ellmann interestingly notes, "especially the celebrated 'Conclusion,' he had by heart" (p. 47). For some echoes in Wilde's own works of the "Conclusion" specifically, see *Miscellanies*, pp. 39, 274; echoes of other *Renaissance* passages in *Miscellanies*, pp. 30–31, 243–44, 262. See also *Oscar Wilde's Oxford Notebooks*, pp. 124, 141, 141–42. For the influence of Pater and other figures (Hegel, Spencer, et al.) on Wilde's formative years, see the introductory material to the *Notebooks* by Smith and Helfand. For Pater and Ruskin as influences on Wilde, see Ellmann, "Overtures to *Salome*," in Ellmann, ed., *Oscar Wilde: A Collection of Critical Essays* (Englewood Cliffs, N.J.: Prentice-Hall, 1969), pp. 73–91. On the "fatal book" topos, see Linda Dowling, *Language and Decadence in the Victorian Fin de Siècle* (Princeton: Princeton University Press, 1986), pp. 164–66, 169–74.

3. Holbrook Jackson's analysis of the relation between Wilde's life and art still seems quite germane: "What he seemed to be doing all the time was translating life into art through himself. His books were but incidents of this process. He always valued life more than art, and only appreciated the latter when its reflex action contributed something to his sensations; but because he had thought himself into the position of one who transmutes life into art, he fell into the error of imagining art to be more important than life. And art for him was not only those formal and plastic things which we call the fine arts; it embraced all luxurious artificialities. 'All art is quite useless,' he said. Such an attitude was in itself artificial; but with Oscar Wilde this artificialism lacked any progressive element: it was sufficient in itself; in short, it ended in itself, and not in any addition to personal power" (*The Eighteen Nineties* [London: Grant Richards, 1913], p. 104).

4. In his *Into the Demon Universe: A Literary Exploration of Oscar Wilde* (New Haven: Yale University Press, 1974), Christopher Nassaar reads this passage as indicative of a "loss of equilibrium" on Wilde's part (p. 147). But it seems more plausible to see Wilde's descent into the depths as a logical outcome of his quest. See also Richard Ellmann's argument for Wilde's fascination with evil as a new form of experience ("The Critic as Artist as Wilde," in Charles Ryskamp, ed., *Wilde and the Nineties* [Princeton: Princeton University Library, 1966], pp. 11–15).

5. In her *Idylls of the Marketplace: Oscar Wilde and the Victorian Public* (Stanford: Stanford University Press, 1986), Regenia Gagnier claims (p. 5) that there is only a negative or inverse relation between Wilde as dandy and the hero of *À Rebours*. Surely, however, the essential affinity between these two lies in their analysis of the psychology of desire.

6. Cf. the speech of the statue in "The Happy Prince": " 'When I was alive

and had a human heart,' answered the statue, 'I did not know what tears were, for I lived in the Palace of Sans-Souci, where sorrow is not allowed to enter. In the daytime I played with my companions in the garden, and in the evening I led the dance in the Great Hall. Round the garden ran a very lofty wall, but I never cared to ask what lay beyond it, everything about me was so beautiful" (*A House of Pomegranates / The Happy Prince,* 171). On Wilde at Oxford, see the reminiscences in E. H. Mikhail, ed., *Oscar Wilde: Interviews and Recollections* (New York: Barnes and Noble, 1979), 1:3–28, esp. those of Hunter-Blair.

7. See the following entry from Wilde's Oxford notebook: "What is morality but the perfect adjustment of the human organism to the actual conditions of Life" (*Oscar Wilde's Oxford Notebooks,* p. 156).

8. So Richard Ellmann too hypothesizes. See his "The Critic as Artist as Wilde," pp. 15–16. See also, more recently, Ellmann's *Oscar Wilde,* pp. 92, 382, in which Ellmann speaks of Wilde's "sense of doom," relating it on the one hand to Wilde's conjectured contraction of syphilis, and, on the other hand, to the reading and remembrance of Aeschylus' *Agamemnon*. One finds some confirmation of this "sense of doom" in Wilde's own remarks to André Gide. Thus, before the catastrophe: "I must go on as far as possible. I cannot go much further. Something is bound to happen . . . something else" (*Oscar Wilde,* p. 51). And after: "of course I knew that there would be a catastrophe, either that or something else; I was expecting it. There was but one end possible. Just imagine—to go any further was impossible, and that state of things could not last. That is why there had to be some end to it, you see. Prison has completely changed me. I was relying on it for that" (p. 59).

See also Gide's own remarks, pp. 46–47, and Wilde's qualification of pleasure (p. 47) as "tragic." For Wilde's sense of tragedy, see his Oxford notebooks: "tragedy breasts the pressures of life · comedy eludes them by its irony · but the ultimate peace and assurance rests with tragedy · that is nothing ever comes of shirking a problem" (*Oscar Wilde's Oxford Notebooks,* p. 108).

In this light it is interesting to consider Wilde's review of Wilfred Scawen Blunt's *In Vinculis* (*Reviews,* pp. 393–96), entitled "Poetry and Prison" and written in 1889—six years before Wilde himself went to prison. On the effect of Wilde's prison experience as a formative influence upon *De Profundis,* see Regenia Gagnier, *Idylls of the Marketplace,* chap. 5, esp. pp. 186–87. With all due respect to the unique and irreproducible quality of prison experience in general, it seems to me one must notice the many points of resemblance between *De Profundis* and Wilde's earlier works. But this epistle "in carcere et vinculis" would also appear to distinguish itself from other prisoners' memoirs in its attempt to impart a form to remembered experiences and hence to all of the author's life—a specific manifestation, I take it, of the Aesthetic quest.

9. In his *Oscar Wilde* (New York: New Directions, 1947), Edouard Roditi equates art with nature in *De Profundis* (pp. 190–91). But nature lacks form, which is the essence of that "Symphony of Sorrow" that constitutes Wilde's life.

10. In rejecting Pater, Wilde also rejects his own earlier ideal (based on Pater): see *Oscar Wilde's Oxford Notebooks*, pp. 141–42.

11. Hence the concluding assertion of "Humanitad": "That which is purely human, that is Godlike, that is God" (*Poems*, p. 228). Here the secularism of Wilde's religion must be emphasized: in his *Into the Demon Universe* Christopher Nassaar argues that Wilde "creates for himself a private Satan—Lord Alfred Douglas—and a private Christ" (p. 148). But ultimately Wilde seems closer to the viewpoint of Renan's *Vie de Jésus*, which affirms the possibilities for human life inherent in one's present existence. For evidence of Renan's influence on Wilde, see the Renan entries in *Oscar Wilde's Oxford Notebooks*, pp. 111, 173, 174.

12. On Wilde's conception of Christ, cf. Nassaar, *Into the Demon Universe*, pp. 156–59; Rodney Shewan, *Oscar Wilde: Art and Egotism* (New York: Barnes and Noble, 1977), pp. 196–97; and Gagnier, *Idylls of the Marketplace*, pp. 189–91. Gagnier's description of Christ as "fully aestheticized and autonomous" (p. 190) seems to me, however, to miss a crucial element of the conception of Jesus in *De Profundis:* "But in a manner not yet understood of the world he regarded sin and suffering as being in themselves beautiful, holy things, and modes of perfection" (*Letters*, p. 486). "Beautiful" because they make possible the kind of intense realization that other experiences do not, hence more "real"—which means, for Wilde, more "romantic."

13. Thus Lord Goring's witty declaration in *An Ideal Husband:* "No, Lady Chiltern, I am not a Pessimist. Indeed I am not sure that I know what Pessimism really means. All I do know is that life cannot be understood without much charity, cannot be lived without much charity. It is love, and not German philosophy, that is the true explanation of this world, whatever may be the explanation of the next" (*An Ideal Husband*, p. 101).

14. Thus in *The Duchess of Padua* the Duchess declares: "And besides, / While we have love we have the best of life . . ." (*The Duchess of Padua*, p. 67). Later Guido opines: "Now then I know you have not loved at all. / Love is the sacrament of life . . ." (p. 97).

15. See George Moore's similar description of Christ in his *Confessions of a Young Man:* "For verily Thy life and Thy fate has been greater, stranger and more Divine than any man's has been. The chosen people, the garden, the betrayal, the crucifixion, and the beautiful story, not of Mary, but of Magdalen. The God descending to the harlot! Even the great pagan world of marble and pomp and lust and cruelty, that my soul goes out to and hails as the grandest, has not so sublime a contrast to show us as this" (p. 124).

16. See Gide's comment: "Wilde did not converse—he told tales" and Wilde's own assertion: "They do not understand that *I cannot* think otherwise than in stories" (*Oscar Wilde*, pp. 23–24, 38).

17. Thus Arthur Symons can remark: "One sees that to him everything was drama, all the rest of the world and himself as well; himself indeed always at once the protagonist and the lonely king watching the play in the theatre emptied for his pleasure" (*A Study of Oscar Wilde*, pp. 84–85).

6. A SENSE OF THE PAST

1. I condense this speech somewhat from James's original notebook entry, rather than the preface. See *The Complete Notebooks of Henry James,* p. 141.

2. On James and Whistler during the novelist's early London years, see Leon Edel, *Henry James* (Philadelphia: Lippincott, 1953–72), 2:335. For a later meeting in Whistler's house in the rue du Bac, see 3:336–37. On the incident which gave rise to *The Ambassadors,* see 4:150–51 and 5:73–74.

3. On the theme of vision in *The Ambassadors,* see F. O. Matthiessen, *Henry James: The Major Phase* (1944; rpt. New York: Oxford University Press, 1963), pp. 30–36 and Nicola Bradbury, *Henry James: The Later Novels* (Oxford: Clarendon Press, 1979), pp. 36–41, 44–46, 53–55. In light of James's emphasis upon the "demonstration" of Strether's "process of vision" as "the precious moral of everything," it seems a mistake to accord equal weight to Chad's destiny and that of the various "attachments" in the novel, as does Laurence Holland in *The Expense of Vision* (Princeton: Princeton University Press, 1964), pp. 231, 248. Here the moral significance of such attachments lies not in the attachments themselves but in Strether's perception of them, which represents the emergence of a moral consciousness. It is the nature of this moral consciousness that lies at the heart of James's moral concerns in *The Ambassadors.* On moral consciousness (and consciousness in general) in *The Ambassadors,* see Paul Armstrong, *The Challenge of Bewilderment: Understanding and Representation in James, Conrad, and Ford* (Ithaca: Cornell University Press, 1987), chap. 2.

4. On the context of Gloriani's garden party and its thematic significance, see Holland, *The Expense of Vision,* pp. 251–53.

5. Thus James's principal notebook entry for *The Ambassadors* speaks of "an elderly man who hasn't 'lived,' hasn't at all, in the sense of sensations, passions, impulses, pleasures" (*Complete Notebooks,* p. 141).

6. On Strether's relation to Madame de Vionnet, see Holland, *The Expense of Vision,* pp. 257–60. Ultimately, however, that relation becomes something more than what Holland terms a "vicarious" one—on account of Strether's own deepening attachment to her. Precisely because of his attachment, Strether will finally leave Paris—so as not to feel he has compromised himself as an "ambassador." See also, on Strether and Madame de Vionnet, Bradbury, *Henry James: The Later Novels,* pp. 60–71.

7. Edith Wharton, *A Backward Glance,* p. 246.

8. We know of James's own passionate interest in (and even identification with) Napoleon; see the curious deathbed dictation (*Complete Notebooks,* pp. 582–84).

9. See James's notebooks: "These delicious old houses, in the long August days, in the south of England air, on the soil over which so much has passed and out of which so much has come, rose before me like a series of visions. I thought of a thousand things. . . . of stories, of dramas, of all the life of the past—of things one can hardly speak of. . . . Such a house as Montacute,

so perfect, with its grey personality, its old-world gardens, its accumulations of expression, of tone—such a house is really, *au fond,* an ineffaceable image; it can be trusted to rise before the eyes in the future" (*Complete Notebooks,* p. 224).

With this one might compare the consciousness of Ralph Pendrel in *The Sense of the Past:* "If his idea in fine was to recover the lost moment, to feel the stopped pulse, it was to do so as experience, in order to be again consciously the creature that he *had* been, to breathe as he had breathed and feel the pressure that he had felt. . . . What he wanted himself was the very smell of that simpler mixture of things that had so long served; he wanted the very tick of the old stopped clocks. He wanted the hour of the day at which this and that had happened and the temperature and the weather and the sound, and yet more the stillness, from the street, and the exact look-out, with the corresponding look-in, through the window and the slant on the walls of the light of afternoons that had been. He wanted the unimaginable accidents, the little notes of truth for which the common lens of history . . . was not sufficiently fine. 'Present' was a word used by him in a sense of his own and meaning as regards most things about him markedly absent. It was for the old ghosts to take him for one of themselves" (*Novels and Tales* 26:48–50). See also James's *The American Scene:* "I draw courage from the remembrance that history is never, in any rich sense, the immediate crudity of what 'happens,' but the much finer complexity of what we read into it and think of in connection with it" (p. 182).

10. See James, *Literary Criticism* [Essays on Literature, American Writers, English Writers], pp. 46, 50, 63–65.

11. See the similar emotions in some of Ernest Dowson's poems, e.g., "Nuns of the Perpetual Adoration": "Calm, sad, secure; with faces worn and mild: / Surely their choice of vigil is the best? / Yea! for our roses fade, the world is wild; / But there, beside the altar, there, is rest." Or in his "Benedictio Domini": "Strange silence here: without, the sounding street / Heralds the world's swift passage to the fire: / O Benediction, perfect and complete! / When shall men cease to suffer and desire?" (*Poems,* pp. 43, 54) See also Lionel Johnson's "Pax Christi": "I / Have mourned, because all beauty fails, and goes / Quickly away: and the whole world must die" (*Poetical Works,* p. 223).

12. For a sense of how James's own appreciation of those "accumulations of expression" has deepened, compare his description of Notre Dame in *The Ambassadors* with that of his earlier *Tragic Muse* (*Novels and Tales* 7:174–76).

13. For a description of the agnostic mood of the *fin de siècle,* see John A. Lester, Jr., *Journey Through Despair 1880–1914: Transformations in British Literary Culture* (Princeton: Princeton University Press, 1968). See also Jerome Buckley, *The Victorian Temper,* chaps. 5 and 10 (pp. 87–108, pp. 185–206).

14. See James's description of John Singer Sargent: "In the brilliant portrait of Carolus Duran, which he was speedily and strikingly to surpass, he gave almost the full measure of this admirable peculiarity, that perception with him is already by itself a kind of execution. It is likewise so, of course, with many another genuine painter; but in Sargent's case the process by which the

object seen resolves itself into the object pictured is extraordinarily immediate. It is as if painting were pure tact of vision, a simple manner of feeling" (*The Painter's Eye,* p. 217).

7. THE TRIUMPH OF FORM

1. For another analysis of the opening of the novel and the theme of *Imperium,* see Mark Seltzer, *Henry James and the Art of Power* (Ithaca: Cornell University Press, 1984), pp. 66–67.

2. See Gabriel Nash's exclamation in *The Tragic Muse:* "Oh the happy moments of our consciousness—the multiplication of those moments. We must save as many as possible from the dark gulf" (James, *Novels and Tales* 7:32).

3. For a criticism of the collector's passion in Adam Verver, see Ruth Bernard Yeazell, *Language and Knowledge in the Late Novels of Henry James* (Chicago: University of Chicago Press, 1976), pp. 121–23. More generally, on the "morality" or "immorality" of Adam's and Maggie's conduct and attitudes, F. O. Matthiessen, *Henry James: The Major Phase* (1944; rpt. New York: Oxford University Press, 1963), pp. 101–4; F. W. Dupee, *Henry James* (New York: Sloane, 1951), pp. 258–60, 266; Dorothea Krook, *The Ordeal of Consciousness in Henry James* (Cambridge: Cambridge University Press, 1962), pp. 250–52; Yeazell, *Language and Knowledge in the Late Novels of Henry James,* chap. 5; Nicola Bradbury, *Henry James: The Later Novels* (Oxford: Clarendon Press, 1979), pp. 139–40; Seltzer, *Henry James and the Art of Power,* pp. 65–66, 94–95.

In her treatment, Yeazell argues that "the direct link between imaginative sympathy and self-sacrifice . . . is in *The Golden Bowl* strangely broken" (p. 114). But in a world in which everyone suffers, suffering ceases to represent the ultimate meaning of experience. The question now becomes one of making such suffering purposive, hence meaningful. Then too, as Nicola Bradbury points out, Maggie's and her father's awareness of the morally problematic aspect of their actions pre-empts criticism to some extent. See Bradbury, pp. 171, 180, 190–91.

Seltzer presents a somewhat different approach, asserting the "interchangeability" of love and power. But are these (in *The Golden Bowl*) really the same? One can conceive of the *exercise* of power for love—but this is not the same as a desire for power. Perhaps the deepest problem springs from the supposed incompatibility of exercising power and feeling genuine love, which seems in contradiction with causing another to suffer. But such a contradiction exists only if suffering is the source of meaning, rather than becoming meaningful through its relation to something else.

For a view that differs somewhat from all of the above, see Martha Nussbaum, "Flawed Crystals: James's *The Golden Bowl* and Literature as Moral Philosophy," *New Literary History* (Autumn 1983), 15:25–50. Nussbaum focuses upon Maggie's progress from innocence to knowledge: from the naïve ideal of a "watertight" morality to becoming "richly conscious" of the suffering of others to recognizing finally that "a deep love may sometimes require an infidelity against even this adult spiritual standard" (p. 39). Her interpretation, however, fails to take into account Maggie's commitment to marriage itself and what it symbolizes—to form, in other words, as a positive value that makes suffering meaningful and hence transforms the whole nature of what is moral.

4. Cf. Nick Dormer's appreciation of "the sanctity of the great portraits of the past" in *The Tragic Muse:* "Empires and systems and conquests had rolled over the globe and every kind of greatness had risen and passed away, but the beauty of the great pictures had known nothing of death or change, and the tragic centuries had only sweetened their freshness" (*Novels and Tales* 8:390–91).

5. In her *Henry James and the Visual Acts* (Charlottesville: University Press of Virginia, 1970), Viola Hopkins Winner documents the impact of Pater's *Renaissance* upon the early James. Pater's relative lack of influence is ascribed to a "lack of energy, robustness, 'manliness' " (p. 45). But perhaps this influence had only required time to germinate. Note, for instance, James's original title of *The Spoils of Poynton—The House Beautiful,* suggesting possibly an echo of Pater's *Appreciations.*

6. Edith Wharton, *A Backward Glance,* p. 174.

7. R. P. Blackmur remarks that Maggie "looms on the consciousness of the other persons as an image of moral beauty, strikes them as conscience (the agenbite of inwit), and teaches them a new possible, impossible (James's own phrase) mode of love in which conscience and moral beauty are joined" (Veronica Makowsky, ed., *Studies in Henry James* [New York: New Directions, 1983], p. 151). Yet it is precisely by *not* acting upon the others directly but playing them off against each other (like a dramatist) that Maggie ultimately compels them to act.

8. On James's dramatic career as preparation for his final novels, see Matthiessen, *Henry James: The Major Phase,* pp. 7–17. See also James's own notebook entries: on the "divine principle of the Scenario," on "the *scenic* method," and the following: "When I ask myself what there may have been to show for my long tribulation, my wasted years and patiences and pangs, of theatrical experiment, the answer . . . comes up as just possibly *this:* what I have gathered from it will perhaps have been exactly some such mystery of fundamental statement—of the art and secret of it, of expression, of the sacred mystery or structure" (*Complete Notebooks,* pp. 115, 167, 127).

9. See James's famous remark in a letter to H. G. Wells: "It is art that *makes* life, makes interest, makes importance, for our consideration and application of these things, and I know of no substitute whatever for the force and beauty of its process" (*Letters* 4:770). On James's concept of aesthetic form, see R. P. Blackmur, *Studies in Henry James,* pp. 125–26. Blackmur speaks of a "theoretic form for feeling, intuition, insight, what I mean by the theoretic form of life itself." But this "theoretic form" does not actually affect or alter life; it consists merely of an intellectual apprehension of it, leaving life itself intrinsically formless.

10. Thus the action of volume 2 of *The Golden Bowl* presents itself not so

much as a "supersession of the aesthetic by the moral" (Dorothea Krook, *The Ordeal of Consciousness,* p. 273) but rather as the supersession of an aestheticism of consciousness by an aestheticism of form. To characterize what Maggie does simply as "good" is misleading—it fails to take sufficiently into account the suffering she causes others. Nor is it feasible, on the other hand, to treat the action simply as "mechanical plot," in contrast to "the action of the soul in its poetic drama" (Blackmur, *Studies in Henry James,* p. 149). What such symbolic "essentialism" fails to take into account is precisely what gives the novel the explicit form and significance of drama.

11. Cf. Blackmur: "there she completes her recognition: that she cannot and will not give them up, but must master them by her goodness, by love, but by a goodness and love which would nevertheless act as a retribution" (*Studies in Henry James,* p. 225). Yet we are told in the novel that the "straight vindictive view" is precisely what Maggie cannot take.

12. Surely in this respect one feels the difference between Maggie's relation to her father and the Prince's to Charlotte—the one based upon giving, the other upon a desire for possession. Yet in *The Expense of Vision* Holland can claim: "Charlotte's and the Prince's affair of passion, and Maggie and Adam's relation, are given the same status in the novel: that of a strained and contorted fusion of what is authentic, normative, and good with what is false, perverted, and evil" (p. 374).

13. See a similar instance in *The Sacred Fount:* "I ventured less than, already, I should have liked to venture: yet I none the less seemed to see her [Mrs. Briss] try on me the effect of the intimation that I was going far. 'Is it your wish,' she inquired with much nobleness, 'to confront me, to my confusion, with my inconsistency?' Her nobleness offered itself somehow as such a rebuke to my mere logic that, in my momentary irritation, I might have been on the point of assenting to her question. This imminence of my assent, justified by my horror of her huge egotism, but justified by nothing else and precipitating everything, seemed as marked for these few seconds as if we each had our eyes on it. But I sat so tight that the danger passed, leaving my silence to do what it could for my manners" (*The Sacred Fount,* p. 250).

14. On the "opacity" of Adam Verver for Maggie, see Yeazell, *Language and Knowledge,* pp. 118–20.

15. For the symbolism of the bowl, see Holland, *The Expense of Vision,* pp. 343–49.

16. Thus on Giotto Berenson writes: "it was of the power to stimulate the tactile consciousness . . . that Giotto was supreme master" (*Italian Painters of the Renaissance,* p. 64). See also Vernon Lee on Masaccio: "With Masaccio began the study of nature for its own sake . . . the passionate wish to arrive at absolute realization" (*Euphorion,* p. 178).

17. In *Henry James: The Later Novels,* pp. 193–94, Nicola Bradbury specifically mentions the "Florentine sacred subject" of the painting, but then neglects to discuss its significance. More generally, Holland in *The Expense of Vision* observes: "The image of society presented in *The Golden Bowl* is built on the pair of fictive marriages, projected first and then achieved, and the

strange family they institute, which are central to both the form and the import of the novel because they are made symbolic not only of marriages in actual life but of other social institutions and processes which are fused with them" (p. 350). But the sanctity of marriage can hardly depend upon its symbolizing "other social institutions and processes"—presumably, there is nothing more sacred in these than in marriage. If emotion alone (as in adulterous love) lacks sanctity, and form alone is meaningless, emotion that passes into form imparts to it a sacred quality. Cf. James's earlier treatment of this theme in *The Portrait of a Lady* (*Novels and Tales* 4:355–57), and, on James's concept of "form" in *Portrait*, William Veeder, *Henry James—the Lessons of the Master* (Chicago: University of Chicago Press, 1975), pp. 84–86, 178–79.

8. THE MUSIC OF TIME

1. For an analysis of the opening line of Proust's novel, see Roger Shattuck, *Proust's Binoculars* (New York: Random House, 1963), pp. 80–83. Shattuck translates: "A long time, I lay me down to sleep at an early hour," emphasizing the indefinite temporal aspect of "longtemps." For an analysis of the opening scene as a whole, see Leo Bersani, *Marcel Proust: The Fictions of Life and of Art* (New York: Oxford University Press, 1965), pp. 21–23. Clearly, the "esquisses" of the beginning of the "ouverture" in the new Pléiade edition of the *Recherche* reveal an emphasis upon the spatiotemporal confusion of the sleeper (see esp. 1:634, 635, 638, 648–49, 654–55). See also on this subject Claudine Quémar, "Autour de trois 'avant-textes' de l'"Ouverture' de la *Recherche:* nouvelles approches des problèmes du *Contre Sainte-Beuve*," *Bulletin d'informations proustiennes* (1976), 3:8. Through its dissociation from external conditions of space and time, the self becomes capable of imaginative reverie.

In one of the "esquisses" the reason for this emerges even more clearly than in the final version: "Qu'elle était reposante pour mes yeux cette obscurité mystérieuse qui me semblait venue là sans que je m'en fusse aperçu, plus reposante encore pour mon esprit qui sentait qu'il était suspendu pour une seconde encore comme dans ce hamac délicieux au-dessus de la terre, sans plus saisir l'enchaînement des effets et des causes" (1:642).

2. On the loss of spatiotemporal orientation in the *Recherche,* see Georges Poulet, *Proustian Space,* tr. Elliott Coleman (Baltimore: Johns Hopkins University Press, 1977), pp. 7–16.

3. An earlier "esquisse" describes a similar experience: "Une sorte de participation à l'obscurité de la chambre, à la vie inconsciente de ses cloisons et de ses meubles, tel était mon sommeil" (1:640). Significantly, previous versions of the opening of the "ouverture" speak of the narrator as reading a "journal" rather than an "ouvrage"—omitting entirely any mention of the three motifs (see, for instance, 1:653). On these three motifs as leitmotivs, see Proust's remark in a letter to Lucien Daudet (early September, 1913) on the similar proleptic function of details in the early part of the *Recherche:* "ce sera comme les morceaux dont on ne sait pas qu'ils sont des leitmotive quand on les a

entendus isolément au concert dans une *Ouverture* sans compter tout ce qui se situera après coup" (*Correspondance* 12:265).

4. On the "église" and its architectural connotations in Proust, see Jean-Yves Tadié, *Proust et le roman* (Paris: Gallimard, 1971), pp. 240–42 and, more generally, on the "architecture of the work," chap. 9. Also Yves Clogenson, "Le thème de la cathédrale dans Proust," *Bulletin de la Société des amis de Marcel Proust* (1964), 14:152–59. In his first letter to Jacques Rivière, Proust writes: "Enfin je trouve un lecteur qui *devine* que mon livre est un ouvrage dogmatique et une construction!" And, later, speaking of his *Recherche:* "Comme elle est une construction, forcément, il y a des pleins, des piliers, et dans l'intervalle des 2 piliers je peux me livrer aux minutieuses peintures" (*Marcel Proust–Jacques Rivière: Correspondance*, pp. 1, 114). See also Céleste Albaret, *Monsieur Proust*, ed. Georges Belmont and tr. Barbara Bray (New York: McGraw-Hill, 1976): "One night he said to me: 'You know, Céleste, I want my work to be a sort of cathedral in literature. That is why it is never finished. Even when the construction is completed there is always some decoration to add, or a stained-glass window or capital or another chapel to be opened up, with a little statue in the corner'" (p. 240). Maurice Duplay records a similar anecdote in *Mon ami Marcel Proust* (Paris: Gallimard, 1972), p. 79.

5. In her *Marcel Proust: théorie pour une esthétique* (Paris: Klincksieck, 1981), Anne Henry depicts architecture as the "lowest" of the arts in the *Gradus ad Parnassum* or hierarchy of the arts represented in the *Recherche,* because of its dependence upon a material substance. But "architecture" in the *Recherche* need not imply a material medium: its principle consists simply of a relation between various points in space—or time. One may indeed take the three motifs (church, quartet, rivalry of François I and Charles V) as suggesting something of a Gradus ad Parnassum. But then its defining motive ought to be something other than the Schellingian-Schopenhauerian concept Anne Henry proposes. In the *Recherche,* moreover, music offers something more than a "synthesis of emotion" (Henry, *Marcel Proust,* p. 302). Insofar as it represents the possibility of experiencing temporality, it defines itself (like other arts in the *Recherche*) by its relation to time.

6. In an interview Gaston Poulet recalled: "Pour Marcel Proust, seule existe véritablement la musique de chambre; pour lui, la musique lyrique compte peu, et il est fort éloigné de la symphonie" ("Proust et la musique," *Bulletin de la Société des amis de Marcel Proust* (1961), 11:428. In letters to Reynaldo Hahn and Louis de Robert from 1912 and 1913, Proust speaks specifically of his intense desire to hear the Beethoven quartets (*Correspondance* 11:309, 12:43).

7. For other analyses of this scene, see Bersani, *Marcel Proust,* pp. 227–29, and Poulet, *Proustian Space,* pp. 77–79.

8. In his *Proust and Signs,* tr. Richard Howard (New York: Braziller, 1972), Gilles Deleuze argues that the narrator's impressions are to be regarded as "signs" (pp. 11–13). But what the impression as a sign really reveals is "essence" (pp. 40–41). In the present passage, however, there need not be any-

thing beyond the impression—the mere feeling of something beyond it suffices to convey to the narrator the intuition of something permanent within the impression itself.

9. See a similar passage in Proust's *Carnet de 1908*, p. 102.

10. On the narrator's artistic vocation as the unifying principle of the *Recherche*, see Tadié, *Proust et le roman*, pp. 246–47.

11. For another instance of Proust's use of the term "ensoleillement," see *Recherche* 1:433. Speaking of the pleasure he anticipates from hearing la Berma recite the famous lines of *Phèdre*, the narrator observes: "mais mon coeur battait quand je pensais, comme à la réalisation d'un voyage, que je les verrais enfin baigner effectivement dans l'atmosphère et l'ensoleillement de la voix dorée." See also *Recherche* 1:574–75.

12. I take this from Céleste Albaret, *Monsieur Proust*, pp. 97–98 and 327–32. For another, quite different version see George Painter's *Proust: The Later Years* (Boston: Little, Brown, 1965), pp. 243–44, based apparently upon the interviews with Gaston Poulet and Amable Massis recorded in "Proust et la musique," *Bulletin de la Société des amis de Marcel Proust* (1961), 11:424–37. A discussion of the different accounts occurs in J. M. Cocking, *Proust* (Cambridge, Eng.: Cambridge University Press, 1982), pp. 188–89, 217.

13. Here we have, I believe, the true meaning of music in the *Recherche*—rather than in the attempts of various commentators to relate the form of the *Recherche* to that of particular musical works. Cf. for instance, J. M. Cocking, *Proust*, pp. 109–29, and esp. 126–29, with his conjecture of Proust's use of Vincent d'Indy's *César Franck* and its diagram of Franck's Quartet as inspiration for the novel's structure. See also Pierre Costil, "La Construction Musicale de la Recherche du Temps Perdu," *Bulletin de la Société des amis de Marcel Proust* (1958), 8:468–89 and (1959), 9:83–110. In this regard it is significant that in the remarks on Vinteuil in Proust's notebooks (esp. Carnets 3 and 4) there are almost no technical descriptions of his music; see on this point Karuyoschi Yoshikawa, "Vinteuil ou la genèse du septuor," *Études proustiennes* (Paris: Gallimard, 1979), 3:298. Similarly, Gaston Poulet recalls: "A vrai dire, il ne s'intéressait pas à proprement parler à l'esthétique musicale; c'est même là un sujet que nous n'avons pour ainsi dire jamais abordé" (from "Proust et la musique," *Bulletin de la Société des amis de Marcel Proust* (1961), 11:426. Hence the emphasis upon Swann's (and later the narrator's) experience of listening to the works of the composer Vinteuil.

14. For a somewhat different view of the relation of music to emotion in the *Recherche*, see Costil, "La Construction Musicale de la Recherche du Temps Perdu," pp. 484–89. Subsequently (pt. 2, pp. 100, 103), Costil argues that the music of Vinteuil offers "la révélation d'une réalité supra-terrestre, sur laquelle le temps n'a pas de prise" (p. 103). But this seems to imply too drastic a distinction between music and life—as if music were something other than the purified emotion it seems to be for Swann and the narrator. Simultaneously, it neglects the profound relation between music and time.

15. On the composite nature of Proust's sources for the Vinteuil sonata, see one of his letters to Antoine Bibesco (*Correspondance* 14:234, 236). In an

earlier letter (Saturday evening, April 19, 1913) to the same friend, Proust describes his own response on hearing César Franck's sonata: "Grosse émotion ce soir. A peu près mort je suis allé cependant à une salle rue du Rocher pour entendre la *Sonate* de Franck que j'aime tant, non pour entendre Enesco que je n'avais jamais entendu (*sicissime*) [.] Or je l'ai trouvé *admirable;* les pépiements douloureux de son violon, les gémissants appels, repondaient au piano, comme d'un arbre, comme d'une feuillée mystérieuse. C'est une très grande impression" (*Correspondance* 12:147). On Proust's musical sources for the Vinteuil sonata (Saint-Saëns, Fauré, Wagner, Franck) see J. M. Cocking, *Proust,* pp. 110–24 and Karuyoschi Yoshikawa, "Vinteuil ou la genèse du septuor," *Études proustiennes* 3:289–347, esp. 297–98, 302–3.

16. Thus later the narrator's experience in hearing the Vinteuil sonata for the first time is also one of confusion that only gradually clarifies itself; see *Recherche* 1:520–21. In her *Proust's Additions* (Cambridge: Cambridge University Press, 1977), p. 23, Alison Winton notes that this passage (forming part of a larger addition, 1:520–25)—like many others relating to Vinteuil—does not figure in Proust's earlier (1913–14) version of the *Recherche.*

17. On the significance of repetition in Proust, see Tadié, *Proust et le roman,* pp. 242–43.

18. In *À l'ombre des Jeunes Filles en fleurs,* speaking of the Vinteuil sonata, the narrator develops a similar analogy between music and life: "Pour n'avoir pu aimer qu'en des temps successifs tout ce que m'apportait cette Sonate, je ne la possédai jamais tout entière: elle ressemblait à la vie" (*Recherche* 1:521). On music and its role in the *Recherche* see Ernst Robert Curtius, *Französischer Geist im neuen Europa* (Stuttgart: Deutsche Verlags-Anstalt [1925]), pp. 24–28.

·19. The thematic importance of this fact appears in an early draft for *Le Temps retrouvé* [*L'Adoration perpétuelle*]: "Depuis que j'ai quitté le monde, puis Paris, tous ces gens-là ont vieilli et cette espèce de crépuscule dont me donnent l'idée toutes ces figures où il semble qu'on ait baissé la lumière intérieure, c'est tout simplement les lumières de la fête de ma vie qui ne sont plus si brillantes qu'au commencement. Tout commence à pâlir, à diminuer, un jour tout s'éteindra" (*Matinée chez la Princesse de Guermantes,* p. 33). And, from the *Bal de Têtes:* "Est-ce du reste le changement de tous ces visages mais tous les yeux me paraissent moins vifs, et comme si je voyais tous ces êtres en effet dans un rêve dont ils n'ont pas conscience, dans un crépuscule où la vie avait baissé" (ibid., p. 190). Originally the Princesse de Guermantes's "matinée" was described as a "soirée."

20. Hence the phenomenon Genette describes as "the *increasing discontinuity* of the narrative" (*Narrative Discourse: An Essay in Method,* tr. Jane E. Lewin [Ithaca: Cornell University Press, 1980], p. 93), for his analysis of which, see pp. 93–94.

21. Thus Walter Benjamin in "The Image of Proust": "Only the *actus purus* of recollection itself, not the author or the plot, constitutes the unity of the text. One may even say that the intermittence of author and plot is only the reverse of the continuum of memory, the pattern on the back side of the tapestry" (*Illuminations,* tr. Harry Zohn [New York: Schocken, 1969], p. 203).

22. As Bersani points out: "The suffering of Proust's lovers comes from their not being able to make those they love 'sit' permanently for them, give up their freedom and live like models posing in a studio" (*Marcel Proust*, p. 78). See also on this point the effect of Proust's late additions, discussed in Winton, *Proust's Additions*, pp. 215–16.

23. On the relation between space and time in Proust's novel (which includes even their "interchangeability"), see Curtius, *Französischer Geist im neuen Europa*, pp. 38–42.

24. See on this point Bersani, *Marcel Proust*, pp. 63–65, and, for the analysis of love in the *Recherche* more generally, chaps. 2 and 3. What is revealing about the narrator's obsession with Albertine is its continuation even after her death—which suggests that the source of his interest in her is not Albertine herself but rather his memory of the emotion she inspired in him, which he now seeks to repossess. See also Alison Winton's description (*Proust's Additions*, pp. 267–83) of Proust's later augmentation of Albertine's lies and the narrator's uncertainty about her. The "principal intention," Winton observes, "is to generate more uncertainty about her actions, and to show the effect this has on Marcel" (pp. 272–73). Earlier, speaking of *La Prisonnière*, she states: "Entirely missing from the main MS are almost all of the present suspicious incidents focussing on Albertine" (p. 45).

25. In one of his drafts for a projected "preface" to *Contre Sainte-Beuve*, Proust writes: "En réalité, comme il arrive pour les âmes des trépassés dans certaines légendes populaires, chaque heure de notre vie, aussitôt morte, s'incarne et se cache en quelque objet matériel. Elle y reste captive, à jamais captive, à moins que nous ne rencontrions l'objet. À travers lui nous la reconnaissons, nous l'appelons, et elle est délivrée. L'objet où elle se cache—ou la sensation, puisque tout objet par rapport à nous est sensation—, nous pouvons très bien ne le rencontrer jamais. Et c'est ainsi qu'il y a des heures de notre vie qui ne ressusciteront jamais" (*Contre Sainte-Beuve*, p. 211).

For Proust, significantly, "every object in relation to us is sensation"—we never possess or apprehend the object itself. Such "sensation" consists of everything that makes up our *experience* of an object—thoughts and emotions as well as sensory perceptions. But if we equate objects with sensations, the ultimate source of our knowledge becomes consciousness and what it retains of these objects through its memory of sensations. In a letter to Jacques Rivière (September 1919), Proust observes: "Vous dirai-je que je ne crois même pas l'intelligence *première* en nous . . . je pose avant elle l'inconscient qu'elle est destinée à clarifier—mais qui fait la réalité, l'originalité d'une oeuvre" (*Marcel Proust–Jacques Rivière: Correspondance*, p. 64). With regard to rational intelligence vs. intuition in Proust, see Shattuck, *Proust's Binoculars*, pp. 86–93, and Cocking, *Proust*, pp. 166–72.

26. Thus Bersani perceptively observes: "For sexuality is both important and unimportant in the novel. We seldom find physical love as something pleasurable in itself in Proust's world. What Marcel desires, for example, is not Albertine, but rather knowledge and control of Albertine's desires. . . . Marcel wants much more than physical possession, but physical possession is

the short-cut to what he wants. It is a way of completely taking over another consciousness" (*Marcel Proust,* pp. 58–59).

27. It is both interesting and revealing to compare the description of this incident in *Le Temps retrouvé* (*Recherche* 3:866ff.) with an earlier version from a projected preface to *Contre Sainte-Beuve.* There, speaking of the experience of the "mémoire involontaire," Proust had written: "Je sentais un bonheur qui m'envahissait, et que j'allais être enrichi d'un peu de cette pure substance de nous-même qu'est une impression passée, de la vie pure conservée pure (et que nous ne pouvons connaître que conservée, car au moment où nous la vivons, elle ne se présente pas à notre mémoire, mais au milieu des sensations qui la suppriment) et [qui] ne demandait qu'à être délivrée, qu'à venir accroître mes trésors de poésie et de vie" (*Contre Sainte-Beuve,* pp. 212–13).

The "pure substance of ourselves" which is "a past impression" indicates a Proustian identification of self with consciousness: a past impression can be equated with the self only if that self consists of experience (rather than some concept of the "I"), in other words, the content of consciousness. To speak of "pure life conserved in its pure state" ("la vie pure conservée pure") reveals a desire to possess as fully as possible the experience of a past moment. But, as Proust recognizes, it is impossible to possess the past in this pure form: at the moment of originally experiencing it, the sensation we now treat as past occurred along with other, conflicting sensations and impressions. Thus in possessing that sensation again, i.e., in re-experiencing it, we know it only as a "conserved" one, distinct from the chaotic actuality of our present sensations or impressions.

But to know it in this fashion is problematic. It makes the experience of a past moment possible, but fails to yield the sensation of that past moment in its totality or essence, which had been the original object of desire. See also a passage from an earlier draft of the Guermantes hôtel episode (*L'Adoration perpétuelle*): "Au moment où mon pied passait d'un pavé un peu plus élevé sur [un autre] un peu moins élevé, je sentis se former obscurément en moi, tressaillir comme un air oublié dont tout le charme touche un instant ma mémoire sans qu'elle puisse encore distinguer son chanteur et le reconnaître, cette félicité qui était en effet aussi différente de tout ce que je connaissais que l'est la musique, spéciale comme une sorte de thème mélodique d'un bonheur ineffable. . . . Quelques autres fois encore à des intervalles souvent longs de plusieurs années tout d'un coup dans ma vie cette musique je l'avais encore entendue . . ." (*Matinée chez la Princesse de Guermantes,* p. 125). Here, in contrast to the final version in *Le Temps retrouvé,* Proust in effect equates the Guermantes hôtel experience with that of music. It must have been yet further reflection upon the nature of music and of time as experienced through the "mémoire involontaire" that led him finally to distinguish between these, as evidenced by his suppression of the references to music (except for the allusion to Vinteuil, a late addition) and by his inclusion of the "rivalry between François I and Charles V" in the "overture" as a third motif, after the "quartet."

28. We now know that the phrase "que les dernières oeuvres de Vinteuil m'avaient paru synthétiser" (3:866) represents a late addition (see Winton,

Proust's Additions, p. 340–41). Winton goes on to comment: "It was structural good sense to juxtapose Vinteuil's music with Marcel's involuntary memories" (p. 341). But surely Proust has a more specific rationale in mind—one that concerns the experience of time's passage in music and the problem of recovering past moments.

29. See the witty and apt aperçu of Samuel Beckett in his *Proust* (rpt. New York: Grove Press, 1970): "Proust had a bad memory—as he had an inefficient habit, because he had an inefficient habit. The man with a good memory does not remember anything because he does not forget anything. His memory is uniform, a creature of routine, at once a condition and function of his impeccable habit, an instrument of reference instead of an instrument of discovery" (p. 17). In a similar fashion Proust himself observes in his "Carnet" of 1908: "Nous croyons le passé médiocre parce que nous le *pensons* mais le passé ce n'est pas cela, c'est telle inégalité des dalles du baptistère de St Marc (photographie du Bap[tistère] de St Marc à laquelle nous n'avions plus pensé, nous rendant le soleil aveuglant sur le canal" (*Carnet de 1908,* p. 60).

30. It is precisely this consciousness which distinguishes an involuntary reminiscence not only from an original experience in the past but also from the impression produced by a work of art. For this reason it seems incorrect to claim, as does Henri Bonnet in his *Le Progrès spirituel dans "La Recherche" de Marcel Proust* (2d ed.; Paris: Nizet, 1979), pp. 291–92, that the "souvenirs involontaires" and aesthetic impressions are equivalent. The specific perception the narrator makes concerning the nature of his own past experiences (i.e., of their eternism) is one that is only possible through their recurrence in an involuntary reminiscence. On "l'intemporal" in the *Recherche,* see Tadié, *Proust et le roman,* pp. 426–28.

31. See on this point Henri Bonnet, *Le Progrès spirituel dans "La Recherche" de Marcel Proust,* pp. 280–81.

32. In *Le Progrès spirituel,* p. 290, Henri Bonnet maintains that the joy the narrator experiences from a "souvenir involontaire" is an *intellectual* one, resulting from the satisfaction of recapturing a moment of the past in its actuality. But surely the narrator's inability to explain the precise nature or cause of his happiness indicates its emotional rather than intellectual source.

33. Thus Shattuck: "The much touted *moments bienheureux* do not bring Marcel to his vocation or confer on him any lasting happiness. They represent an important step toward both those ends, or more accurately, they are the guideposts which show him the right direction without themselves taking him to his goal except by anticipation. The multiple sequence they contribute toward the end functions as a preliminary to the *dénouement* of the book, not as its true climax. . . . *The ultimate moment of the book is not a* moment bienheureux *but a recognition*" (*Proust's Binoculars,* pp. .36–37). Shattuck then goes on to maintain that the essence of this recognition is a "self-recognition." See also Proust's first letter to Jacques Rivière: "Non, si je n'avais pas de croyances intellectuelles, si je cherchais simplement à me souvenir et à faire double emploi par ces souvenirs avec les jours vécus, je ne prendrais pas, malade comme je suis, la peine d'écrire" (*Marcel Proust–Jacques Rivière: Correspondance,* p. 28).

And earlier in the same letter: "J'ai trouvé plus probe et plus délicat comme artiste de ne pas laisser voir, de ne pas annoncer que c'était justement à la recherche de la Vérité que je partais, ni en quoi elle consistait pour moi" (p. 2).

34. See Georges Poulet, *Proustian Space,* p. 102.

35. See on this point Curtius, *Französischer Geist,* pp. 42–47.

PRIMARY SOURCES

Adams, Henry. *The Education of Henry Adams,* ed. Ernest Samuels. Boston: Houghton Mifflin, 1973.

——*History of the United States of America during the Administrations of Jefferson and Madison,* ed. Earl N. Harbert. 2 vols. Library of America. New York: Literary Classics of the United States, 1986.

——*Novels, Mont Saint Michel, The Education,* ed. Ernest Samuels and Jayne N. Samuels. Library of America. New York: Literary Classics of the United States, 1983.

Banville, Théodore de. *Mes souvenirs.* Paris: Charpentier, 1882.

——*Les Stalactites,* ed. E. M. Souffrin. Paris: Didier, 1942.

Barbey d'Aurevilly, Jules. *Oeuvres romanesques complètes,* ed. Jacques Petit. 2 vols. Bibliothèque de la Pléiade. Paris: Gallimard, 1964–66.

Baudelaire, Charles. *Correspondance,* ed. Claude Pichois and Jean Ziegler. 2 vols. Bibliothèque de la Pléiade. Paris: Gallimard, 1973.

——*Oeuvres complètes,* ed. Claude Pichois. 2 vols. Bibliothèque de la Pléiade. Paris: Gallimard, 1975–76.

Beardsley, Aubrey. *The Story of Venus and Tannhäuser or "Under the Hill,"* ed. Robert Oresko. London: Academy Editions and New York: St. Martin's Press, 1974.

Beerbohm, Max. "A Defence of Cosmetics." In *The Yellow Book: Quintessence of the Nineties,* ed. Stanley Weintraub. Garden City, N.Y.: Doubleday-Anchor, 1964.

Berenson, Bernard. *The Italian Painters of the Renaissance.* Rpt. New York: World, 1957.

Burckhardt, Jacob. *Gesammelte Werke.* 10 vols. Basel: Schwabe, 1955–56.

Dowson, Ernest. *The Poems of Ernest Dowson,* ed. Mark Longaker. Philadelphia: University of Pennsylvania Press, 1962.

Fredeman, William, ed. *The P.R.B. Journal.* Oxford: Clarendon Press, 1975.

Gautier, Théophile. *Émaux et Camées,* ed. Claudine Gothot-Mersch. Paris: Gallimard, 1981.

——*Mademoiselle de Maupin,* ed. Adolphe Boschot. Paris: Garnier, 1955.

——*Poésies complètes de Théophile Gautier,* ed. René Jasinski. Rev. ed. 3 vols. Paris: Nizet, 1970.

Gide, André. *Oscar Wilde: A Study,* tr. Stuart Mason. Oxford: Holywell Press, 1905.

Goncourt, Edmond and Jules de Goncourt. *Oeuvres complètes.* 21 vols. Geneva and Paris: Slatkine Reprints, 1986.

Gosse, Edmund. *Father and Son: A Study of Two Temperaments.* London: Heinemann, 1907.

Hunt, William Holman. *Pre-Raphaelitism and the Pre-Raphaelite Brotherhood.* 2 vols. 1905. Rpt. New York: AMS Press, 1967.

Huysmans, Joris-Karl. *Oeuvres complètes de J.-K. Huysmans.* 18 vols. Paris: Crès, 1928–34.

James, Henry. *The American Scene.* Introd. and notes by Leon Edel. Bloomington: Indiana University Press, 1968.

——*The Complete Notebooks of Henry James,* ed. Leon Edel and Lyall H. Powers. New York: Oxford University Press, 1987.

——*Henry James Letters,* ed. Leon Edel. 4 vols. Cambridge: Harvard University Press, 1974–84.

——*Literary Criticism,* ed. Leon Edel and Mark Wilson. 2 vols. Library of America. New York: Literary Classics of the United States, 1984.

——*The Novels and Tales of Henry James.* 24 vols. (+2 vols.). New York: Scribner's, 1907–9. [The New York Edition.] (Both *The Ambassadors* and *The Golden Bowl* are cited from this edition, but simply by individual title, with the designation vol. 1 or 2 for each novel.)

——*The Painter's Eye: Notes and Essays on the Pictorial Arts,* ed. John L. Sweeney. Cambridge: Harvard University Press, 1956.

——*The Sacred Fount.* London: Methuen, 1901.

Johnson, Lionel. *Poetical Works of Lionel Johnson.* New York: Macmillan and London: Elkin Mathews, 1915.

Leconte de Lisle, Charles Marie René. *Oeuvres de Leconte de Lisle,* ed. Edgard Pich. 4 vols. Paris: Les Belles Lettres, 1976–78.

Lee, Vernon [Violet Paget]. *Euphorion: Being Studies of the Antique and the Mediaeval in the Renaissance.* 2d ed., rev. London: T. Fisher Unwin, 1885.

Moore, George. *Confessions of a Young Man,* ed. Susan Dick. Montreal: McGill-Queen's University Press, 1972.

Newman, John Henry. *Apologia Pro Vita Sua,* ed. Martin J. Svaglic. Oxford: Clarendon, 1967.

Nietzsche, Friedrich. *Werke: Kritische Gesamtausgabe,* ed. Giorgio Colli and Mazzino Montinari. 22 vols. to date. Berlin: De Gruyter, 1967– .

Pater, Walter. *Letters of Walter Pater,* ed. Lawrence Evans. Oxford: Clarendon, 1970.

——*The Renaissance: Studies in Art and Poetry,* ed. Donald L. Hill. Berkeley: University of California Press, 1980.

——*The Works of Walter Pater.* 10 vols. Library Edition. London: Macmillan, 1910. (Cited in text and notes by individual titles.)

Proust, Marcel. *À la recherche du temps perdu,* ed. Jean-Yves Tadié. 2 vols. to date. Bibliothèque de la Pléiade. Paris: Gallimard, 1987– .

——*À la recherche du temps perdu,* ed. Pierre Clarac and André Ferré. 3 vols.

Bibliothèque de la Pléiade. Paris: Gallimard, 1954. (In both texts and notes, I cite where applicable the new Pléiade edition in progress, otherwise the earlier edition by Clarac and Ferré.)

——*Le Carnet de 1908,* ed. Philip Kolb. Cahiers Marcel Proust, No. 8. Paris: Gallimard, 1976.

——*Contre Sainte-Beuve, Pastiches et mélanges, Essais et articles,* ed. Pierre Clarac and Yves Sandre. Bibliothèque de la Pléiade. Paris: Gallimard, 1971.

——*Correspondance,* ed. Philip Kolb. 17 vols. to date. Paris: Plon, 1970– .

——*Marcel Proust–Jacques Rivière: Correspondance 1914–1922,* ed. Philip Kolb. 2d ed. Paris: Gallimard, 1976.

——*Matinée chez la Princesse de Guermantes,* ed. Henri Bonnet and Bernard Brun. Paris: Gallimard, 1982.

Renan, Ernest. *Oeuvres complètes de Ernest Renan,* ed. Henriette Psichari. 10 vols. Paris: Calmann-Levy, 1947–61.

Rossetti, Dante Gabriel. *Letters of Dante Gabriel Rossetti,* ed. Oswald Doughty and John Robert Wahl. 5 vols. Oxford: Clarendon Press, 1965–67.

——*The Works of Dante Gabriel Rossetti,* ed. William Michael Rossetti. Rev. ed. London: Ellis, 1911.

Rossetti, William Michael. *Dante Gabriel Rossetti: His Family-Letters with a Memoir.* 2 vols. Boston: Roberts Brothers, 1895.

Ruskin, John. *The Correspondence of John Ruskin and Charles Eliot Norton,* ed. John Lewis Bradley and Ian Ousby. Cambridge: Cambridge University Press, 1987.

——*The Diaries of John Ruskin,* ed. Joan Evans and J. H. Whitehouse. 3 vols. Oxford: Clarendon, 1956–58.

——*The Ruskin Family Letters (1801–1843),* ed. V. A. Burd. 2 vols. Ithaca: Cornell University Press, 1973.

——*Ruskin in Italy: Letters to his parents 1845,* ed. H. I. Shapiro. Oxford: Clarendon, 1972.

——*Ruskin's Letters from Venice 1851–1852,* ed. John Lewis Bradley. New Haven: Yale University Press, 1955.

——*The Works of John Ruskin,* ed. E. T. Cook and Alexander Wedderburn. 39 vols. Library Edition. London: George Allen, 1903–12.

Swinburne, Algernon. *The Complete Works of Algernon Charles Swinburne,* ed. Edmund Gosse and Thomas James Wise. 20 vols. Bonchurch Edition. London: Heinemann and New York: Gabriel Wells, 1925–27.

Symonds, John Addington. *Renaissance in Italy: The Age of the Despots.* New York: Holt, 1888.

Symons, Arthur. *Studies in Two Literatures.* London: Smithers, 1897.

——*A Study of Oscar Wilde.* London: Charles Sawyer, 1930.

——*The Symbolist Movement in Literature.* London: Constable, 1908.

Verlaine, Paul. *Oeuvres poétiques complètes,* ed. Y.-G. le Dantec, rev. and completed by Jacques Borel. Bibliothèque de la Pléiade. Paris: Gallimard, 1962.

——*Oeuvres en prose complètes,* ed. Jacques Borel. Bibliothèque de la Pléiade. Paris: Gallimard, 1972.

Wharton, Edith. *A Backward Glance.* New York: D. Appleton-Century, 1934.

——*Novels,* ed. R. W. B. Lewis. Library of America. New York: Literary Classics of the United States, 1985.

Whistler, James Abbott McNeill. *The Gentle Art of Making Enemies.* Rpt. New York: Dover, 1967.

Wilde, Oscar. *The Letters of Oscar Wilde,* ed. Rupert Hart-Davis. London: Hart-Davis, 1962.

——*Oscar Wilde's Oxford Notebooks,* ed. Philip E. Smith II and Michael S. Helfand. New York: Oxford University Press, 1989.

——*The Picture of Dorian Gray,* ed. Donald L. Lawler. Norton Critical Edition. New York: Norton, 1988.

——*The Works of Oscar Wilde,* ed. Robert Ross. 14 vols. London: Methuen, 1908. (Cited in text and notes by individual titles.)

INDEX

ILLUSTRATIONS